Is the UK Becoming a Failed State?

Is the UK Becoming a Failed State?

Intelligence Diversity, Domestic Governance,

Accountability and Devolution of Powers

Musa Khan Jalalzai

Vij Books India Pvt Ltd

New Delhi (India)

Published by

Vij Books India Pvt Ltd
(Publishers, Distributors & Importers)
2/19, Ansari Road
Delhi – 110 002
Phones: 91-11-43596460, 91-11-47340674
Mobile: 98110 94883
e-mail: contact@vijpublishing.com
www.vijbooks.in

Copyright © 2022, *Musa Khan Jalalzai*

ISBN: 978-93-93499-23-3 (Hardback)
ISBN: 978-93-93499-24-0 (Paperback)
ISBN: 978-93-93499-25-7 (ebook)

Contents

Introduction

The drawing powers and attractiveness of the welfare state are government-protected minimum standards of income, health, security, housing, and education. The British welfare state has been enmeshed in multifaceted crises, including poverty, racism, lack of coherence, and a smattering of social and political infrastructure. The Westminster thank tank for public services reforms (Reform-20 November-2020) has judged degenerating and decaying health of the British state from the discontenting facts and certitudes of depressed disconsolate feelings of on the dole British citizens: "Many of those losing their jobs will be shocked to find just how bare bones the welfare state is. For those earning even the median salary, benefit rates appear woefully inadequate, providing no buffer to allow for an adjustment of outgoings or time to find a comparable job". Notwithstanding all commentaries, and interpretations, 'the welfare state (Esra Dundar Aravacik, IntechOpen-28 November 2018) still regulates and implements social policies. Exposed to some transformations and to some extent replaced by neoliberal policies as a result of changes caused by the globalization and information age, the welfare state is predicted to continue its existence in new forms'.

These challenges have debilitated and infirmed communication of our state on international forums, and incapacitated its enforcement capabilities. After the COVID-19 and African Omicron virus's well-built attacks, and Britain's disaffiliation with the EU, the state is facing economic and political challenges. The Labour government had failed in yesteryears, to address mistrust between government and communities. Correspondingly, and for that reason, the Conservative government continued to affix its footprints to goof up and blunderism. Politicians and parliamentarians have asked very unusual questions about the future of the United Kingdom. Some whooped the UK on the brink, and some depressed by the deteriorating health conditions of the nation. The Scottish independence movement is getting stronger, the Wales body-temperature is steaming up, while with the security crisis in Northern Ireland is going to sharpen.

Now, politicians, bureaucrats, think-tanks, intelligence agencies and parliamentarians also confused how to prevent the proliferation of social and political diseases, and put a stop to the decaying British state. Britain's National Security Council in the past consistently played a vital role in fighting the Pandemic by adopting a professional approach to national crisis management. The basic function of the Joint Committee on National Security Strategy (JCNSS) is to consider the National Security Strategy and its operational mechanism, but in yesteryears, performance of National Security Council had been contended. From Iraq to Afghanistan and domestic governance, the NSC never played a constructive role in addressing these challenges. The role of National Security Council, National Security Adviser, and National Security Secretariat in the Cabinet Office is to manage national security crises, but neither the function of domestic government improved nor foreign operational mechanisms of these organisations.

National Security Council (NSC) is a cabinet committee to highlight government's objectives on national security strategies. Chaired by the Prime Minister, it brings together senior Ministers from different departments to coordinate a whole-of-Government approach to national security. The exponentially growing nature of all these national security threats coming from safe distances, and weaknesses of security organs forced government to publish the Integrated Review of the UK's Defence, Security, Development and Foreign Policy on 16 March 2021-with a speech from the Prime Minister to the House of Commons. Experts and policy makers hoped that this review may help state institutions to manage national crises, but things decamped and aggravated. These and other second thoughts have crippled business of the UK government to organise a fight of competent forces against the COVID-19, Omicron virus, domestic unrest, and unemployment.

The Covid-19 exposed credibility of government and surveillance agencies and their interest in tackling the disease. As pandemic still dancing in our towns and cities, online discussions, newspapers reporting, brutal killing of George Floyd, and emergence of Black Lives Matter movement were developments that spotlighted weakness of western states in fighting Covid-19-related national security threats. These fears were compounded by getting cold feet of Britain's foremost anti-terrorism strategy, "The Prevent". In a more direct way, too, the pandemic proved fertile ground for radical propagandists bent on spreading hate. Fundamentalists, for instance, were known to have used social media to profile Muslims as the prime source of spreading Pandemic. Newspapers, periodicals and journals in Britain have paid little attention to the question of how to reorganise and reinvent the vulnerable British state. The 20th-century British state was among the most stable states, but with the inception of the 21st century, things changed abruptly. The state remained in crisis as its political problems caught up with its economic challenges.

In their recent research paper, Sean Healy and Brigid Reynolds have warned, "If the welfare state cannot be funded in the future, then it will not survive. In fact, the political acceptability of any development in the welfare state is closely linked to economic sustainability." The welfare state in the UK is under pressure from all sides. State institutions are not delivering properly, and literacy rate is going down by the day. The three terrorist attacks of 2017 increased public's lack of confidence in the authorities for a variety of reasons, including police failure to disrupt terrorist plots, deteriorating law and order situation, and media criticism of the government's lack of a strategic approach to security threats. The threat of extremism and terrorism expanded as radicalized elements who had joined conflicts in Middle East, the Persian Gulf, and South Asia, returned to the country with new ideas and ways of thinking. Until 2020, there were thousands of registered extremist and radicalised elements representing a range of sectarian groups in British towns and cities. However, by any reasonable barometer, the level of security of the United Kingdom in 2017 was inauspicious. That year, terrorists carried out three attacks, in which innocent civilians were killed.

As the COVID-19 and Omicron continue to inflict huge social and health fatalities on communities, popularity of Prime Minister Boris Johnson is enfeebled. The state and government powers of managing the COVID-19 crisis have also been tested. Citizens demanded a competent crisis management institution to respond to national security challenges. In every chapter of this book, I have made a point of the need for institutional reforms to make the British state high-spirited and competent. All these issues, domestic crisis and social inequalities have also been documented by Daniel Wincott in his well-written analysis. He also emphasised on constitutional reform to address countrywide protestations and indispositions of the civilian population. Professor Daniel Wincott, in his paper (UK in a Changing Europe: The possible break-up of the United Kingdom) documented issues relating to Scotland, Northern Ireland, Wales and England:

"Is Westminster the sovereign source of political authority in a unitary nation-state? Or is the UK a voluntary union of nations? Equally, Brexit and Covid-19 have exposed a peculiar mix of thin simplification and tacit knowledge showing that Johnson's political misreading is not limited to the UK's Sphinx-like multinational hybrid state. Even across England, when Westminster asserts its sovereignty the result can prove counterproductive. Some political scientists see the UK as particularly prone to policy fiasco and folly, whether we are talking about the battle against Covid-19, the introduction of the Poll Tax or the abolition of the Greater London Council. Number 10's difficulty reading Scotland is, in one sense, understandable. UK wide institutions still govern England, and England contains the vast bulk –85% plus – of the entire UK population and economy. But as a result when dealing with the UK's territorial arrangements, successive Westminster governments have been guilty of neglect, limited imagination and constitutional failure…….The UK constitution is in a state of deep disrepair. Its governing system does not 'do' systematic constitutional reform. The Johnson administration's search for autonomy and control rests on very thin simplifications of a complex reality. Having shown undeniable skill at reading England electorally, it is locked into campaign mode and, for the purposes of government, is poorly equipped to make sense of UK. In the search for a cure, the tendency is to double-down on the causes of fiasco and constitutional fracture – and in so doing to deepen the constitution's disrepair. Faced with a deep existential challenge, political leaders across the UK would do well to work much harder on the totality of relationships among the peoples – and nations – of these islands–whatever constitutional form those relationships may come to take".

We are onlooker to incidents of terrorism, extremism, targeted attacks, knife-crime and radicalization by the day, but never tried to help police administration in fighting this hydra. Sarah Dix, Karen Hussmann, and Grant Walton in their paper (Risks of corruption to state legitimacy and stability in fragile situations-U4 Issue-May 2012 No 3, Anti-Corruption Resource Centre) have defined fragility of the state: "A state in a fragile situation has by definition not yet established a stable political and security environment in which the government can extend its influence and deliver core services over the entire territory. Political instability is of particular concern in fragile states because of the potential for widespread violence with devastating social, political, and economic effects". Within the two years (2020-2021) period, things shaped differently, while performance of the union became weak. Wales, and Scotland demanded a referendum, while unrest in Northern Ireland demonstrated the strength of local militias that disrupted normal function of provincial administration. The COVID-19 attacks further complicated mutual relationships across the country over respective responsibilities of regional governments. Concerns about the future of the UK are being expressed across the political spectrum. In May 2021, Sir David Lidington in his lecture on the future of the British constitution and function of the Union of four provinces, warned that the future of the country was in danger.

Brexit casted shadow over relationship between Westminster and other provinces. Moreover, relationship between the UK and European Union also deteriorated over trade and the border altercation of Northern Ireland. The Teresa May government was unaware of the looming flares but relied on persisting mechanism of intergovernmental relations to mobilise devolving regional governments to effectively respond to the looming crisis. On 21 June 2020, Westminster arranged a meeting of conveners and representatives of Committees scrutinising Brexit-related issues in the Scottish Parliament, National Assembly for Wales, House of Commons and House of Lords to discuss the future of the UK after Brexit, and relationship with the EU member states. The meeting warned that persisting intergovernmental relations in the UK was not fit for purpose" and called for substantial reform.

Prime Minister Johnson's decision to centralise power after the COVID-19 attacks in 2019, to take all decision making processes into his own hands was criticized in press. Newspapers highlighted his intentions with different perspectives. On 11 November 2020, government introduced a long-anticipated National Security & Investment Bill. On 20 July 2021, Government published new guidance and updated draft sector definitions for mandatory notification under the National Security and Investment Act 2021. Announcement of these legal measure was a big step forward, but politicians expressed reservations on deteriorating economic crisis. Former Prime Minister, Gordon Brown warned in January 2021, that the UK could become a failed state without reform. Brexit and the COVID-19 crisis have weakened the ties that bind England, Wales, Scotland and Northern Ireland, Brown said. BBC reported his commentary on 25 January 2021, in which he warned: "Unless the United Kingdom is fundamentally reformed, it could swiftly become a failed state because of rising concerns that the country is governed by a London-centric elite acting in its own interest. "I believe the choice is now between a reformed state and a failed state." Brown wrote in the Daily Telegraph newspaper. "It is indeed Scotland where dissatisfaction is so deep that it threatens the end of the United Kingdom." In his article Gordon Brown warned:

"Whoever in London thought of that is a common refrain, reflecting the frustration of people in outlying communities who feel they are the forgotten men and women, virtually invisible to Whitehall," wrote Brown, who served as Labour Prime Minister from 2007 to 2010. Boris Johnson should reform the way the UK is governed, warning the country must "urgently rediscover what holds it together", or risk fracturing. In his article (Boris Johnson's perfect storm: The UK faces supply shortages, an energy crisis and a government at war with itself- The New Statement (13 October 2021), Tim Ross noted a series of crisis that pressure economy and trade:

"Multiple crises are now combining to put unprecedented pressure on the economy and the institutions of the state: food supplies, factories, courts, farms, hospitals, restaurant chains and power grids are all being pushed towards breaking point. Parallels are being drawn with the 1970s, when daily life was blighted by blackouts and industrial action. For a few days in September 2021, an ageing Nottinghamshire coal-fired power station, which is due to close next year, was one of the last things keeping the lights on. "There is no single argument to be made about what is happening, it's a whole series of interconnected issues all at once," one minister said. "It's the perfect storm." As they grapple with the fallout from Brexit and the pandemic, Johnson and his team are taking policy decisions they accept will cause pain for many people but insist these are worth it for the longer term. On every front, Johnson faces a battle with members of his own party. His critics range from right-wingers who oppose state intervention in markets to MPs who fear the pain that savage welfare cuts will inflict on millions of voters in parts of the north and the Midlands that only recently converted to conservatism. Johnson chose to raise taxes to fund the health and social care sector from spring 2022".

As documented earlier, persisting machine of state and government has become weak and unable to meet political and economic demands of citizens, while Parts of the state machine have become unfashionable to positively respond to economic and social challenges. Economic and social crisis deeply divided society on poor and rich, sectarian, and racism bases. The state and government response to these crises has been weak during the fight against the pandemic. Lessons from an extensive range of crises suggest the need to tighten accountability and transparency. Emerging evidence suggests that this is already a significant concern for both economic recovery and for rolling-out the COVID-19 vaccine. The failure of the state response to this biological war means that an unreformed state cannot manage a crisis with old strategies. Newspapers, and social media in Britain, unfortunately, focussed on ethnic inequalities and health consequences of the pandemic itself. The viruses triggered a wide range of direct risks to health and health-care systems. Saffron Karlsen and Rosie Nelson in their research paper (Staying "One Step Ahead of a Racist": Expanding Understandings of the Experiences of the Covid-19 Pandemic among People from Minoritized Ethnic Groups Living in Britain-November 2021) documented the UK government response to the pandemic, political, social and economic crises:

"The evidence regarding the disproportionate impact of the Covid-19 pandemic on those in minoritized ethnic groups living in Britain and elsewhere is irrefutable (Aldridge et al., 2020; Haque et al., 2020; Larsen et al., 2021; PHEd 2020a; 2020b; Platt and Warwick 2020a; Sze et al., 2020; WEC, 2020). In particular, studies have shown those with Bangladeshi, Black African, Black Caribbean, Indian and Pakistani ethnicities to experience higher rates of infection, hospitalisation and death compared with the white British population. But it is clear that the impact of the pandemic on society has not only been in relation to increased illness and death. Increasingly, empirical evidence has exposed other ways in which the pandemic, and the measures introduced to mitigate its effects, have disadvantaged those in minoritized ethnic groups, often by exacerbating pre-existing inequalities (Karlsen et al., 2020; Li and Heath, 2018, Longhi 2018). For example, people in ethnic minority groups already struggling to make ends meet found themselves in occupations more vulnerable to the economic consequences of social distancing measures or less open to working at home or furlough (BSWN, 2020, Platt and Warwick, 2020a,b). The "digital divide" (and implications of overcrowded accommodation) became even more significant in a world where work and study were conducted almost entirely online (Baker et al., 2020). These negative experiences will, in turn, exacerbate persistent ethnic inequalities in health (Bambra et al., 2020; John et al., 2021; Maddock et al., 2021). For example, in the United Kingdom, people in Black, Asian (and "other white") groups reported poorer mental health and an increased sense of worry following the first pandemic lockdown1 (Barnes and Hamilton, 2020). Research from the US has also indicated higher risk of food scarcity as a consequence of the pandemic among marginalised ethnic groups which is likely to be replicated in the United Kingdom (Siddiqi et al., 2021)".

As I have illuminated earlier, without complete devolution, political and security sector reforms, the UK may possibly become a fragile, or a failing state. The issues of Islamophobia, reforms, and racism within the state institutions of the country have been widely discussed by experts and commentators, in order to divert the attention of government in power to the looming danger. I have already highlighted this hydra in my newspapers articles and research papers, but political parties of the country never realised the importance of security sector reforms. Director of Governance after Brexit and Blackwell Professor of Law and Society at Cardiff University, Professor Daniel Wincott in his article (The possible break-up of the United Kingdom, UK in Changing Europe, 19 Dec 2020) has noted important aspects of the failing UK state:

"National devolved institutions in Scotland and Wales did remarkably smoothly. By contrast, London has failed to consider, in the round, how territories and peoples across the UK should be governed. The institutional arrangements to manage relationships between the UK Government and those in Northern Ireland, Scotland and Wales are inadequate. Belying its name, the UK is far from united. Its disunity reveals that the Kingdom is a mystery to itself. Belying standard accounts of nation-statehood, surprisingly little effort has been made to create or sustain a shared state-wide identity or the institutions that might underpin it. There is little evidence of the shared 'imagined community' that is vital for any nation. On the contrary, recent research on relative territorial identities – how individuals view their sub-state and Britain-wide identities – casts new light on the character of apparently shared British identity. It turns out to work in very different ways across Britain. In the Brexit referendum, those who emphasised British national identity were more likely to vote Remain in England, but Leave in Scotland and Wales. The greater propensity of predominantly British identifiers in Wales and Scotland (although at a lower level) shows similarity to those emphasising English identity in England. The UK constitution is in a state of deep disrepair. Its governing system does not 'do' systematic constitutional reform. The Johnson administration's search for autonomy and control rests on very thin simplifications of a complex reality. Having shown undeniable skill at reading England electorally, it is locked into campaign mode and, for the purposes of government, is poorly equipped to make sense of UK".

Musa Khan Jalalzai
January 2022, London

Chapter 1

The United Kingdom in Danger of Becoming a Failed State

A state with an incapacitated and fractured body of national critical infrastructure, unhealthy political and social stratification, and failed foreign and domestic policies, normally, demonstrates the other way around, or unable to speak for all social colours. Fragile urban infrastructure, unemployment, racism, poverty and social disobedience also contribute to the weakness of the state. There has been no attempt in yesteryears to mix unmatched and peerless social colours in European states. Hatred, abomination, abhorrence and racism deeply disturbed their social stratification, and now, in the UK government circles, there has been a substantial debate about the revocation and termination of passports and nationality of criminas and terrorists. The clefts have expanded and social life has been disturbed by statements of government Ministers about the integration of social colours. We have two kinds of states; weak states and strong states. Weak states are of weak capacity to deliver, and strong states are competent, resourceful and reformed. These kinds of states and their institutions deliver services properly. As a matter of fact, every nation-state fails due to its internal breakdown, social and economic collapse.

When states are unable to deliver positively-due to their weak control over society and financial resources, they are called staggering states. We have so many examples of state failure in Asia and Africa, where conflicts and civil wars caused migration, human fatalities and economic breakdown. In August 2021, Afghan state and government collapsed as a consequence of corruption, Talibanization, nepotism, jingoism and Pakistan's military interference. Robert I. Rotberg, in his well-written book *"Failed States, Collapsed States, Weak States: Causes and Indicators"*, has noted some causes of state failure: "In times of terror, moreover, appreciating the nature of and responding to the dynamic of nation-state failure have become central to critical policy debates".[1] We have more than dozen of weak states in South and Southeast Asia, where citizens live in hardship, but corruption and detachment of successive governments further added to their pain. Robert I. Rotberg is of the opinion that weak states typically harbour-ethnic, religions, linguistic, or other intercommunal tensions that have not yet, or not yes thoroughly, become overtly violent.[2]

The chemistry and philosophy of a welfare state is government-protected minimum standards of income, health, housing, and education. The British welfare state is under threat and embroiled in multifaceted crises, such as poverty, lack of coherence, unemployment and fractions of social and political infrastructure. Government's strategies to address grievances of citizens led to social and economic crises. Many of those losing their jobs will be shocked to find just how bare bones the welfare state is. M. Weir, "International Encyclopaedia of the Social & Behavioural Sciences,-2001", noted some aspects of welfare state in his paper: "A welfare state is a state that is committed to providing basic economic security for its citizens by protecting them from market risks associated with old age, unemployment, accidents, and sickness. The term 'welfare state' first emerged in the UK during World War II. It has since been used much more broadly to describe systems of social welfare that have developed since the nineteenth century. Welfare state studies have sought to create typologies that group countries into categories based on variations in the role that state, market, and family play in ensuring well-being. A second line of research has sought to account for welfare state development and variation, by examining economic, political, institutional, and ideological factors. These studies are broadly cross-disciplinary. Contemporary research examines welfare state restructuring as economic globalisation, and changes in the family and gender roles have placed new pressures on welfare states".[3]

Moreover, K.W. Moore, in his comment (International Encyclopaedia of the Social & Behavioural Sciences, 2001) highlighted the crisis of the welfare state. As we read in newspapers every day about the fragility of the welfare state, successive governments in Britain have struggled to introduce different political and legal strategies to address greivances of citizens:

"Welfare states throughout Western Europe have cut their benefits, and face fiscal and demographic crises of varying degrees. Ageing populations create a shift from system contributors to recipients, deindustrialization and 'Eurosclerosis' have produced high unemployment, and the labour market has been transformed by the growing proportion of nonstandard work and the mass entrance of women into the workforce. Central to recent literature on the welfare crisis are issues of gender and family. Feminist

10

scholars have criticized the political economy approach to welfare state studies because in concentrating its attention on the state and market, it ignores the family and the structural ramifications of women's unpaid domestic work, and in focusing on 'equity' without considering gender, it falsely universalizes equality. At an even more fundamental level, Orloff (1993) asks whether welfare state scholarship is correct to assume that welfare states actually promote overall social well-being and security, since its premises are putatively sexist".[4]

Failed or failing states cause concern to their neighbours. They are an unquestionable and authentic source of terrorism, organized crime, drug trafficking, violence, disease, and economic breakdown. Afghanistan is an example of such a troubled state, which collapsed over again in 1992 and 2021. The Afghan state remained shattered and failed on account of inattention of international coalition and its neighbours interference. In modern intellectual forums, most of the failed-state discourses are centred on lack of a state's capacity to carry out basic services for which it is responsible, such as the rule of law, good governance, and effective border control against external threats.

State failure in Afghanistan, Somalia, Yemen, and to some extent in Pakistan, causes headache to their neighbouring states. These kinds of states proliferate and escalate violent conflict, terrorism, and extremism. Unfortunately, the role of international community has been underwhelming to turn failed states into prosperous and modern states, but instead they destroyed and tortured failed states. The United States and its NATO allies destroyed Afghanistan, looted its mineral resources, and extrajudicially killed innocent women and children in villages and cities. Saudi Arabia and Dubai destroyed Yemen, Sudan, Mali, Somalia and South Africa, but never strived to bring peace and stability to these states. Associate Professor of Law, University of Virginia School of Law, Rosa Ehrenreich Brookst (Failed States, or the State as Failure? The University of Chicago Law Review, Volume 72 Fall 2005 Number-4, the University of Chicago) has chronicled responsibilities of international community in building failed states:

"In the absence of effective governmental control, both violence and illicit economic activity flourish, and both terrorist groups and the leaders of rogue states take ready advantage of the prevailing anarchy. Failed states also pose legal challenges: in an international order premised on state sovereignty and state consent, societies lacking functioning governments create a range of problems. They cannot enter into or abide by treaties;

11

they cannot participate in the increasingly dense network of international trade, environmental, or human rights agreements and institutions; they cannot enforce contracts between their citizens and foreigners or protect settled property interests. For these reasons and more, failed states have increasingly been viewed as a cause for concern by the international community, and a variety of international responses have been attempted and pro-posed. In response to state failure, international actors and institutions, from international and regional organisations to nongovernmental organisations (NGOs) and states, have taken steps to address the immediate humanitarian and security problems characteristic of failed states, through means that range from food aid to the deployment of peacekeeping forces".[5]

The state in United Kingdom is in a deep crisis. Corruption, racism and Islamophobia have fractured the body of the British state that is now experiencing a backbreaking burden of challenges. These challenges have debilitated its voice on international forums, and incapacitated its enforcement capabilities to energetically respond to the waves of terrorism, foreign espionage, and extremism. After the COVID-19 and African Omicron virus's well-built attacks, and its disaffiliation with the EU, the state in Britain has become fragile and frustrated. The Labour government had failed in yesteryears to address mistrust between government and communities. Now, government, politicians, think-tanks and parliamentarians have become frustrated to address proliferation of social diseases, and failed to prevent the state from decaying. In his thesis on "Failed or Fragile States in International Power Politics", Mr. Nussrathullah W. Said (City College of New York, 2013) has documented causes of state fragility:

"System failure in a state has grave consequences. It affects people's physical safety, which includes depriving them or restricting them from accessing social facilities, legal rights, political rights, and social opportunities. Public safety is a key requirement in sovereign territories, and the survival of a state is dependent on security. Lack of social safety contributes to failures of systems in a state. The authorities of failed states cannot maintain public safety, because they cannot control the emerging violence and the collapse of the overall system in their countries. Insecurity thus becomes inevitable. State security not merely implies the end of a war, but it implies maintaining a functioning social structure. In failed states, people cannot continue their businesses in a safe environment; they cannot have a job and travel or provide for the education of their children and they cannot feel safe that their families will not be harmed in the course of their daily affairs. People in failed states have no guarantee that what they have gained today will not be taken away and destroyed tomorrow. Citizens in failed states cannot make decisions to make choices close to their heart. In other words, people want safety and dignity in their daily lives, and this is lacking in failed states".[6]

External interference damages the state's fundamental institutions. There have been several types of interference in the UK that complicated security of citizens. Foreign espionage, cyberterrorism, intelligence operations, and targeted killings have badly damaged domestic governance and public administration. Lack of a coherent society also prompted instability, financial disorganisation and an insecure political and economic environment. Domestic debt and dilapidated relationship with the EU member states, and weak international engagement on different fronts, prompted many challenges. Expert Stewart Patrick in his paper (Working Paper Number 73, January 2006. Weak States and Global Threats: Assessing Evidence of "Spill overs". Centre for Global Development) noted challenges of failing states:

"The growing concern with weak and failing states is premised on the belief that such states are responsible for, or implicated in, new transnational threats that increasingly define the national and international security agenda. There are really two propositions here: first, that traditional concepts of security as interstate violence should be expanded to encompass cross-border threats driven by non-state actors (e.g., terrorism), activities (e.g., crime) or forces (e.g., pandemics, environmental degradation); and second, that such threats have their origins in large measure in weak governance in the developing world. Before scrutinising the latter claim, a few comments about the former are in order".[7] Expert Heather Rawling in the Socialist newspaper analysis, (Poverty increasing. Welfare state in crisis. Do we need a new Beveridge Report?-28 April 2021) noted increasing poverty, socioeconomic crisis and power politics in the UK that further generated energy and transportation crises. The state faced different types of crisis such as violence, terrorism, unemployment, diseases, homelessness and domestic violence. War against the pandemic exposed weaknesses of the British state. Failure to lockdown early enough, failures of effective test and trace, lack of PPE, inadequate benefits to enable people to self-isolation:

"The pandemic has revealed stark inequalities in today's society. The poorest areas have been hit hardest by Covid, with about twice as many deaths as in the richest areas. Child poverty is on the rise and those already in 'deep poverty' have seen the biggest reduction in their earnings, either being furloughed, having their hours reduced, or being laid off. So do we need another Beveridge Report? Is it possible to restore the welfare state to its original mission of caring for people 'from cradle to grave' and creating a safety net to prevent destitution? Or do we want to create something better? In truth, the post-war welfare state was not ideal. There was still poverty, and there was still homelessness. We had a National Health Service but the pharmaceutical industry was left in private hands. Even so, it was a huge improvement on the past. However, the welfare state was created at the beginning of one of the biggest and most sustained economic booms the world has ever seen...In 2020, the UK economy recorded its worst economic performance for over 300 years-worse than the slump after the First World War and the Spanish flu. The original report outlining a universal welfare state was written by a liberal, William Beveridge, and published during the Second World War. It promised to overcome what he patronisingly called the 'five giants' of Want, Disease, Ignorance, Squalor and Idleness. But why would a liberal pen such a report? It was written when the Labour Party was in coalition with the Conservative Party. The two main classes in society - the ruling class owners of finance and big business, and the working class - had different reasons for supporting it".[8]

The fact is, COVID-19 has badly affected the UK economy, travel industry, agriculture, trade, transportation and curtailed social movements and interaction. This disease has killed millions of people across the globe. Its surprise attack disrupted society and challenged public sector. It has also affected education and trade mobilisation, and put a massive burden on hospitals and care homes. In public sector, the attack of COVID-19 caused massive flooding and drought induced by global warming, and global financial crisis. The UK state institutions have been under a deep pressure due to the abrupt attacks of these viruses. State and its regional partners demanded decentralisation and reforms, and called for cross-border collaboration to meet national security challenges. Challenges of climate change, terrorism, extremism, energy and transport are due to ill-equipped public sector. When COVID-19 was detected in the UK, the unprepared hospitals and industry became under pressure and failed to address virus related problems. Analysts and experts, Christopher Ansell, Eva Sørensen & Jacob Torfing in their research paper (The COVID-19 pandemic as a game changer for public administration and leadership? The need for robust governance responses to turbulent problems-2020) highlighted problems of public sector and urged understanding of the concepts of turbulence and robustness-how they challenge the traditional thinking about public governance:

"The virus was a mutated SARS virus that proved to be more contagious but less lethal than previous iterations. It was always expected to mutate again. It apparently affected those it infected very differently, but the pattern and reasons were unknown, and those who got seriously ill could not be offered effective treatment. The conventional government response to the pandemic was a near-total lockdown of society that disrupted the economy and forced poor people without welfare support to choose between hunger and infection. Other solutions, such as social distancing, were more experimental and there was little evidence that wearing a facemask would reduce the risk of infection. However, it was clear that public, private, and third-sector actors, including the citizens themselves, must mobilise in the effort to curb the health crisis and the resulting social and economic crisis. Finally, the massive public debt incurred during the COVID-19 crisis is likely to come at the cost of future health standards and lead to more deaths".[9]

These and other second thoughts have crippled business of government to organise a fight of competent forces against the COVID-19, Omicron virus, domestic turmoil, poverty and unemployment. The British state needed attention of politicians, parliamentarians, think tanks, communities and armed forces to address multifaceted crisis that made lives of citizens insecure, but unfortunately, their rols has been shamelessly underwhelming. We are witnessed to incidents of terrorism, extremism, targeted attacks, knife-crime and radicalization by the day, but never tried to help police administration in fighting this hydra. Experts Sarah Dix, Karen Hussmann, and Grant Walton in their paper (Risks of corruption to state legitimacy and stability in fragile situations-U4 Issue-May 2012 No 3, Anti-Corruption Resource Centre), have defined fragility of the state. "A state in a fragile situation has by definition not yet established a stable political and security environment in which the government can extend its influence and deliver core services over the entire territory. Political instability is of particular concern in fragile states because of the potential for widespread violence with devastating social, political, and economic effects".[10] However, Analyst Mario Silva (Failed and Failing States: Causes and Conditions-June 2012) has highlighted security in failed and fragile states:

"In failed states, human security is constantly threatened with widespread violence, internal conflict and, at the extreme spectrum, civil war and terrorism. These conditions inevitably lead to a loss of territorial control and political instability attributed usually to authoritarian rule that lacks legitimacy among the population, with no separation of powers and with an ineffective justice system. Under such circumstances, there is a provision of impunity to those who commit serious criminal violations of human rights. Failed states result from temporary or prolonged loss of the structural competency of the state to provide security and basic political goods. Adding to the seemingly overwhelming misery of the situation is widespread poverty, rampant corruption and a loss of social cohesion and development. The characteristics of state failure are not homogeneous and vary from region to region. Failure is attributed to the structural incompetency of the state and its genesis is to be found in the historical realities of both Cold War politics and the effects of colonialism. Leaders who have lost the legitimacy to govern and who provide for no social and economic development, using clan and elite sections of society to maintain power, have also undoubtedly paved the way for state failure".[11]

Politicians and parliamentarians have often asked a very unusual question about the future of the United Kingdom. Some whooped the UK on the Brink, the reason that the Scottish independence movement is getting stronger, while security crisis in Northern Ireland has intensified. To save the Union by different social and administrative strategies, Westminster's centralisation of power, and plans to introduce a law that may strengthen inter provincial relationship, was criticized in newspaper. The Wales province complained that it has been side-lined by Westminster. One of the key issues on new government's agenda was constitutional reform in order to improve how existing devolution settlement works, but provinces have showcased reservation. Later on, British governments developed a political system to address complaints of provinces, and in March 2018, review of Joint Ministerial Committee presented an opportunity to make system fit for challenges.[12]

There are four provincial administrations in operation in Britain. Each of these administrations have different political and social responsibilities, principles of governance and regional security mechanisms. Complicated relationships between these four provincial administrations and the role of Westminster have further complicated issues of trust and mutual respect. Within the two years (2020-2021) period, things shaped differently, while performance of union became controversial. Wales, and Scotland demanded referendum, while civil war in Northern Ireland demonstrated the strength of local militias that disrupted normal function of provincial administration. In Wales, question of independence is still on the table.

Former adviser to David Cameron on devolution once said; "no room for complacency" about the support for the union in Wales. The COVID-19 attacks further complicated mutual relationships across the country on respective responsibilities of regional governments. Concerns about the future of the UK are being expressed across political spectrum. In May 2021, Sir David Lidington in his lecture on the future of British constitution and function of the Union of four provinces warned that the future of the country was in danger.[13] The Wales government published a report full of protestation and complaints (Reforming our Union: Shared governance in the UK June 2021. The 2nd edition of the Welsh Government's views on the reforms needed to put the Union on a sustainable footing for the future):

"The UK government published Lord Dunlop's review of the UK government's union capability. His report includes recommendations on the constitutional and intergovernmental relations agenda, which overlaps with ongoing work on the joint Review of Intergovernmental Relations. While helpful in some ways, the context in which the review was completed (2019) and date of issue by the UK government (24 March 2021) has since changed. The recommendations to establish a UK Intergovernmental Council, supported by a standing independent secretariat, and to improve the transparency and accountability of intergovernmental relations, are reforms we have been calling for over a number of years. But, the UK government's interpretation and selective approach will result in potential tensions which may arise from, for example, UK government financial instruments, communication and branding, as well as establishing offices in the devolved nations, particularly if these are in competition with devolved government responsibilities and priorities……. Beyond coronavirus, the UK Government appears to have rejected a four nation approach, in favour of a greater emphasis on the strength of the Union expressed through an 'aggressive unilateralism'– most clearly manifested by the United Kingdom Internal Market Act 2020 for example–and it has down-played the multi-national character of the UK. It seems that the UK Government perceives a tension between these two visions of the UK, and is seeking to assert one at the expense of the other; our view is that these two visions are entirely compatible with one another, and that an acknowledgement of that will actually strengthen the Union".[14]

According to the BBC report (February-2021); "Elsewhere, rows have broken out between UK and Welsh Ministers over who should control funds replacing EU aid and a new trade law that the UK government said will protect Welsh businesses. Welsh Ministers said Westminster-Cardiff relations have worsened since Lord Dunlop said reforming intergovernmental relations was one of the key recommendations in his unpublished report. "It needs to be less ad-hoc, more predictable, a flow of meetings, I think the agendas need to be more about joint decision-making. It needs to feel jointly owned. He said people in Wales should not get carried away by individual polls but there was not any room for complacency. There's been some suggestion devolution has failed because it hasn't killed nationalism. Whereas my view is devolution isn't a failed project-it's an unfinished project'. BBC reported.[15] BBC (February 2021) also reported Political analyst Laura McAllister's standpoint about the Welsh independence, a topic on all parties radars: "We know at the moment independence in Wales remains a minority interest," she said. One senior UK government told BBC: "There's definitely an increased recognition within No-10 that Wales was a strong unionist nation, and that there was an opportunity to build upon the 2019 general election result by levelling up the Welsh communities that have felt left behind by both the Welsh Government and previous UK governments. BBC reported.[16]

Brexit has deeply impacted Britain's economy, agriculture and financial market, and still continues to inflict catastrophe on its social life. During the past two years, local governments tried to tackle this crisis with different measures and strategies, but devolution of powers, centralization of powers, lack of coordination and majoritarian democracy generated different types of challenges. Analysts and experts Vivien Lowndes, and Alison Gardner in their research paper (Local Government under the Conservatives: Super-austerity, devolution and the 'smarter state', Institute of Local Government Studies-2016) highlighted power devolution approach of the conservative government: "The Conservatives are promoting devolution as a strategy to stimulate economic growth based on greater sub-regional autonomy and increased competitiveness across and between English localities. 'Combined authorities' have the opportunity to champion local identities and acquire new economic development powers from Whitehall. But devolution could be a strategy to decentralise austerity, shifting responsibility to the local level for deeper cuts (56% by 2020) and inevitable service reductions. Local government confronts 'super-austerity', where new cuts come on top of previous ones, compounding original impacts and creating dangerous (and unevenly spread) multiplier effects. The Conservatives' 'smarter state' policies, aimed at delivering 'more for less', amount to little more than a recycling of new public management diktats".[17]

Institutionalisation of the devolution process caused consequences of pandemic management, the reason that provincial governments were only in control of health, housing and social care, they were unable to make fiscal and economic policy. These powers remained with England. The Scotland Acts have expanded its fiscal autonomy, but the scope for large-scale borrowing remained limited in size and purpose for both Scotland and Wales. In their research paper, Karlo Basta & Ailsa Henderson (2021 Multinationalism, Constitutional Asymmetry and COVID: UK Responses to the Pandemic, Nationalism and Ethnic Politics) have noted challenges faced by the devolution program:

"The manner in which devolution has been institutionalised has had important consequences for the management of the COVID-19 pandemic. The devolved governments have control over health, housing, education, and social care, but do not possess comprehensive fiscal or economic policy autonomy. Successive Scotland Acts (2012 and 2016) have broadened Scottish fiscal autonomy, but the scope for large-scale borrowing remains limited in size and purpose for both Scotland and Wales. This means that while the devolved governments were in a position to pursue independent policy choices on many public health dimensions of the pandemic response in their territories, the UK government took the lead on the same in England and developed and implemented the fiscal response across the UK. At the same time, the relationship between the devolved governments and the central administration has been poorly institutionalised, suggesting the relative lack of importance that the central government attaches to the multi-level character of the UK polity....The Joint Ministerial Committee system, the UK's principal intergovernmental forum, is consultative and does not meet on a sufficiently regular basis to facilitate productive coordination in policy-making. While the early response to the pandemic was coordinated, though not through the JMC, the central government subsequently charted its own course with far less collaboration with the devolved governments. The pandemic, combined with devolution in health care, but without strong institutionalisation in the intergovernmental domain, shaped the devolved government response. While devolved governments implemented largely the same public health policies as the central government, and with similar health outcomes, they distinguished themselves from Westminster largely through differentiated timing in the implementation of those policies".[18]

In 2020, the devolution power has been concealed in England by the process of levelling up. In 2017, the government white paper on devolution had promised to expedite the process, but now its intentions have changed. Analyst and expert, Mark Sandford, (Is this the way to English devolution? Voice, delegation, levelling up? UK in a Changing Europe, 06 Sep 2021) has briefly highlighted devolution of powers and resolve of Whitehall: "In the last year, devolution of power in England has been eclipsed by the agenda of 'levelling up'. The government's white paper on English devolution, first promised in late 2017, will now be incorporated into a white paper on levelling up, anticipated in late 2021. This generated speculation that the government had cooled on the idea of devolving power to local areas. That speculation was exacerbated by the range of centrally-managed funding programmes created or expanded under the Johnson administration: the Future High Streets Fund, the Towns Fund, the Levelling up Fund, the Community Renewal Fund."[19]

Whatever the UK's historical origin may be, the country had a well-functioning state in the past in case of a voluntary association of nations taking the form of a multinational state. Wales, and Scotland were contributing their share in governance, economy and legislation, and Northern Ireland was maintaining good relationship with England. In its recent report (Reforming our Union: Shared Governance in the UK-2021), the Wales government has shared so many complaints in the field of judicial, administrative and financial decision making, and protested on some other issues. It also complained against the devolution process and its representation in Parliament. As reported by newspapers, and electronic media since the 2020 lockdowns and restrictions, intergovernmental relationships improved between Westminster and provinces. To tackle the crisis, Boris Johnson needed to call the COBRA meetings but he didn't perceive it necessary. Provincial governments were not invited to attend the new committees meetings. The Welsh Chief Minister, Mark Drakeford, complained that he had only one telephone conversation with Prime Minister Johnson in 2020.

Some political parties supported referendum and some rejected it. Brexit complicated relationship between Westminster and other provinces, where they expressed reservations on some regional issues. Moreover, relationship between the UK and European Union also deteriorated over the trade and border issue of Northern Ireland. The Teresa May government was unaware of the reality of looming flares but relied on persisting mechanism of intergovernmental relations to mobilise devolving regional governments to effectively respond to the looming crisis. Analysts and experts, Michael Kenny, Philip Rycroft and Jack Sheldon, in their joint research paper

(Union at the Crossroads: Can the British state handle the challenges of devolution? The Constitution Society-2021) documented weaknesses of the UK Union and reservations of regional government on various political and economic issues:

"Relations deteriorated further over the legislation required to execute the UK's withdrawal from the EU. The judgement offered by the Supreme Court in the iconic Miller case, in January 2017, reflected the enduring primacy of the doctrine of parliamentary sovereignty and rejected the notion that conventions, whatever their political force, had a legal basis. This confirmed in particular that the Sewel convention–the practice whereby the UK government did not usually legislate on devolved matters without the consent of the devolved legislatures–was not legally binding. And the 'not normally' caveat in the relevant clause of the Scotland Act 2016 meant what it said; if the UK government deemed the circumstances not to be normal, then the UK parliament could override the refusal of a legislative consent motion by any of the devolved legislatures. The significance of this point was brought home during the fraught passage of the European Union (Withdrawal) Act–the legislation that repealed the European Communities Act 1972, and paved the way for the UK's formal extrication from the European legal order.....Both the Scottish and Welsh governments were strongly opposed to the bill that was introduced to the Westminster parliament in October 2017, which sought to 'freeze' the powers that would otherwise flow to the devolved legislatures as the UK left the EU. The rationale for this was to preserve the stability of cross-UK law until such time as the respective governments could agree a way forward that would protect the integrity of the UK's internal market".[20]

On 21 June 2020, Westminster arranged a meeting of conveners and representatives of Committees scrutinising Brexit-related issues in the Scottish Parliament, National Assembly for Wales, House of Commons and House of Lords to discuss the future of the UK after Brexit, and its relationship with the EU member states. The meeting warned that persisting intergovernmental relations in the UK was "not fit for purpose" and called for substantial reform. However, power centralization further exacerbated the pain of devolving governments. The process generated debates in intellectual forums that this cannot address regional issues and warned that this action of central government can undermine and marginalise the role of both the devolved governments and legislatures. The Wales government report (Reforming our Union: Shared governance in the UK June 2021), highlighted these and other issues relating to Wales and Northern Ireland:

"Under the traditional understanding of parliamentary sovereignty, legislative devolution does not mean the transfer by the UK Parliament of legislative powers to the devolved legislatures. Currently, the UK Parliament continues to have unlimited legislative competence in respect of all parts of the UK (including, in respect of the devolved territories, competence about devolved matters), and the devolved legislatures are additional legislatures for their territories, with competences overlapping that of the UK Parliament. If legislative devolution is to have real meaning, this situation, therefore, requires the UK Parliament to adopt a self-denying ordinance in respect of legislation on matters in the devolved sphere, thereby acknowledging the primary responsibility of the devolved legislatures for legislation in their territories on devolved matters. In the case of Northern Ireland, provision is made for periodic "border polls", and in certain circumstances the Secretary of State is statutorily obliged to arrange for the holding of one. There are no equivalent standing statutory arrangements for Scotland or Wales for the holding of referendums on continuing membership of the Union, but it remains our view that, provided a government in either country has secured an explicit electoral mandate for the holding of a referendum, and enjoys continuing support from its parliament to do so, it is entitled to expect the UK Parliament to take whatever action is necessary to ensure that the appropriate arrangements can be made".[21]

Moreover, Chief Minister of Wales, Mark Drakeford expressed concern over the attitude of Whitehall towards provinces and the future of the Union. In his commentary in the foreword of the report of his administration (Reforming our Union: Shared Governance in the UK-2021), he warned that 'in some important ways the Union failed to keep pace with the full and real implications of the creation of legislatures in Wales, Scotland and Northern Ireland'. He also regretted aggressive action in a unilateral way on behalf of the whole UK without perceiving the status of provinces and their democratic mandates. He also warned that if Whitehall didn't change its attitude towards provinces, the country will be overtaken by competing loyalties and the lure of separatism:

"Beyond slogans, buildings and flag flying, the current UK Government has contributed little to thinking about an energised and viable future for the Union. The Welsh Government has actively tried to stimulate wider debate about UK reform. This document, containing our proposals to protect and reform the Union, was first published in October 2019. We have by no means all the answers. However, it is a contribution to a debate that needs to happen on a range of issues as seen from a Welsh Government perspective. Things move quickly and much has happened since the first publication, and we have updated the document accordingly. Following our election the people of Wales have given a broad endorsement to the Welsh Government's vision and the need to revitalise our Union. In the period ahead we will be engaging directly with civil society and citizens to think through the issues we need to progress in greater detail. I hope that the UK Government in particular will accept the role it needs to play in cooperating with us and others to mould a forward-looking Union, fit-for-purpose and capable of earning the goodwill and respect of all its peoples. In the election of May this year the choice could not have been clearer. I shared a platform with leaders of parties which argued to abolish devolution on the one hand, and to take Wales out of the UK on the other".[22]

Having shared his concern on government in the UK, on 25 January 2021, former Prime Minister Gordon Brown warned that the public's trust in the way the UK was run was breaking down. He said Covid-19 had exposed "tensions" between Whitehall and the nations and regions, who were often treated by the centre as if they were "invisible". He urged Boris Johnson to set up a commission to review how the country was governed and powers shared. "Mr. Brown's intervention comes amid a looming clash between Mr Johnson and Scottish First Minister Nicola Sturgeon, who demanded the UK agree to another Scottish independence referendum if the SNP wins a majority in elections". BBC reported.[23] "Whoever in London thought of that?' is a common refrain, reflecting the frustration of people in outlying communities who feel they are the forgotten men and women, virtually invisible to Whitehall?" Brown said British Prime Minister Boris Johnson should reform the way the UK is governed, warning the country must "urgently rediscover what holds it together, or risk fracturing. He called on Johnson, head of the ruling right-wing Conservative Party, to set up a commission and review how the country is run. Al Jazeera reported.[24]

The UK is facing threat of foreign espionage, political interference, assassination and disinformation warfare. The only way to meet these challenges is to introduce security sector reforms to make law enforcement and intelligence agencies competent. The NHS has failed to tackle national health security challenges. Unnecessary surveillance and facial recognition measures have proved the inability of provincial governments to address dynamics of national security challenges. Now citizens realised that their own privacy has been discarded in the name of international security.[25]

Since the partition of Ireland, Northern Ireland adopted domestic rules in 1920, and in 1972, amidst civil unrest, direct rule was re-established. In Scotland and Wales, political parties demanded devolution in 1970s but after a tiresome struggle, the devolution process happened in the 1990s. Devolution of executive and legislative powers may have contributed to increased support for independence in the constituent parts of the United Kingdom. The evidence of the period since the election of a Labour Government in 1997 was more mixed. "While there is some evidence of relaxation of controls, (Centralisation and Decentralisation of Power in the United Kingdom, 1992-2002, Professor Alan Page Department of Law University of Dundee.www.parliament.uk. October 2003) the more general picture in relation to the areas already examined was of the retention and, in some cases, extension of the powers of direction and control acquired under previous administrations". Between 1997 and 1999, directly-elected lawmaking bodies and executives were generated for London, Scotland, Wales and Northern Ireland, (Centralised Power and Decentralised Politics in the Devolved UK. Akash Paun and Robert Hazell, University College London) and established provincial assemblies for nine regions of England. The unsettled altercation of British territorial politics came to the fore in 2007. Former Prime Minister Theresa May kicked off process of centralisation in policy and administrative decision making within Whitehall, while Boris Johnson accelerated these tendencies after the Pandemic war on British society. Expert and analyst Martin Ivens (Japan Times, 27 May, 2020) in his article highlighted centralisation of powers in Britain:

"The new coronavirus has changed everything. It has seen Johnson dither over using his executive power to lay down the law. True, most democratic leaders find life-and-death decisions unnerving, but the Prime Minister has made too many missteps for Britain's emergence as "the sick man of Europe" to be seen as mere bad luck. The U.K. has an unwelcome lead in the continent's league table of fatalities, in part due to its role as a transport and business hub. But Johnson's administration bears the blame for failing to lock down as quickly as Germany, for prematurely terminating track and tracing of the infected in March, and for allowing hospital patients to be discharged untested into care homes for the elderly......Britain's muddled approach to immigration, a central policy area for the Conservatives, is equally perplexing. While the contagion was still spreading, the U.K.

permitted free entry from China, Italy, Iran and other countries with high infection rates. Johnson's Brexit vision is of an outward-looking Global Britain, not the protectionist Little England imagined by his enemies, and that rendered him reluctant to pull up the drawbridge. Now his government has lurched in the opposite direction, devising a draconian regime that will force all U.K. arrivals to self-isolate for 14 days. The policy looks unworkable. Today, the machinery of state needs a clarifying moment and clearer division of roles than the present buck-passing. The modus operandi of the current government is that civil servants must be kept in check, lest a "blob" of resistance hobble Johnson's and Cummings's plans on Europe or anything else. That is no recipe for cohesion.[26]

The state body has been tortured by wrongly designed strategies and policies of politicians, governments and asymmetrical religious and sectarian cultures, and now it has become sick and tired to tolerate burden of weak economy, social and political inequalities. Brexit, COVID-19, racism, and Islamophobia have further weakened its roots and ties in Northern Ireland, Scotland, Wales and England. Former Prime Minister Gordon Brown (Al Jazeera-25 January 2021) warned that the UK was becoming a failing state: "I believe the choice is now between a reformed state and a failed state," Brown wrote in Daily Telegraph newspaper. "It is indeed Scotland where dissatisfaction is so deep that it threatens the end of the United Kingdom." 'Whoever in London thought of that?' is a common refrain, reflecting the frustration of people in outlying communities who feel they are the forgotten men and women, virtually invisible to Whitehall," Brown noted.[27] The state's voice has enfeebled internationally while its reputation as a competent and high-spirited state splotched. Law enforcement is in crisis, criminal culture generated consternation and fear, and police has failed to deliver. Brown said Johnson should convene "Citizens' Assemblies in each region and nation so that he could listen to what the public were saying". He also proposed replacing the UK Parliament's unelected upper chamber, the House of Lords, with a "senate of the regions.[28]

British extra-nationalism has gone wrong, regionalism and centralisation of power has become a real danger. Citizenship of British citizens can be removed by the Home Office without warning following a new clause added to the Nationality and Borders Bill in November 2021. The updated bill made the government exempted from giving Britons notice of any citizenship removal. Clause 9 of the Nationality and Borders Bill was added in November 2021, and it exempted the government from giving notice of a decision to deprive a person of citizenship if it is not "reasonably practicable" to do so, or in the interests of national security, diplomatic relations or "in the public interest". The Guardian reported Home Office (Al Jazeera-06 December-2021) in response to the new clause: "British citizenship is a privilege, not a right. Deprivation of citizenship on conducive grounds is rightly reserved for those who pose a threat to the UK or whose conduct involves very high harm. These new clauses and policy of government ultimately prompted reservations of communities, and it created a huge cleft between government and ethnic minority communities in case of privilege, not a right politics. In January 2021, George Osborne in one of his articles asked an extraordinary question that 'how can Boris Johnson avoid disaster–and ignoble title of the worst Prime Minister ever?' On 25 January 2021, Gavin Esler in his article (Is the UK really about to become a 'failed state'? The National News) also quoted Mr. Osborn and noted signs of dismemberment of the British state on account of government's weak approach to governance and autonomous rights of provinces:

"By "this disaster", Mr .Osborne was talking of the breakup of the UK. It came as I was signing orders for the first copies of my new book How Britain Ends, which takes up the same theme. I was stunned that Mr. Osborne, a leading thinker in "the Conservative and Unionist party" agreed that Prime Minister Boris Johnson has put the union of the UK at risk. In the book I argue that the UK has survived Scottish, Welsh and even violent Irish nationalism, but cannot survive resurgent English nationalism plus the incompetence of the Johnson government. Mr. Osborne wrote: "By unleashing English nationalism, Brexit has made the future of the UK the central political issue of the coming decade. Northern Ireland is already heading for the exit door." I agree. Scotland voted overwhelmingly against leaving the EU. Scotland's First Minister Nicola Sturgeon insists Mr Johnson may have a mandate to take England out of the EU but has no mandate for Scotland to Leave. Ms. Sturgeon wants another independence referendum. Northern Ireland also voted Remain. British Prime Minister Boris Johnson speaks to US President Joe Biden from London on January 23. Downing Street handout via Reuters. Now thanks to Mr Johnson's incompetence, there is a customs border in the sea between Northern Ireland and the rest of the UK. That has meant empty supermarket shelves in Belfast and furious exporters and importers who cannot get their goods in and out......The former UK prime minister Gordon Brown appears to agree with much of Mr Osborne's argument. He said that rows over the handling of Covid-19 showed the UK risked becoming a "failed state," because the pandemic has "brought to the surface tensions and grievances that have been simmering for years" between Downing Street and the various parts of the UK".[29]

Every head of state wants his country to be strong and capable of administrative and political structure. Thus, every state needs security sector reforms to make competent law enforcement agencies, but in the UK, packages have been prepared, strategies are designed and legal procedures are expedited, but in reality, all these measure are saved in files and libraries.[30] In The SIPRI Yearbook 2002, (The challenges of security sector reform, Dylan Hendrickson and Andrzej Karkoszka) importance of security sector reforms have been highlighted in detail and noted that these reforms can intercept the risk state weakness or failure: "Where states are unable to manage developments within their borders successfully, the conditions are created for disorder and violence that may spill over onto the territory of other states and perhaps ultimately require an international intervention. Restoration of a viable national capacity in the security domain, based on mechanisms that ensure transparency and accountability, is a vital element of the overall effort to strengthen governance. Security sector reform aims to help states enhance the security of their citizens. There has been a shift from state- and military-centric notions of security to a greater emphasis on human security. This has underscored the importance of governance issues and civilian input into policy making. Security sector reform has potentially wide-ranging implications for how state security establishments are organised and for how international security and development assistance is delivered. These implications are only just starting to be understood and translated into policy and are eliciting mixed reactions from both the international actors that provide security assistance and the recipients of aid".[31]

BBC noted the intervention of Mr. Brown during the cold war between Wales and Scotland Chief Ministers and Boris Johnson. In his Daily Telegraph article, Mr. Brown noted that the pandemic brought to the surface tensions and grievances that had been simmering for years between Downing Street and various parts of the UK. He also noted sharp differences over issues such as lockdown restrictions and furlough and said; "unless underlying tensions were resolved, the UK risked becoming a failed state". However, in his Press TV analysis, (Brexit is propelling Britain towards the door marked 'failed state'-24 September 2021) analysts John Wight noted: "When Boris Johnson succeeded in replacing Theresa May as the country's leader in 2019, in his first speech to Parliament he set out a vision of Brexit Britain so utopian you could have lapsed into believing the country was on the cusp of a new golden age. Johnson even used the term 'golden age' in the speech, declaring that "we will look back on this period, this extraordinary period, as the beginning of a new golden age for our United Kingdom.".…… The threat to the Belfast/Good Friday Agreement threatens peace in Ireland, what with the loyalist and Unionist community up in arms over the border down the Irish Sea that Johnson and his acolytes had pledged would not be established, bringing the UK-controlled Six Counties in the North of Ireland into the EU's trading and customs orbit in order to ensure than a hard border is not reintroduced between Northern Ireland and the Irish Republic".[32]

Brexit caused financial, economic and trade confusion. Britain decided to leave the European Union and live alone to manage its affairs of the state, but things went wrong when Scotland and Northern Ireland exhibited their reservation to leave the project. A country with a strong industrial infrastructure faced multi-branches challenges, including food shortage, energy crisis, transportation challenges, NHS crisis, and deterioration of its relationship with the EU member states is now standing in hot water. Brexit and COVID-19 hit the UK financial market, society and employment sector, and still continues to inflict fatalities and misadventures. Now, Prime Minister Boris Johnson decided to devolve powers to the local governments in order to enable them to take bold and radical steps to tackle major challenges, including climate crisis and rising inequality of wealth. Experts and analysts, Luke Raikes and Dr. Arianna Giovannini, in their joint paper (The Progressive Policy Think Tank 20 November, 2019) have highlighted centralization of power politics in the United Kingdom:

"The UK is a uniquely centralised country: both political and economic power are hoarded in London to a disproportionate extent. Despite recent efforts to decentralise power through 'devolution deals', England–a nation of 55 million people living in diverse towns, cities and villages–is still mostly governed from the capital in the corner. Our analysis shows that centralisation of spending has increased in the last five years, with local governments in England forced to cut spending by £9.5 billion since 2014/15 (in real terms 2018/19 prices). No comparable country endures such an imbalance of power. This centralisation has enabled regional inequalities to deepen across the country. For decades, successive governments have focused on London and the South East as if it's the 'economic engine' of the country and the golden goose for public finances–this region is treated like the Treasury's business investment, where spending is justified on the promise of short-term GDP growth and tax returns. Most obviously this deprives other regions across England of essential investment, and makes it difficult for them to become productive and inclusive economies. But London's dominance affects Londoners too – the capital's housing crisis has helped create the highest levels of poverty in the country".[33] On 15 July, 2021, in his address to the nation, Prime Minister Boris Johnson highlighted his vision of levelling up the United Kingdom:

"There are difficult days and weeks ahead as we deal with the current wave of the delta variant there will be, sadly, more hospitalisations and sadly there will be more deaths but with every day that goes by we build higher the wall of vaccine acquired immunity, a wall that is now higher and stronger in this country than almost anywhere else in the world, and with every day that goes by our economy is slowly and cautiously picking itself up off the floor, businesses are opening their doors, you will see the employment figures this morning, people are slowly coming back to the office and over the next few weeks more and more people will find themselves back on their daily commute and as Andy Haldane of the Bank of England has said – there is every prospect that this country is poised to recover like a coiled spring and it is the mission of this government to ensure that in so far as COVID has entrenched problems and deepened inequalities – we need now work double hard to overturn those inequalities so that as far as possible that everyone everywhere feels the benefits of that recovery and that we build back better across the whole of the UK."[34]

About his levelling up strategy, the Prime Minister said the goal can only be achieved with a strong economy and Levelling up can only be achieved with a strong and dynamic wealth creating economy. "There has got to be a catalytic role for government, and government is there to provide a strategic lead but that requires consistency from government–not chopping and changing-in the last 40 years we have had 40 different schemes or bodies to boost local or regional growth- we had the Abercrombie plan in London, the new towns, the economic development committees, the urban regeneration corporations, the new deal for communities, the regional development agencies, and yet none of these initiatives have been powerful enough to deal with the long term secular trends-de-industrialisation or the decline of coastal resorts and that basic half-heartedness has been coupled with an unspoken assumption by policy makers that investment should always follow success- so that to use a football metaphor the approach has always been to hang around the goal mouth rather than being the playmaker" In his Japan Times article, Martin Iven (Britain's Prime Minister has centralised power, but he doesn't seem to want to use it-May 27, 2020) has taken issue of centralization and fight against the COVID-19:

"An awkward question hangs over the COVID-19-shuttered world of Downing Street. At his daily morning meeting, Boris Johnson, back to full duties after suffering a serious bout of the virus, recently asked who was in charge of relaxing Britain's lockdown plan, with all of the risks and uncertainties that entails for a government. "There was just silence," an insider told the Sunday Times newspaper. "He looked over at Mark Sedwill (his top civil servant) and asked, 'is it you?' The official replied, 'No, I think it's you, Prime Minister.'" Sedwill was right. The United Kingdom's leader enjoys some of the strongest centralised powers in Europe—and yet, paradoxically, the man who fought so hard to gain control of his party and Britain's destiny is reluctant to take responsibility. Before the crisis, Johnson ruled as a near-absolute monarch, often through his eccentric but effective adviser (and key Brexit strategist) Dominic Cummings. In a tale familiar to English court politics down the centuries, the arrogant outsider resented by lesser talents has himself become a hindrance to the man he serves. Cummings, one of the architects of Britain's lockdown, bent the rules by driving his sick wife and child 400 km to his family's northern home where he may or may not have breached self-isolation to walk in local beauty spots. Hitherto, an 80-seat majority in the House of Commons and the trouncing of Jeremy Corbyn's Labour Party in the December election had boosted the Prime Minister's natural self-confidence, and a Cabinet largely composed of inexperienced unequal's reinforced his dominance".[35]

British economy appears to have weathered the initial shock of Brexit in 2021, and the value of Sterling Pound remained near a 30-years low. The EU single market was seen by its advocates as a great achievement but present political and financial ruckus across the continent has put it in danger. The market which was completed in 1992 facilitated free movement of goods and other related materials across Europe, but recent borders restrictions and terrorist attacks in some EU member states, future of the single market has become bleak.[36] Major political, economic, and technological developments in the continent and distrust between Britain and the EU project have prompted a questionable situation in the market of the country, which is very much dependent on imports from the European Union. The UK's 58 percent exports went to the EU, which was the biggest trade volume in the continent. Germany, Netherland and France were its bigger trade partners, while the United State also boosted the UK market by investing billions of dollars in various sectors.[37]

International trade is undoubtedly, the exchange of capital, products and import and export-related activities across borders, but as is evident from the fact, the UK economy is dependent on foreign trade and domestic taxation, for that reason the country is active in a multifaceted trade activity worldwide. John Dudovskiy's recent study spotlighted some global impacts on the UK business organisation and elucidated that these impacts increased the level of multiculturalism in the country's organisations, and level of interdependence of national economies.[38]The impact of global forces on the British market, as he noted, are political, economic, social, technological, legal and ecological, while global environment and competitions are the main actors. These factors give us an unbelievable understanding of lifestyle patterns and tastes of any population.[39]

Law and regulations are factors that can also affect British business strategies where business organisations need to find ways they can react to the change of law affecting their way of business within the EU member states. However, in the EU market, the UK organisations also needed to regulate them. Political and global insecurity, Russian and Chinese role in the world market, weak growth, and China's recent economic reforms are factors that can influence the spending habits of consumers in Europe. The revolving nature of the European economy, banking and monetary systems, EU tax rate, money supply system, cash reserve-ratio and fiscal policies can leave the same impact on the British market economy. However, market structures in Europe such as perfect competition, monopoly and others can also impact the UK market, if business organisations did not meet marketing standards of every state, maintaining better quality standards, and fixing a reasonable price for the local customers are important requirements of the EU single market.[40]

On 18 April 2019, journalist Lyra McKee was killed by a new IRA terrorist. There were three other attacks by the group in 2019. The other failed attacks were primarily directed at security service personnel within Northern Ireland, including an under-vehicle IED targeting the parked car of an off-duty police officer at Shandon Park Golf Club. Recent Rioting was seen in Northern Ireland as the worst in years. During several hours of violence, police officers were attacked, petrol bombs were thrown and a bus was burnt. Eight officers were injured at an interface between loyalist and nationalist areas in west Belfast. The Ulster Volunteer Force (UVF) was suspected of involvement in the rioting in Belfast according to police sources. The PSNI was concerned at the potential for further trouble in the days ahead. It was believed the PSNI was paying close attention to interface areas and the risk of further clashes between communities. The activities of dissident republicans were monitored as routine and the police were wary of any attempt to escalate the situation. Assistant Chief Constable Jonathan Roberts was asked at a press conference if he feared weapons could come on to the streets. Northern Ireland politics and bigger events like Brexit are all in play here but there is no single straight forward reason. There is a lot of fury over the attendance of Sinn Féin politicians at a funeral of a former IRA leader in 2020 summer which appeared to blatantly flout Covid-19 rules. Unionist political leaders-including Democratic Unionist Party (DUP) leader and First Minister Arlene Foster said, PSNI Chief Constable Simon Byrne should resign over the force's handling of the funeral of senior republican Bobby Storey in June 2020.[41]

BBC reported violence in Belfast and involvement of different stakeholders: "The leaders of the Democratic Unionist Party (DUP), UUP, Traditional Unionist Voice (TUV) and Progressive Unionist Party (PUP) have said Mr. Byrne's position is untenable over the PSNI's handling of the funeral. On Wednesday, Jonathan Powell, the former adviser to Tony Blair at the time of the Good Friday Agreement, said politics has got "quite hot" again in Northern Ireland and people are "playing with matches".[42]"Politicians trying to second guess the police when they're making operational decisions is really a mistake and I hope that the first minister will back off on this and allow the police to proceed with their job," Mr. Powell said"[43] The DW news reported crowds of mostly young men in a pro-British area of the Northern Irish city of Belfast set a hijacked bus on fire with petrol bombs and attacked police with stones. Videos circulating on social media showed the bus being hit with incendiary devices and later completely burning out. British writer and analyst of politics and international relations, Tom Fowdy (07 April 2021) in his analytical and critical article noted:

"Northern Ireland is a conflict of identities. Catholic and Protestant. Republican and Loyalist. Irish and British. The instability in the country is a product of a century-long dispute over to whom Ulster belongs. The largely Catholic Republicans argue that there should be a 'United Ireland', and that Northern Ireland is a longstanding occupation of the island's northern third by the British Crown. The predominantly Protestant Loyalists, on the other hand, descendants of Scottish settlers into the territory, pledge their allegiance to the United Kingdom, and were instrumental in leading the six counties of Ulster to break from the newly formed Irish state and re-join Britain nearly a century ago. The latter group were subsequently favored and actively suppressed the Republican-leaning population, creating the longstanding instability the area is infamous for and led to 'the Troubles' of the 70s, 80s, and 90s. Then, in 1998, the landmark Good Friday Agreement was reached and saw the groups and communities compromise for peace, a new power sharing model, and an open border with the Republic. However,

Britain's departure from the European Union has placed this open border in jeopardy. Brexit coverage has for the past four years been synonymous with the words 'Northern Ireland', particularly because leaving the EU customs union means an open border between Northern Ireland the Republic has become untenable, threatening the agreement's terms".[44]

Chapter 2

Domestic Governance, Intelligence Diversity, and Surveillance

The Home Office Web-Spying Powers and its collaboration with Internet Providers who helped its networks and National Crime Agency in tracking websites-visits is a matter of great concern. No doubt, our privacy is under threat. It also involved providers creating Internet connection records to show who visited this and that websites. On 11 March, 2021, BBC reported (Home Office tests web-spying powers with help of UK internet firms) uneasiness of privacy rights organisations on web-spying business of Home Office: "The power to spy on the websites people visit comes from the Investigatory Powers Act, which critics called it a "snoopers' charter" on account of widespread concerns about its scope. The act gives the secretary of state the power, with a judge's approval, to order internet providers to keep their records for up to a year. The definition is so broad that critics believe all ISPs will simply be issued with such orders to cover all their customers. Those records can include which websites a customer visits, when, and how much data they download, as well as the relevant Internet Protocol) addresses-but not what pages or exactly what content they read on those sites." BBC reported.[1]

When Theresa May became Prime Minister of the UK, the CAGE article (13 July, 2016) highlighted the most damaging policies her government put to parliament. An independent grassroots organisation striving for a world free of injustice and oppression, the CAGE in its article noted inflicted harassment of Mass Surveillance in British society: "Mass surveillance not only is the antithesis to a free and open society where controversial ideas can be debated and refined, it also serves to silence dissent and promote conformist behaviours. In a study, Assistant Professor at Wayne State University, Elizabeth Stoycheff found that "government's online surveillance programs may threaten the disclosure of minority views and contribute to the reinforcement of majority opinions". Even those who regarded government mass surveillance programs as necessary, "readily conform their behaviour—expressing opinions when they are in majority, and suppressing them when they're not".[2]

Unescorted strategies and measures cannot help maintain security and stability unless practical steps are taken on different fronts. The state in Britain faces numerous threats, and implicated in different boiling issues; such as centralization of powers, slow process of devolution, regionalism, international terrorism, extremism and foreign intelligence war. Government still fighting terrorism and radicalization with changing approaches. Radicalised elements from Pakistan, Central Asia and the Arab world are free to challenge the authority of the state. After every five years, the UK Government conducts a strategic review of defence and security, but specific objectives haven't been achieved as the insects war emaciated its economy and domestic governance. National security strategy from the UK Cabinet Office set out how the government could address and manage security challenges the country faces, but the Cabinet office could not identify accurate dynamics of national security challenges. Only reports and strategies on paper are not a permanent panacea, more strength is required. The British State is facing greater challenges of COVID-19, and African Omicron virus attacks that once more started inflicting catastrophe and pain on civilian population. Analysts and experts, Mariana Mazzucato, Rainer Kattel, Giulio Quaggiotto and Milica Begovic, in their research paper, (United Nations Development Programme: COVID-19 and the Need for Dynamic State Capabilities: An International Comparison) highlighted capacity of the state and societal challenges:

"The COVID-19 pandemic presents a massive challenge for societies, and specifically governments, worldwide. "COVID-19 is far more than a health or socio-economic crisis; it is also a governance crisis, testing not only the resilience of governance systems and public sector institutions to adapt, function, and innovate in their delivery of public services, but also exposing underlying vulnerabilities in the social contract."Governments in emerging markets are particularly tested, having to address dilemmas such as how to ensure compliance with social distancing in high-density areas like urban slums, how to provide social protection for returning migrant labourers, or how to tackle the compound effects of the pandemic and natural hazards (from locusts to typhoons). The pandemic response also requires an unprecedented level of collaboration between public and private sectors domestically and internationally, from the race for a vaccine to rethinking global supply chains. One of the biggest lessons is that public-sector capabilities to manage a crisis of this proportion are dependent on the cumulative investments that a state has made in its capacities to govern and manage. These prior investments in the form of institutions, infrastructure, human resources and public-private partnerships provide the public sector with a greater set of options to choose from when facing emergency conditions such as a pandemic response".[3]

Major terrorist attacks in Britain have been planned by home-grown extremists that support violence and recruit young fighter for their cause.[4] Prime Minister Boris Johnson in his front matter on Policy paper of Cabinet Office (Global Britain in a Competitive Age: The Integrated Review of Security, Defence, Development and Foreign Policy-16 March 2021) noted: "As the attacks in Manchester, London and Reading have sadly demonstrated, the terrorist threat in the UK remains all too real—whether Islamist-inspired, Northern Ireland-related or driven by other motivations. We will continue to invest in this essential work, through increased funding for the intelligence agencies and Counter Terrorism Policing in 2021-22 and our drive to recruit an extra 20,000 police officers. And we will maintain constant vigilance in protecting British citizens from serious and organised crime".[5] Britain has been subjected to a series of terrorist attacks in yesteryears. In 2005 and 2009, homegrown extremist groups targeted both government installations and public places in London. In 2013, attacks on mosques in Birmingham generated significant consternation, and in 2014, the Woolwich attack on a British army soldier casted doubts on the credibility of law enforcement that failed to retrieve advance intelligence information about the suspected terrorist.

The three attacks of 2017, increased in public's lack of confidence on authorities for a variety of reasons, including police failure to disrupt terrorist plots, deterioration of law and order situation and media criticism on the government's lack of a strategic approach to security threats. The threat of extremism and terrorism expanded as radicalized elements who had joined conflicts in the Middle East, the Persian Gulf, and South Asia, returned to the country with new ideas and way of thinking. Until 2020, there were registered thousands of extremist and radicalized elements representing a range of sectarian groups in British towns and cities. However, by any reasonable barometer, the level of security of the United Kingdom in 2017 was inauspicious. That year, terrorists carried out three attacks that killed several civilians.[6]

Dr Javier Argomaniz, Dr Oldrich Bures and Dr, Christian Kaunert, (A decade of EU Counterterrorism and Intelligence: A critical assessment) have

36

described the threat of terrorism in different perspectives: "high density of factors affecting the incidence of terrorist violence and the difficulty in isolating the short and long-term impact of individual variables has clear implications for counter-terrorism, both at the domestic and international level. It undermines the capacity that national and supranational actors have in other public policy arenas to deliver evidence-based policies that are sustained by meaningful cost-effectiveness analyses and whose overall impact and implications can be measured in a thorough and credible manner".[7] The Policing and Crime Act-2019 also introduced some changes in the system, but these changes were not fully implemented.[8] Home Office and the British Parliament's Intelligence and Security Committee (ISC) remained in deep pain with limited capacity for maintaining and conducting oversight over a powerful intelligence infrastructure. The editors of The U.K.'s Changing Democracy noted some aspects of security sector reforms as they pertain to the ISC and surveillance operations:

"Choreographed evidence sessions between the committee and the service heads suggest an over-cooperative, too close relationship. So too does the past willingness of the committee to very promptly exonerate the GCHQ petabytes of the Snowden revelations and the charges of data collection and surveillance exceeding the agency's remit—a clearance that occurred while the revelations were still emerging. Although the ISC criticised the lack of privacy safeguards in the Investigatory Power Bill, it did not secure major changes in the final act. Security Sector Reforms (SSR) is a complex process. Narrowly defined, it can encompass institutions and organizations established to deal with external and internal threats to the security of the state and its citizens. At a minimum, therefore, the security sector includes military and paramilitary forces, the intelligence services, national and local police services, border, customs, and coast guards. However, it is increasingly understood that SSR is broader than these institutions."[9]

When I first read news and comments in newspapers, watched different TV channels that demonstrated and made perfectly clear the idea of intelligence reforms in the United Kingdom, I exclusively began searching for reports and articles to make my book more comprehensive. Recruiting diverse talent by spy agencies to protect modern Britain is a proficient and multifaceted approach. Policy experts and intelligence analysts wholeheartedly wrote numerous papers and articles-stressing security sector reforms to fit intelligence to the fight against terrorism, foreign espionage and the intelligence war in Europe. The agencies are responsible for collecting and producing foreign and domestic intelligence, providing military intelligence, performing espionage and counter-espionage. In part, I wrote several articles on security sector reforms in the UK, in order to make our intelligence agencies vibrant and high-spirited, but now, I am confident and see our agencies in the frontline. The Intelligence and Security Committee of Parliament with statutory responsibility for oversight of the UK Intelligence Community must be given credit for its tireless, unremitting and indefatigable efforts that put together all necessary pieces in one basket:

"Under Justice and Security Act 2013, (Intelligence and Security Committee-13 November 2021) the Committee oversees policies, administration and operations of MI5, MI6, GCHQ, Defence Intelligence, the Joint Intelligence Organisation, the National Security Secretariat (NSS) and Homeland Security Group. The National Security Secretariat comes up with coordination on issues of strategic importance. By supporting the work of the National Security Council and the Joint Intelligence Committee respectively, the NSS yield advice to the Prime Minister and senior Ministers[10]. Intelligence and Security Committee of Parliament, in its report, (Diversity and Inclusion in the UK Intelligence Community Presented to Parliament pursuant to section 3 of the Justice and Security Act 2013, 18 July 2018), highlighted different aspects of diversity:

"The Civil Service Diversity and Inclusion Strategy, launched in 2017, is a targeted plan of action to take this forward and increase the representation of under-represented groups at all grades across the Civil Service. It has a dedicated programme for improving the representation of ethnic minority staff at senior levels, a revised Disability Inclusion programme, and a Diverse Leadership Task Force reporting to the Cabinet Secretary. The Strategy also commits the Civil Service to having specific plans to ensure working environments are LGBT inclusive. Highlighting accountability as a critical factor in driving improvement, the Strategy states that diversity and inclusion will be embedded within Single Departmental Plans so that it is central to the assessment of every Government department. It will clearly take time for some of these measures to have the desired effect and the Civil Service cannot afford to be complacent. In particular, progress continues to be slow on the appointment of BAME staff to senior positions….To gain a clear understanding of diversity across the intelligence community, robust data is essential. Until an organisation knows where it stands and how it is performing, it cannot define and deliver progress. This means that no organisation's commitment to diversity and inclusion can be taken seriously until it collects, scrutinises and is transparent with its workforce data and can measure its progress accordingly. Unfortunately, the current data across the intelligence community is not sufficiently robust. In addition, the Committee has not, with the notable exception of MI5, been provided with the declaration rates for new recruits and entrants to the Agencies and organisations. This makes it difficult to properly evaluate BAME, LGBT and disability figures for those embarking on, or continuing, their careers in the intelligence community"[11]

Intelligence and Security Committee (Diversity and Inclusion in the UK Intelligence Community Presented to Parliament pursuant to section-3 of the Justice and Security Act 2013, 18 July 2018)) in its report noted comments of intelligence leaders and experts on diversity strategy: Alex Younger, Chief of Secret Intelligence Service remarked: "Diversity, equality and inclusion are strategic enablers for SIS to succeed in fulfilling our increasingly challenging and complex mission. However, Jeremy Fleming, Director, Government Communications Headquarters said: "Diversity and inclusion (D&I) is at the heart of GCHQ's mission and the organisation we aspire to build. We know if we get this right, we will be better at keeping the country safe – there is no more powerful motivation. Air Marshal Philip Osborn, Chief of Defence Intelligence stated: "I believe it would be professionally negligent not to realise the clear benefits gained from promoting diversity and inclusion in all we do. National Security Adviser in the National Security Secretariat, Mark Sedwill declared: "We are committed to ensuring that the most talented people join the National Security Secretariat and that we support them to develop the most robust policy advice for the National Security Council. Our ways of working must embed creativity and challenge, which is why we have changed the way we develop policy advice for the NSC.[12]

Director General, Office for Security and Counter-Terrorism, Tom Hurd said: "I want OSCT to be a diverse and inclusive workplace, where everyone feels part of the team and can reach their full potential. I recognise that unconscious bias and discrimination still exist in OSCT and the wider Civil Service, and that they hold us back from being the best we can be". In the tail-end, Charles Farr, Chair, Joint Intelligence Committee, stated: "We want the Joint Intelligence Organisation (JIO) to be fully representative of the UK working population. This is not only legally and morally the right thing to do, but it is also key in ensuring the success of the organisation. A diverse workforce will ensure we produce better reports for our readers, bringing to bear a range of views and perspectives and better ensuring continuous internal challenge. Diversity requires that we dispel the myths about working in the national security community and create an environment that is genuinely inclusive".[13]Expert and analyst Daniel W. B. Lomas in his research paper on diversity in the UK intelligence agencies, (ForgetJamesBond: diversity, inclusion and the UK's intelligence agencies, Intelligence and National Security) has highlighted diversity and professional reforms within the UK intelligence infrastructure:

"In February 2021, The Times reported that Britain's foreign intelligence agency, the Secret Intelligence Service (SIS or MI6), was relaxing rules to allow applicants with dual UK nationality, or with one parent being a UK national or having 'substantial ties to the UK', to apply. Sources told the paper it was just the latest move to access a 'larger talent pool', adding: 'We want a diversification of thought, a diverse workforce, not people who all think in similar ways'. Later, marking LGBT History Month 2021, SIS's Chief ('C') Richard Moore followed other agency heads in apologising for the historical treatment of LGBT (Lesbian, Gay, Bisexual and Transgender) officials and the bar to gay men and women serving in SIS. In a video shared on his Twitter feed, Moore said the ban deprived SIS of 'some of the best talent Britain could offer' and was 'wrong, unjust and discriminatory'. PinkNews also interviewed two LGBT SIS officers. 'I think the legacy of the ban has been . . . helping people understand that LGBT+ people aren't inherently untrustworthy', said 'Leia', a member of SIS's LGBT+ Affinity Group. 'It's drawn a line in the sand', she added. The statements and media coverage mark just the latest in a series of announcements on the agency's commitment to diversity and change. In January 2021, tabloid newspapers reported on an SIS recruitment drive, specifically an advert, headlined 'Tell me a secret', calling for 'individuals with diverse skill sets and life experiences' to apply for part-time and consulting roles. Responding, Moore tweeted his service's commitment to 'flexible working' and 'diversity'. 'ForgetJamesBond', he added, acknowledging that Bond often shaped perceptions of the ideal intelligence officer. Sir Colin McColl, 'C' from 1989 to 1994, once described the fictional intelligence officer as, in his view, 'the best recruiting sergeant in the world', yet successive Chiefs, like Moore, have tried to distance themselves, seeing Bond's legacy as both a blessing and a curse. In October 2016, Moore's predecessor, Alex Younger, admitted he was 'conflicted' about Bond, on the one hand creating a 'powerful brand', although one that seemed exclusively white and male. 'For too long–often because of the fictional stereotypes I have mentioned – people have felt that there is a single quality that defines an MI6 officer', Younger told journalists in his first public speech in SIS's Vauxhall Cross headquarters, 'be it an Oxbridge In July 2018, the Intelligence and Security

Committee reported on Diversity and Inclusion in the UK intelligence Community".[14]

The idea of recruiting Women, Lesbian, Gay, and Transgender (WLGT) for intelligence infrastructure is the best decision in order to make intelligence powerful and professional. Speaking to the CyberUK conference in April 2018, the GCHQ Director, Jeremy Fleming noted; 'we don't always do enough to make a career accessible to everyone who could contribute to our mission. Former MI5 Director General, Andrew Parker remarked: "committed to gender diversity on boards and senior management teams, that MI5 needed the 'richest mix of talents". Expert Daniel W. B. Lomas, in his research paper on diversity in the UK intelligence agencies, (ForgetJamesBond: diversity, inclusion and the UK's intelligence agencies, Intelligence and National Security) spotlighted professional approach to reforms within the UK intelligence infrastructure:

"There have been significant efforts to change internal culture and promote change, all three agencies having well established networks for women–SIS (DEUCE) and MI5 (GENIE)–and BAME groups- SIS (EMBRACE), MI5 (My5), GCHQ (REACH). LGBT and disability networks have also been formed. For GCHQ, the REACH network has 'led to increased engagement across the organisation, a change in approach to recruitment and traction with BAME communities across the country'. Thanks to internal work the Security Service was named best employer of the year by Stonewall in 2016, remaining in the organisation's top 100 LGBT list of employers. Both SIS and MI5 were also listed in The Times top fifty employers for women in 2018. There are also factors outside agency control. GCHQ's difficulties can be explained by a general shortage of women in STEM subjects; according to UCAS and HESA data just 35% of STEM students were women. Representation in 'Computer Science' and 'Engineering and Technology' was just 19% and GCHQ has been forced to reach out and promote women in STEM subjects to develop a talent pipeline. Equally, the collapse of languages in UK higher education is worrying; according to a January 2020 report in the Financial Times, university language departments were downsized or cut entirely thanks to a significant drop in student numbers. The report also warned that just 32% of 16–30 year olds can read and write in another language. 'We are looking for people with top end language skills', 'Chris', a GCHQ linguist told the BBC in 2011, adding: 'we are not finding as many as we were finding at the beginning of the 2000s'. Though speakers of French, German and other European languages with language aptitude still form a core of GCHQ's intake, speakers of Arabic, Mandarin

Chinese, Mirpuri, Russian, Urdu and other sought after languages are still hard, placing a growing focus on candidates that may not pass nationality rules".[15]

The role of Interception Communications Commissioner (IoCC) is widely discussed throughout intellectual forums in the UK. The IoCC's role, and oversight mandate was seen as controversial and serving to alienate citizens from the state and government. The commissioner claimed that, under Part-1, Chapter-1 of the Regulation of Investigatory Power Act 2000, its role was to provide independent statutory oversight over the lawful interception of communication, and also asserted that it also investigated complaints.[16] Civil Society and intellectual groups didn't agree with this assessment. The functions of the Office of Surveillance Commissioners (OSC) are not so different from that of Intelligence Surveillance Commissioner (ISC). The OSC uses human intelligence sources under the Police Act-1997, as well as under Part-11 and Part-111 of the Regulations of Investigatory Power Act of 2000 (RIPA). These institutions help the state to maintain security and stability as well as provide important information to intelligence agencies. Further expanding functions of the Intelligence Surveillance Commissioner was the Justice and Security Act of 2013.[17]

The introduction of Mass Surveillance programs by British and European intelligence services prompted nationwide debate on the rights of civilians to be protected from illegitimate or warrantless collection, and analysis of their data and metadata.[18] British newspapers and human rights forums published numerous reports, in which experts expressed concerns about the diminishing privacy of citizens. However, the growing concern of citizens about the right of their privacy has also been reported in print and electronic media, but their voice was never heard. Google, YouTube, Twitter, and Facebook continue to violate the rights of their users. They are operating shamelessly like intelligence Agencies, collecting and noting every aspect of a user's interactions and conversations to expand their data businesses.[19] The "Don't Spy on US," coalition of organizations released a policy paper in September 2014 highlighting surveillance and intelligence operations and their impact on the privacy of citizens in the EU and U.K.: "In summer 2013 it was revealed that GCHQ was routinely intercepting submarine fiber-optic cables containing private communication of millions of British residents (the 'TEMPORA' program). The reported scale of the interception is staggering: each day, GCHQ accesses some 21 petabytes of data—the equivalent of downloading the entire British Library 192 times."[20]

The bigger barrel is TEMPORA, a surveillance tool used by Government Communication Headquarters (GCHQ). The TEMPORA intercepts communications—collecting information from fibre-optic cables. The system is able to access the data of large amounts of internet users, including personal data, regardless of individual suspicion or targeting. Edward Snowden noted in 2016 that TEMPORA maintained two principal components: Mastering the Internet (MTI) and Global Telecoms Exploitation (GTE).[19]Some intelligence experts argued that GCHQ was more effective in the business of mass-surveillance than the U.S. National Security Agency (NSA) because TEMPORA has access to all telephone and internet communications—including Facebook and email—across Europe.[21] The TEMPORA is comprised of different components codenamed; POKERFACE and the XKEYSCORE. In his 2016 television interview, Edward Snowden revealed that the NSA and GCHQ were using a new surveillance system called MUSCULAR, one of at least four other similar programs that relied on a trusted second party. The programs together were known as WINDSTOP. According to newspaper reports, over a 30-day period from December 2012 to January 2013, MUSCULAR collected 181 million records, while INCENSER, another WINDSTOP program, collected over 14 billion records over the same period. MUSCULAR can collect information without needing warrants, and also supports the NSA's PINWALE data collection system.[22]

On 01 July, 2015, the Investigatory Powers Tribunal (IPT), which investigates complaints of unlawful contacts of the UK intelligence agencies, notified Amnesty International that the British government agencies had spied on organization by intercepting, accessing and storing its communications.[23] The IPT previously identified one of two NGOs which it found had been subjected to unlawful surveillance by the U.K government as the Egyptian Initiative for Personal Rights (EIPR).[24] The other NGO which was spied on was the Legal Resources Centre in South Africa.[25] The Investigatory Powers Tribunal said that until December 2014, GCHQ failed to provide clear enough details of how it shared data collected from Mass Internet Surveillance. It was the IPT's first ruling against an intelligence agency in its fifteen-year history.[26]The inquiry was prompted by the revelations from information leaked by former CIA contractor Edward Snowden.[27] The committee concluded that there was no bulk surveillance and gave a lengthy defence on it: "We have established that bulk interception cannot be used to search for and examine the communications of an individual in the U.K. unless GCHQ first obtain a specific authorization naming that individual, signed by a secretary of state."[28] The time, the government was attempting to restore control orders, but the very concept of control orders had already failed.[29] Unless extremist returnees are de-radicalized at the community level, no control order can prevent them from joining the ISIS terrorist network.

In the United Kingdom and some European states, strict surveillance measures have been adopted to control population, maintain law and order and counter foreign espionage, but these measures caused social unrest and mental torment. In the UK, we have experienced different types of watchdogs, spy networks and private intelligence and surveillance agencies collecting information and data by illegal means. Privacy and human rights organizations have filed numerous cases against the state surveillance swords in courts, and trying to convince stakeholders that this way of privacy interference can alienate citizens from the state, but state, notwithstanding domestic pressure, resorted to Blanket Surveillance, in which every kind of privacy is being plundered. On 07 October 2020, the Register (Kieren McCarthy) reported Britain, France and Belgium's spying networks ruled illegal by courts:

"Mass surveillance programs run by the UK, French and Belgian governments are illegal, Europe's top court has decided in a huge win for privacy advocates. The European Court of Justice (CJEU) announced on Tuesday that legislation passed by all three countries that allows the government to demand traffic and location data from internet and mobile providers in "a general or indiscriminate way" breaks EU data privacy laws - even when national security concerns are invoked. "The directive does not authorise the Member States to adopt, inter alia for the purposes of national security, legislative measures intended to restrict the scope of rights and obligations provided for in that directive, in particular the obligation to ensure the confidentiality of communications and traffic data, unless such measures comply with the general principles of EU law, including the principle of proportionality, and the fundamental rights guaranteed by the Charter," the court decided. The ruling is significant because it directly addresses the issue of national security-something that has been used for years to bypass existing personal data protection legislation. It also states categorically that EU privacy laws still apply in such circumstances, almost always. The decision includes a specific carve-out when it comes to national security, noting that "in situations where a Member State is facing a serious threat to national security that proves to be genuine and present or foreseeable, that Member State may derogate from the obligation to ensure the confidentiality of data relating to electronic communications by requiring, by way of legislative measures, the general and indiscriminate retention of that data for a period that is limited in time to what is strictly necessary, but which may be extended if the threat persists."[30]

In November 2015, the UK government promulgated the Investigatory Powers Bill, which generated countrywide debate. Having commented on this bill, Alice Wyss, the UK Researcher at Amnesty International, noted: "The entire surveillance system in the UK desperately needs dragging out of the shadows and into the light of day. An overhaul of these powers is long overdue, so we're glad they're being subjected to proper parliamentary and public scrutiny finally, and we'll be having a close look at the details. "Wider snooping powers will take the UK closer to becoming a surveillance state. "Just a few months ago the government admitted through gritted teeth that they'd been spying on Amnesty International and another NGO".[31] On 06 November 2015, Investigatory Power Bill was introduced by the government that threatened to institutionalise some highly intrusive surveillance powers, the likes of which the UK has never seen before. Blanket, Indiscriminate Interception and retention of people's communications by any other name is still mass surveillance and it can never be proportionate.

Moreover, on 07 October 2020, following the Privacy International initiated lawsuit, the European Court of Human Rights ruled that the UK government's Mass Interception Program violated the rights to privacy and freedom of expression because of insufficient safeguards and lack of oversight. Privacy International, on 08 January 2021, reported the UK court judgement on its case and quashed a previous decision by the Investigatory Powers Tribunal (IPT). The court signalled that fundamental constitutional principles still needed to be applied in the context of surveillance and that government agencies cannot circumvent traditional protections afforded by the common law. On 06 October 2020, Privacy International noted the court ruling repudiated mass surveillance regime in the UK:

"The Court of Justice of the European Union (CJEU) ruled that the mass surveillance programmes conducted by British, French and Belgian security agencies are not tenable under EU law. The ruling stated that instead of being the norm, bulk retention of communications data should only be permissible in the presence of a clear danger to national security. Aspects of EU law such as proportionality, fundamental rights to privacy, data protection, and freedom of expression should also be respected. Caroline Wilson Palow, legal director of Privacy International, said in a statement: "Today's judgement reinforces the rule of law in the EU. In these turbulent times, it serves as a reminder that no government should be above the law. Democratic societies must place limits and controls on the surveillance powers of our police and intelligence agencies." National security–which bulk data retention purportedly falls under–has typically been left up to member states. This latest ruling overturns this assumption and says that this activity should also be in line with EU law. However, the ruling offers some wiggle room to snooping states. It stipulates that if a member state is facing a serious threat to national security, through appropriate legislative measures it can conduct general and indiscriminate retention of data. However, this is only acceptable for a limited period during which time it's strictly necessary".[32]

These all-embracing developments forced British Intelligence Chiefs to explain the importance of Britain's intelligence sharing and security cooperation with the EU. On 20 June 2018, in a speech in Brussels, the GCHQ Chief Jeremy Fleming's statement was evident of his irritation about the dilapidating security crisis. He firmly demanded intelligence cooperation with the EU allies. In his speech, Fleming said; "After Brexit, the UK will continue to work with the EU. Fleming stated. On 14 May 2018, former Chief of MI5, Mr. Andrew Parker consistently demanded cooperation with the EU intelligence agencies: "In today's world, we need that shared strength more than ever. I can say confidently that the way we work together has prevented loss of life in the EU." These statements were clear signs of irritation.[33]

The Prime Minister did not bring to bear the concerns of intelligence Chiefs about the consequences of Brexit. In the aftermath of these criticisms, the government introduced National Security Capability Review (2018) to tackle national security challenges, but growing influence of extremist forces across the country[34], casted doubt on the credibility of law enforcement agencies, and highlighted the weak approach of the May government to national security. The first major strategic failure of the review was that it didn't elucidate security road-map. This lack of strategic clarity has been highlighted by the Joint Committee on the National Security Strategy (JCNSS), the main parliamentary body scrutinising its implementation". The country's National Security Strategy also missed the boat to keep momentum with emerging threats and didn't adequately respond to the exponentially growing threat of radicalization.[35] In its 04 June 2018 version, the U.K. Counter-Terrorism Strategy highlighted many vulnerabilities, citing the proliferation of jihadism, and a growing number of terror networks across the country, which prompted negative perceptions about its operational effectiveness, and popularity.[36], However, several new amendments were added to the National Security Strategy, Strategic Defence and Security Review, and Cyber Security Strategy, to make effective law enforcement and intelligence infrastructure against radicalized forces, lone wolves and foreign espionage, but these amendments were not a proper panacea to the looming security crisis.[37]

From January to June 2019, more than 100 people in England were killed, and 100 more were injured in different incidents, but police and law enforcement agencies never realised how to address concerns of communities. Interestingly, no single Muslim was found behind these attacks, while former Home Secretary Sajid Javed shamelessly linked terrorism to Islam. His verboseness against Islam appeared in a recent report of Christian Today newspaper: "Islam has been responsible for terrorist attacks in Britain....... "It is 'lazy' and 'wrong' to suggest terror has nothing to do with Islam. But I think it is absolutely fair to say that there is a special burden on Muslim Communities because whether we like or not these terrorists call themselves Muslims, the newspaper reported.[38]The Home Secretary acted irresponsibly and did not take into account the concerns of Muslim communities.

Intelligence agencies in the UK are playing an important role in fighting serious organised crimes and the UK police is a competent organization in its fight against extremism, terrorism and domestic violence, but political interference, racism, and discrimination has emaciated its infrastructure, resolve and engagement. In newspapers and social media, we read news of our police involvement in crimes, murder and racism that damaged its abilities and professional approach in dealing with challenges of national security and law enforcement. We also need to improve tradecraft approach, it requires the application and compliance of organisational practises in a diverse range of operating environments. The emergence of different types of national security challenges, insect war, and foreign involvement in the country's domestic affairs damaged and emaciated our whole system of governance. Experts Ian Stanier and Jordan Nunan in their recent analysis (The impact of COVID-19 on UK informant use and management, Policing and Society) have highlighted the impact of Pandemic on the work and performance of intelligence informants:

"Understanding the consequences of a failure to collect intelligence on a society is important. The collection of information is a core role of policing (Ericson and Haggerty 1997) and can improve the quality of decision-making at all levels of an organisation and is key to organisational understanding (James 2016). Intelligence-based decision-making reduces ambiguity (Betts 1978), it can influence organisation target selection, determine operational priorities and inform tactical choices to be applied against threats. Any reduction in the supply of informant intelligence may weaken law enforcements' operational response capability, thereby threatening community safety, and trust and confidence in policing. The use and management of informants are not without its challenges. Informant deployment is undertaken within a complex and dynamic operational environment. Abuses, including entrapment by informants have previously undermined judicial and public confidence in the collection capability (Aaronson, 2013, Harfield and Harfield 2018, Norris, 2019). Nonetheless, the informer plays a central role in threat identification and harm reduction across a range of offending types, such as tackling volume crime, burglary, youth crime and gangs (Balsdon 1996, Neyroud and Beckley 2001, IPCO 2019). Informants are pivotal to law enforcement efforts to tackle drug supply (Williams and Guess 1981, Dorn et al. 1992, Bean and Billingsley 2001), domestic extremism and terrorism (Hewitt 2010). In Northern Ireland, their use as a key source of information against loyalist and nationalist terrorism was, and still is, critical (Bamford 2005, Charters 2013)".[39]

In March 2021, anti-protest measures, or highly controversial covert human intelligence act became law in the UK, while the government proposed a police, crime, sentencing and court bill that contains new powers to clamp down on the right to protest. Statewatch, monitoring the state and civil liberties in Europe (11 March 2021) in its report noted the covert human intelligence sources (Criminal Conduct Act). Covert Human Intelligence agents might be secret police officers, informers and state agents. They will be instructed from police departments and intelligence offices. One of the most controversial aspects of the law, Statewatch noted is the fact that it contains no human rights safeguards of its own, and instead refers to the Human Rights Act 1988:

"With the CHIS Act on the books, the government has now published the Police, Crime, Sentencing and Courts Bill. This contains a whole host of measures, some of which may have positive effects, such as further laws on child abuse. However, it also plans stricter sentencing rules, new stop and search powers, and provisions that would criminalise trespass (currently a civil offence), which appears to be primarily targeted at gypsy and traveller groups but could also have serious negative effects for protesters, ramblers, wild swimmers and many others. The campaign group Friends, Families and Travellers (FFT) notes that: "Whilst the majority of over 26,000 responses to the Government's consultation did not support the proposals, the Government announced that it planned to still go ahead with plans to strengthen police powers against roadside camps. Under the Government's plans, a new criminal offence will be introduced for people living on roadside camps which could result in people being imprisoned, fined or having their home removed from them." Existing powers will also be extended -despite even the police stating that they don't need new powers to deal with unauthorised encampments, FFT underscores. The Bill also contains specific measures to crack down on protest. The government says these new powers will keep people safe and "ensure that they can get on with their daily lives peacefully and without unnecessary interference."[40]

Policing in the UK is at a turning point as government is trying to harness its digital opportunities, persisting technologies, or intending to modernise police services. The UK policing forces do not operate in nothingness, police is already active and visible on roads and streets. The policing strategy outlined commitments to develop ethics for national data and governance models, and establish core principles, providing clear lines of accountability on data use. This strategy also tests operational deployment of new capabilities which approach ethical boundaries. In 1993, the Audit Commission had identified "a vicious cycle of failure to address crime" and subsequent enquiry revealed that there was in fact a huge variation nationally of intelligence practises which inhibited the flow of information locally, regionally and nationally. In 1999, the National Criminal Intelligence Service (NCIS) created (National Intelligence Model-NIM) which is based upon the "collective wisdom and best practice" nationally and internationally. However, national policing digital strategy: Digital, data and technology strategy-2020-2030 has established policing principles and morals to fulfil their functions and duties:

"A number of the priorities set out in this strategy are underpinned by data; from sharing information across forces and partners, to collecting new data sources provided by digital channels and platforms, and applying data analytics, and AI to assist decision making. Appropriate and transparent consideration of ethics in pursuing these priorities is critical to maintaining the integrity of our policing service and the trust of the public. We will be faced with decisions on what information we choose to acquire, the methods used to transfer and store it, and how we use it to inform actions. These decisions will need to be guided by collective debate, and made open to scrutiny to maintain public trust".[41]National intelligence model with focus on operational policing, is an expert of crime prevention agencies. National Ballistics Intelligence Service is another policing agency that performs a crucial part in UK policing working with the police forces of England, Wales, and Scotland. The Home Office National Centre for Policing Excellence, in its published policing strategy about the operational mechanism of National Intelligence Model has highlighted important aspects of the agency effectiveness:

"At the heart of the business process is the Strategic and Tactical Tasking and Coordination Group Meetings. The process is conducted at three levels to correspond with the specified levels of incidents: Level 1 represents local crime capable of being managed by local resources (which may include the most serious crime) and anti-social behaviour; Level 2 represents force, inter-force and regional criminal activity usually requiring additional resources; and Level 3 represents the most serious and organised crime. The purpose of the Strategic Tasking and Coordination Group Meetings is to agree a control strategy which establishes the intelligence requirement and sets the agenda for intelligence, prevention and enforcement priorities. The purpose of the Tactical Tasking and Coordination Group Meetings is to apply a planned response to the control strategy. The National Intelligence Model is not confined to or restricted for specialist usage. It is relevant to all areas of law enforcement: crime and its investigation, disorder and community safety. Overall, it is a model for operational policing. As such, effective application of the National Intelligence Model should enable police forces to trace the continuum between anti-social behaviour and the most serious crime and then to identify those local issues in most urgent need of attention. The model is compatible with other operational policing methodologies, in particular those which focus on problem solving by using analytical techniques".[42]

European Union introduced its common security policy more than two decades ago. The interconnectedness of violent threats and their mounting effect pose grave dangers to the aptitude of a state to professionally secure its territorial integrity. Home-grown extremism and radicalization continue to expose a significant threat to the National Security of the EU and Britain. The risks from state-based threats have both grown and diversified. The unmethodical and impulsive use of a military-grade nerve agent on British soil is the worse unlawful act of bioterrorists. Research associate, National Centre for Scientific Research, Paris, France, Dr Hager Ben Jaffel and Senior Lecturer, University of Sunderland, Dr Jeremy Pearson, (Intelligence,

Law Enforcement and Brexit-26 Feb 2021) in there analysis highlighted function of intelligence and law enforcement in Britain:

"Over the past years, the heated debates over Brexit have only reinforced the widespread belief that Britain is an awkward partner in EU affairs. However, no matter how controversial Brexit is, Brexit is not the end of Britain's ties with the EU. Rather, it's the continuation of these. This is particularly true in the field of intelligence cooperation. Paying attention to practises – what those in charge of intelligence 'do'–sheds light on long standing intelligence ties between Britain and the EU that will persist despite Brexit. To understand this, it is necessary to take a look at who does intelligence. Today, intelligence is no longer just about intelligence services, spies and espionage but involves an increasing number of law enforcement bodies with responsibility for countering terrorism, organised crime and other security threats. One telling example is the police and its intelligence units located in each of the 43 police forces across the UK, among which the late Special Branch of the Metropolitan Police (before its merger with the Anti-Terrorist Branch into the Counter-Terrorism Command) is the most famous example.......Brexit is a mechanism similar to that of the opt-out: it's an in-and-out process which involves leaving the EU while forging a new relationship with the EU on security issues. This is demonstrated by the deal reached last December, which retains the participation of UK law enforcement in a number of EU arrangements. Second, we need to think about how UK law enforcement responds to a political decision like Brexit. Brexit, like the opt-out from JHA, suggests that security issues are also political. Politicians recognise the need to maintain security cooperation with the EU, but this does not prevent them from defining it according to political arguments such as 'national sovereignty'."[43]

Adding insult to injury was the country's Snoopers Charter Surveillance (SCS) and the government's war on civilian privacy. Liberty, a British human rights organization noted the powers of the Snoopers Charter Surveillance and data collection methods that were causing communities irksomeness: "When the U.K. government passed a law allowing the mass collection of data from all U.K. citizens.....The Investigatory Power Act, more popularly known as the 'Snoopers' Charter,' allow for the indiscriminate collection of data".[44]The police practically started using Snooper Charter Surveillance on a borough-level to monitor communities and their activities by the day. Recently, Liberty and Privacy International called on local communities to report the negative impacts of this consternating and offensive surveillance of local policing authorities, to the Police and Crime Commissioner. The way local police stations use modern surveillance technologies in streets and markets have put our privacy at risk. From car surveillance to mobile phone and drone technologies, the police forces have an unparalleled view into the lives of ordinary British citizens.

Individual liberty and human rights groups recently warned that excessive and offensive use of surveillance tools by the police might alienate communities from the state and government: "From facial recognition in streets to monitoring social media and mobile phones, the police are not open and honest about what tech they use, where they use it, who they use it against and what laws allow them to do so. However, surveillance tech is being used without the public knowledge or consent, on the ground that 95% percent civilians know nothing about the evolving and changing operational mechanism of police surveillance in cities, towns, and streets".[45]More worrisome is the unauthorised surveillance in which South Asian intelligence agencies are using their spies (students, political activists and local resident) against their political opponents, writers and journalists. They are cruising in cities, high streets, markets, mosques and towns with impunity, and receive their salaries through a third person, or from their embassies. Intelligence and policing units of Pakistan, India and Bangladesh embassies are spying on their opponents and critics.[46]

The British Counter-Extremism and Counter-Intelligence capabilities have broken to control these illegal activities of Pakistani and Indian embassies in London. British law enforcement agencies are facing multifaceted crises, including the lack of public confidence, common operational mechanism, and a lacklustre technical approach to domestic security.[47] The UK National Security Council also lacked professional capacity to implement policy properly. Since the UK voted to leave the EU in 2016; huge questions surrounding its place in the international community were left unanswered. Former Prime Minister Theresa May sacked her defence Minister, Gavin Williamson over the leaks of security secrets of the discussion of National Security Council about the Chinese Huawei crisis. This act of the Prime Minister proved that many things were not going in right direction within her government.[41] Iinar research paper underlined crucial aspects of the NSC and its significance to national security. Institute for Government research associates Dr. Joe Devanny and Josh Harris assert that:

"The NSC is a relatively new committee, but it is only the latest iteration of over a century of Prime-Ministerial efforts to coordinate national security issues from the centre. To date, there have been few sustained attempts to examine the NSC and its performance. Four and a half years of different

Prime Ministers choose to approach the issue, structure, and appointment of senior advisors in different ways. It is important that the centre of government can accommodate each Prime Minister's preferred way of working. Few Prime Ministers now take office with much experience of National Security issues, and National Security coordination is rarely a key theme in general election campaigns. But no Prime Minister needs to reinvent the wheel once in office; their predecessors have grappled with similar problems of coordination for over a century."[48]

The Covid-19 hydra tested the resolve and strength of the UK's Asian and Black Communities amidst shameless propaganda of British newspapers about their vulnerability against the Covid-19, but all strategies and plans failed to terrify and profile them as a source of spreading virus. In a report, Public Health of England (PHE) acknowledged the disproportionate effect the pandemic has had on black, Asian and minority ethnic (BAME) people, including making us more likely to become critically ill, and to die. BBC (02 June 2020) quoted two reports which noted vulnerability of Black people-almost four times more likely to die of Covid-19, according to the Office of National Statistics, while Asians were up to twice as likely to die, but they failed to profile them as a source of virus spread. As the crisis thrust British society into unfamiliar contexts, from panic to social distancing and restrictive state rules, it pitted individual interests against the groups and skepticism against trust. Tej Parikh, (Asia Times, 15 June 2020) highlighted several aspects of the racism campaign organized by British media against Black and Asian communities.

In 2020, the UK National Health Service (NHS) shamelessly refused to treat elderly patients during the lockdown. A Sunday Times investigation revealed the extent to which the elderly were neglected by the NHS during the full lockdown. There were 59,000 extra deaths in England and Wales compared to yesteryears. This consisted of 26,000 excess fatalities in care homes and another 25,000 patients in their own homes. Politicians realized the deep pain of these deaths. They were in remonstrance and challenged the authority of the government. Territorial Support Group–the paramilitary wing of the Metropolitan Police was dispersing peaceful anti-lockdown protestors. The abrupt prevalence of Covid-19, followed by lockdowns and restrictions across the country, reduction in political and financial activities, empty highways, and curtailment in travel, air, and land transport, caused pain and consternation. A considerable number of British and European nationals put forward the court cases of their mothers, grand-mothers, fathers and grands-father, sisters and brothers-

died in care homes due to the negligence of health workers, doctors and care home owners. Analyst Clare Dyer in his BMJ commentary (on 15 June 2020, Covid-19: Woman whose father died in care home launches legal review over government's "litany of failures") noted a woman whose father died in a care home launched a judicial review in the High Court over the government's "litany of failures" in protecting the vulnerable elderly residents who were most at risk from covid-19:

"Cathy Gardner accused England's health and social care secretary, Matt Hancock, NHS England, and Public Health of England of acting unlawfully in breaching statutory duties to safeguard health and obligations under the European Convention on Human Rights, including the right to life. Her father, Michael Gibson, who had Alzheimer's disease, died aged 88 of probable covid-19 related causes on 03 April 2020 at Cherwood House Care Centre, near Bicester, Oxfordshire. She claims that before his death the care home had been pressured into taking a hospital patient who had tested positive for the virus but had not had a raised temperature for about 72 hours. "I am appalled that Matt Hancock can give the impression that the government has sought to cast a protective ring over elderly residents of care homes, and right from the start," Gardner said. "The truth is that there has been at best a casual approach to protecting the residents of care homes. At worst the government has adopted a policy that has caused the death of the most vulnerable in our society." The case was filed at the High Court on 12 June 2020, the day the National Audit Office published a report confirming that around 25 000 patients were discharged from hospitals to care homes at the height of the pandemic before testing became routine. The application for judicial review accuses Hancock, NHS England, and PHE of failure to take into account the vulnerability of care home residents and staff to infection and death and the inadequacy of testing and personal protective equipment availability at the time. It contends that there was a "disproportionate, discriminatory, and irrational" focus on freeing hospital capacity at the expense of risking the lives of care home residents and staff".[50]

The global pandemic, and the wider governmental and societal response, is certainly bringing health inequalities into sharp focus. Factors such as age, gender, ethnicity and socioeconomic deprivation are all known to be important. Critically, these factors combined in complex ways to put some people at much greater risk. The Covid-19 lockdowns politics well consecutively exacerbated our pain and anxiety about our social and economic prospects. We must think that a sharp economic downturn has already begun, and we could be facing the worst depression as the government has failed to adopt a positive approach towards the deepening crisis. On 05 November 2020, Prime Minister Boris Johnson imposed a second national lockdown for England and said: "Christmas is going to be different this year, perhaps very different, but it's my sincere hope and belief that by taking tough action now we can allow families across the country to be together."[51] However, he admitted in a Downing Street news conference that he was wrong in his opinion. Prof Neil Ferguson, who's modelling was crucial to the decision to impose the first lockdown, said keeping universities and schools open meant infections would decrease more slowly this time. The month-long lockdown had to suppress the virus, but what was less clear was the No-10 approaches that whether the government could be in a better position to stop it rebounding. There were calls to fix the test and trace service, but that was easier said than done.

The lockdown decision for England comes as scientists warned the NHS could be "overwhelmed within weeks", and documents suggested the UK was on course for a much higher death toll than during the first wave. Sir Jeremy Farrar, director of the Wellcome Trust, said restrictions were not enough to stop the virus spreading and without action, "there's absolutely no doubt that many more of us would have seen loved ones die, suffer with long-term Covid symptoms or from other illnesses". Analyst Jeff Harris, (Global Research, October 30, 2020) critically argued: "Ever since the alleged pandemic erupted this past March 2020, the mainstream media spewed a non-stop stream of misinformation that appears to be laser-focused on generating maximum fear among the citizenry. But the facts and the science simply don't support the grave picture painted of a deadly virus sweeping the land. Yes we do have a pandemic, but it' a pandemic of ginned up pseudo-science masquerading as unbiased fact. Here are nine facts backed up with data, in many cases from the CDC itself that paints a very different picture from the fear and dread being relentlessly drummed into the brains of unsuspecting citizens".[52]

On 04 Nov, 2020, Prime Minister Boris Johnson was criticised after he walked out of the House of Commons as soon as his predecessor former Prime Minister Theresa May started presenting her criticism of his handling of Covid-19 restrictions. Johnson was filmed leaving the chamber as May took aim at England's new four-week lockdown."This pandemic has challenged governments across the world, and Ministers have been under relentless pressure in dealing with this issue," May said. "Boris Johnson is such a petty, ungracious character, "said Labour's Shadow Health Secretary

Jonathan Ashworth, reacting to the incident and tweeting footage of it unfolding. The SNP's Neil Gray labeled Johnson's act "graceless to say the least."[53]

On 06 November 2020, Lockdown Sceptics quoted an article of Professor Carl Heneghan and Dr Tom Jefferson from the Oxford Centre for Evidence-Based Medicine in Daily Telegraph criticizing government's failures in presenting clear, honest, reliable data to justify its decisions. "The data failures in this pandemic have been considerable: continually they have overestimated the numbers going to die miscategorised COVID-19 deaths, exaggerated the impact on hospitals, and missed some 16,000 cases because of an Excel blunder". Lockdown Sceptics reported former Prime Minister Theresa May statement: "For many people, it looks as if the figures are chosen to support the policy rather than the policy being based on the figures." Lockdown Sceptics noted. The growing number of errors seems to occur in only one direction (the worst case scenario) which underpins the point. The combination of loneliness, lockdown, and denial of a cheap and evidence-based treatment amounts to an abysmal failure of the most vulnerable members of our society. Lockdown Sceptics reported Chris Whitty and others claims that the restrictions had an impact on helping curtail the spread.[54]

Chapter 3

Facial Recognition Technology, Biological Terrorism and Mass Surveillance

The UK police and intelligence agencies are using facial recognition technology systems to identify criminal and terror suspects. Facial recognition technology could be seen as a logical extension of technology-based surveillance. Recent rise in these technologies in Britain have received countrywide criticism from different experts and intellectual forums that police has failed to get a satisfactory result when these computationally extracting facial technology capture a picture of a wanted person on a digital video image. In states like Australia, US and UK, these technologies have been fitted to factories, airports, shopping malls, and government buildings. Human rights organizations have demanded that live facial recognition technology should not be used in public spaces. More than thirty human rights groups including Statewatch, and Amnesty International demanded the British parliament to take action and ban the public deployment of live facial recognition technology. By installing these technologies, a huge shift in relations between the state and citizens occurred.

The CoronaVirus (Insects War) impacts on national security have been immeasurable since March 2020 when the government imposed all round-sweeping mass-surveillance on the civilian population to monitor their daily life, movements, and businesses. British intelligence got a good time and iron in the fire to exercise its powers and update data and surveillance related operational mechanisms. From the beginning, both MI5 and GCHQ were on the waterfront to practically demonstrate their expertise and test their own capabilities on civilian ground. Some intelligence experts argued that GCHQ was more effective at mass-surveillance due to TEMPORA's access to all telephone and internet communications—including Facebook and email—across Europe. The TEMPORA is composed of different components codenamed POKERFACE and the XKEYSCORE. In his

2016 television interview, Edward Snowden revealed that the NSA and GCHQ were using a new surveillance system called MUSCULAR, one of at least four other similar programs that rely on a trusted second party. While the virus spread in February 2020, Surveillance Agencies and the army Brigade-77 concentrated information gathering on the spread of Covid-19 and its fatalities. Analyst Paul Rogers (UK security services face some awkward questions when the pandemic is over, OpenDemocracy-30 March 2020) in his well-written article noted failure of intelligence agencies in tackling the virus:

"The failures in the British response to the pandemic goes deeper than the Prime Minister's personal flaws. They are rooted in an entrenched misunderstanding of international security, defence and the role of intelligence and security services, as well as wider issues of political culture. The new investigative reporting organization, Declassified UK, which I advise, has in the past month published a series of hugely informed analyses of some of these failures. Analyst Nafeez Ahmed pointed out that six years ago the UK Cabinet Office's National Risk Register for Civil Emergencies warned that "a global disease outbreak was likely within five years. Despite that, the government's subsequent pandemic planning remained unfit for purpose. That very year, the UK's Centre for Health and the Public Interest, a public health think-tank, warned that Britain's National Health Service (NHS) was unprepared for the impact of such a pandemic. "In a further Declassified UK report, Matt Kennard wrote that there was little if any evidence that MI5 or MI6 have taken the risk of a pandemic seriously, even though the heads of these security services in recent years have tended to make public statements about their priorities. This lack of concern is striking, given that the government's own National Risk Register for Civil Emergencies noted in 2017 that "consequences... for pandemic flu [may include] up to 50% of the UK population experiencing symptoms, potentially leading to between 20,000 and 750,000 fatalities and high levels of absence from work".[1]

The Covid-19 exposed the credibility of our intelligence and surveillance agencies and their approach to tackle the disease. The fact is, by changing national security and espionage mechanisms in Britain, agencies spied on every citizen regardless of his/her political and religious background, they used technology, private partners and people from minority groups who used surveillance on communities with impunity. They were collecting data, personal information and analysing government efforts across the country. Gordon Corera (April 2020) in his paper uncovered all these illegal and unethical means of spying on civilian population:

"In the past, it might have contained details about a planned terrorist attack-perhaps a cell in the Middle East looking at a new way of taking down an airline. This would lead to the well-practised national security machine cranking into gear. But in the future, that report may instead be about an outbreak of a virus in a far-off country which was being concealed by its government. Since the 9/11 attacks nearly 20 years ago, national security has been dominated by terrorism. But there have been voices over the years who have argued the notion of 'security' should be broadened and the coronavirus crisis has raised a significant question about whether global health security should be a more central part of national security. Under the last review, an international pandemic was classed as a Tier 1 national security risk in the UK-meaning it was judged to be of the highest priority - but that has not been reflected in the resources or the way in which the issue has been tackled when compared with the other three threats at the same level-terrorism, war and cyber-attacks. For spy agencies, adapting may take a significant gear change. A priority for policy-makers will be to know the ground-truth about the health situation in another country. For agencies like MI6 and the CIA that recruit human sources, it may mean ensuring you have agents in the right place who can report back on what is really happening. There may also be shifts in what agencies who intercept communications look for and in technical intelligence, satellites may be tasked to look at medical or even burial sites. Just as technology was developed to remotely 'sniff' for traces of nuclear material, new devices may be required to scan for health and bio-threats. But that is still largely the traditional world of intelligence gathering. The real future may be in the use of more complex data sets and artificial intelligence to spot, understand and predict developments in a population."[2]

The exponentially growing number of crime and terrorist incidents in Europe and the UK forced local governments to implement measures and strategies to prevent proliferation of anti-state elements. Member States police and law enforcement agencies were countering terrorist nests and cooperated with each other in case of data and intelligence sharing, but this sharing proved ineffective when terrorists targeted London, Paris and Nice. The pandemic economy presented new business opportunities for criminals attempting to capitalise on goods high in demand and the fear induced by the COVID-19 virus. As the pandemic still dancing in our towns and cities, online discussions, and newspapers reporting on

Asian and Black minority communities, in which they attempted to profile these communities as a source of spreading virus, the brutal killing of George Floyd, and the emergence of Black Lives Matter movement were developments that spotlighted government's weakness in fighting Covid-19-related national security threats. These fears were compounded by the faltering of Britain's foremost anti-terrorism strategy, "The Prevent." Designed to intercept extremist violence by presenting would-be attackers with a peaceful counter-narrative, the program was designed and delivered locally by teachers, and healthcare practitioners. In a more direct way, too, the pandemic proved fertile ground for radical propagandists bent on spreading hate. Hindu and Christian fundamentalists, for instance, were known to have used social media to profile Muslims as the prime source of spreading Pandemic.

On 03 November 2020, BBC reported elevation of the UK's terrorism threat level from "substantial" to "severe". In November 2021, the threat level was again elevated after suicide attacks. We have been experiencing severe, substantial and other levels of terrorism threat levels in the UK since the last 20 years, but never seen practical approach and professional demonstration for eliminating terror networks. Intelligence Chiefs believed that an attack was highly likely but there was no specific intelligence of an imminent incident. Home Secretary Priti Patel said the British people should be "alert but not alarmed". "This is a precautionary measure following the horrific events in France and Austria and is not based on a specific threat."[3] However, head of UK counter-terrorism policing Assistant Commissioner Neil Basu echoed the Home Secretary's comments that there was no intelligence to link any of the attacks in France or Austria to the UK but said his officers were working with international partners. The BBC security correspondent Frank Gardner said "given events in Austria and France, it would have been "remiss" of the government not to raise the threat level. He said the JTAC, which brings together analysts from across transport, health, intelligence and the military, were constantly analysing the ongoing threat to UK citizens anywhere in the world, and will have looked at what has happened in Vienna and at all the postings from al-Qaeda and the Islamic State group, encouraging people to carry out attacks."[4]

Terrorists executed attacks in the UK and Europe by different means, and used assorted tactics in order to deceive law enforcement agencies. Communication and information technologies that covered every aspect of our lives were of great importance for a digitalized economy, but this time they failed to recognize terror suspects. The development of hardware and software facilitated an interconnected digital environment, prioritized efficiency, cost and the convenience of the user. The aggrandisement of computers and Internet into a smart system was extending the threat of remote exploitation to a whole host of new technologies. The UK National Cyber Security Strategy (2016-2021) supported all these developments and changing medical technologies, satellite and traffic control systems that connected to the Internet and, therefore, potentially vulnerable to interference. The threat of cyber terrorism in the UK stretched out attacks from a safe distance caused financial damages. National security—in its traditional sense—is associated with the protection of the territorial integrity and sovereignty of a state, as well as its critical interests abroad. However, the lethal nature of pandemics is increasingly raising scientific awareness about their national security dimensions.[5]

Terror incidents in France and Vienna forced the Johnson administration to impose immediate lockdown in England to prevent terror attacks. On 18 April 2019, in Northern Ireland, journalist Lyra McKee was fatally shot when a 'new IRA' gunman opened fire during rioting in Londonderry's Creggan area. There were three other attacks by Dissident Republican (DR) groups in 2019. In January, a vehicle-borne Improvised Explosive Device (IED) was detonated outside the courthouse in Londonderry, shortly after police received a warning and moved to evacuate surrounding buildings. In March, a postal IED sent to Heathrow Airport partially functioned, and, in August, police were called to a hoax device near Wattle bridge, County Fermanagh, where a concealed secondary device exploded as officers investigated. No one was injured in these incidents. Other attacks in 2019 failed. Three further small, basic postal IEDs which were sent to targets in London and Glasgow while another device discovered at a postal depot in Ireland failed to function. According to the MI5 report; "new IRA" "has represented the main dissident threat for a number of years" and "it is at the forefront of our minds that the 'new IRA' could become a still more dangerous threat". While there was "an initial public backlash [against the 'new IRA'] in the aftermath of the murder of Lyra McKee", MI5 told us that the group had "rallied almost immediately".[6]

British police and intelligence agencies are undoubtedly well-trained, but their ranks have dwindled. Over the past two decades, police have been a less visible presence in the streets, relying on technology to provide them with visibility in towns and cities. Since 2005, intelligence collection has been mostly dependent on CCTV, mobile phones, and surveillance technology to deal with threats like foreign espionage and international terrorism. Conversely, in a majority of EU member states, human intelligence accompanied by a technical approach to national security challenges was of great importance. In the U.K., changes were proposed to improve professionalism and competence of police intelligence (National Intelligence Model, Special Branch, MI5, CID, Cyber Forces) and counter-espionage programs, but political and bureaucratic stakeholders resisted every reform package. Live facial recognition surveillance cameras in the UK, demonstrated as biometric identification checkpoints, are a threat to our privacy. The UK Information Commissioner's Office once stated: "the blanket, opportunistic and indiscriminate processing, even for short periods, of biometric data belonging to thousands of individuals in order to identify a few minor suspects or persons of interest would not meet the high bar required by the law". However, the Surveillance Camera Commissioner said: "overt use of such advancing technology is arguably more invasive than some covert surveillance techniques." The Information Commissioner's Office has acknowledged that live facial recognition surveillance can "affect large numbers of people, in many cases without their knowledge.

The Independent Police Complaints Commission (IPCC) was the only oversight institution designed to improve the competence of the police force, but its efforts went unacknowledged. The commission was established in 2004 to investigate the conduct of police forces. On January 8, 2018, the Independent Police Complaints Commission was renamed as the Independent Office for Police Conduct (IOPC), because it's past performance and achievements were not satisfactory. The Policing and Crime Act 2019 also introduced some changes in the system, but these changes were not implemented. The Home Office and the British Parliament's Intelligence and Security Committee (ISC) remained imperfect with limited capacity for maintaining and conducting oversight over a powerful intelligence infrastructure. Recent reforms were necessary, notwithstanding the ISC remains a weak body over which the Prime Minister and government exercise their influence. The editors of The U.K.'s Changing Democracy noted some aspects of security sector reforms as they pertain to the ISC and surveillance operations:

"Choreographed evidence sessions between the committee and the service heads suggest an over-cooperative, too close relationship. So too does the past willingness of the committee to very promptly exonerate the GCHQ petabytes of the Snowden revelations and the charges of data collection and surveillance exceeding the agency's remit—a clearance that occurred while the revelations were still emerging. Although the ISC criticized the lack of privacy safeguards in the Investigatory Power Bill, it did not secure major changes in the final act. Security Sector Reforms (SSR) is a complex process. Narrowly defined, it can encompass institutions and organizations established to deal with external and internal threats to the security of the state and its citizens. At a minimum, therefore, the security sector includes military and paramilitary forces, the intelligence services, national and local police services, border, customs, and coast guards"[7] The introduction of mass surveillance programs by British and European intelligence services prompted a nationwide debate on the rights of civilians to be protected from illegitimate or warrantless collection, and analysis of their data and metadata. "Don't Spy on US," a coalition of organizations released a policy paper in September 2014 highlighting surveillance and intelligence operations and their impact on the privacy of citizens in the EU and U.K: "In summer 2013 it was revealed that GCHQ was routinely intercepting submarine fibre-optic cables containing private communication of millions of British residents (the 'TEMPORA' program). The reported scale of the interception is staggering: each day, GCHQ accesses some 21 petabytes of data—the equivalent of downloading the entire British Library 192 times."[8]

British counter-extremism and counter-intelligence capabilities have now broken after Brexit. They no more receive fresh intelligence information from Europe, and face difficulties in fighting extremism and terrorism. They also face a multifaceted crisis, including the lack of a common operational mechanism, and a lacklustre technical approach to domestic security. The U.K National Security Council also lacks professional capacity to implement policy and update the government on important matters. Since the U.K. voted to leave the EU in 2016; huge questions were unanswered surrounding its place in the international community. Prime Minister Theresa May sacked her Defense Minister, Gavin Williamson over the leaks of security secrets of the discussion of the National Security Council about the Chinese Huawei crisis. This act of the Prime Minister proved that many things were not going in the right direction within her government. Iinar research paper underlining crucial aspects of the NSC and its significance to national security. Institute for Government research associates Dr. Joe Devanny and Josh Harris assert that:

"The NSC is a relatively new committee, but it is only the latest iteration of over a century of Prime-Ministerial efforts to coordinate national security issues from the centre. To date, there have been few sustained attempts to examine the NSC and its performance. Four and a half years of different Prime Ministers choose to approach the issue, structure, and appointment of senior advisors in different ways. It is important that the center of government can accommodate each Prime Minister's preferred way of working. Few Prime Ministers now take office with much experience of National Security issues, and National Security coordination is rarely a key theme in general election campaigns. But no Prime Minister needs to reinvent the wheel once in office; their predecessors have grappled with similar problems of coordination for over a century. "There are a number of national security and law enforcement agencies performing different stabilization roles in the country. However, if one examines their cycle of information, analysis, and operational mechanism, one can conclude that, without the introduction of meaningful security sector reforms, they will be unable to respond to looming national security challenges.[9]

Chapter 4

Forget James Bond: Diversity, Inclusion and the UK's Intelligence Agencies

Daniel W. B. Lomas

Abstract

Diversity and inclusivity remain top priorities for UK intelligence, having been much maligned for the largely white, male stereotype. The Intelligence & Security Committee of Parliament has published a number of reports suggesting that, even in 2018, the UK's agencies were still behind Whitehall. Historically, there have been issues with female, BAME and LGBT representation, with the article placing today's criticism of the agencies in historical context with a particular focus on the period after 1945. The article also examines the position now and the steps taken by the agencies to promote change, suggesting there are grounds for cautious optimism.

In February 2021, the Times of London reported that Britain's foreign intelligence agency, the Secret Intelligence Service (SIS or MI6), was relaxing rules to allow applicants with dual UK nationality, or with one parent being a UK national or having 'substantial ties to the UK', to apply. Sources told the paper it was just the latest move to access a 'larger talent pool', adding: 'We want a diversification of thought, a diverse workforce, not people who all think in similar ways'.[1] Later, marking LGBT History Month 2021, SIS's Chief ('C') Richard Moore followed other agency heads in apologizing for the historical treatment of LGBT (Lesbian, gay, bisexual and transgender) officials and the bar to gay men and women serving in SIS. In a video shared on his Twitter feed, Moore said the ban deprived SIS of 'some of the best talent Britain could offer' and was 'wrong, unjust and discriminatory'.[2] Pink News also interviewed two LGBT SIS officers. 'I think the legacy of the ban has been . . . helping people understand that LGBT+ people aren't inherently untrustworthy', said 'Leia', a member of SIS's LGBT+ Affinity Group. 'It's drawn a line in the sand', she added.[3]

The statements and media coverage mark the latest in a series of announcements on the agency's commitment to diversity and change. In January 2021, tabloid newspapers reported on an SIS recruitment drive; specifically an advert, headlined 'Tell me a secret', calling for 'individuals with diverse skill sets and life experiences' to apply for part-time and consulting roles.[4] Responding, Moore tweeted his service's commitment to 'flexible working' and 'diversity', he added, acknowledging that Bond often shaped perceptions of the ideal intelligence officer.[5] Sir Colin McColl, 'C' from 1989 to 1994, once described the fictional intelligence officer as, in his view, 'the best recruiting sergeant in the world', yet successive Chiefs, like Moore, have tried to distance themselves, seeing Bond's legacy as both a blessing and a curse.[6] In October 2016, Moore's predecessor, Alex Younger, admitted he was 'conflicted' about Bond, on the one hand creating a 'powerful brand', although one that seemed exclusively white and male. 'For too long – often because of the fictional stereotypes I have mentioned – people have felt that there is a single quality that defines an MI6 officer', Younger told journalists in his first public speech in SIS's Vauxhall Cross headquarters, 'be it an Oxbridge education or a proficiency in hand-to-hand combat. This is, of course, patently untrue'. There was 'no standard MI6 officer'.[7]

Such statements show a clear determination by the UK's agencies to promote diversity and inclusivity, an issue that has received limited attention from academics. This article explores several themes. Firstly, it assesses inclusivity and diversity today, drawing on the reports of the Intelligence and Security Committee of Parliament (ISC) and from wider government to look at how the UK's agencies have responded to criticism on the recruitment, career pathways and the opportunities open to women, BAME (Black, Asian and minority ethnic), and LGBT groups. It compares the performance of the UK agencies against the performance of the wider civil service, concluding that the agencies have charted a similar pathway to analogous departments and that, although attracting criticism on occasion, they have moved a long way. Secondly, it also offers insights into how agency performance now is a prisoner of the past, suggesting that the late avowal has had a lasting effect that has been hard to overcome. It also offers insights into the position of such groups in the post-war British intelligence community, making the argument that the experiences of women, LGBT and ethnic minority groups – subjects that are worthy of articles in their own right –need to be studied under the broader subject of diversity as framed by the ISC's July 2018 report to fully understand progress. Thirdly, the article looks at UK agency efforts to promote diversity and change, arguing that the challenge has forced MI5, GCHQ and SIS to think in new ways about recruitment and to increasingly open up to break down traditional stereotypes.

The study of inclusion and the experiences of women, BAME, and LGBT groups across the history of the agencies is patchy and sporadic, the current literature generally conforming to what Jessica Shahan has called a 'white, male, well-spoken and educated' stereotype, that does little to add to perceptions of the social history of intelligence more widely, often confirming to many that the intelligence world reflects the traditional Bond-like cliché.[8] These stereotypes have real world impact; as Tammy Proctor observes, traditional views of who does intelligence 'still plague the women who try to work for intelligence'.[9] In April 2019, the polling organization YouGov asked whether people would like to join the UK intelligence agencies, just 39% of women (compared to 52% of men surveyed) saying they would consider a career in intelligence.[10] A follow up poll in June asked whether respondents would want to join MI5 or SIS; although 33% of men and women said they would join the Security Service, a minority of women (24%) wanted to join SIS compared to men (30%).[11]

Whereas those studying intelligence have been quick to use new file releases to broaden the history of the UK's agencies and the role of intelligence on policymaking, they have been relatively slow to focus on contemporary social history and themes of diversity and inclusion. Although the 'British school' of intelligence studies deserves plaudits for expanding the subject beyond the narrow 'missing dimension' it was – the subject now described as 'booming'[12] there has been little examination of the agencies' workforce and how representative it is of contemporary British society. If anything, researchers have been guilty of treading a familiar path that focuses on the operational and policy impact of intelligence, overlooking those 'doing intelligence' and the legacy of past practices still felt by the agencies now. To some extent, although it could be suggested that it has been necessary for intelligence academics to first establish an institutional framework to underpin the social history of the UK's agencies, the field of intelligence studies has been relatively slow to pick up on the work of Proctor and others to study the role of women and minority groups generally, though such themes have started to emerge.[13]

To fully understand UK intelligence, academics must expand beyond what the agencies do and the influence they have on policy. In short, the subject needs to 'diversify'.[14] It is also fair to say that the 'British school' has not been helped by the continued closure of records for much of the Cold War and access to data on who made up the agencies or the policies governing the recruitment and progression. Although the study of women in the Security Service (MI5) and the Government Code & Cipher School (GC&CS) is possible pre-1945 thanks to file releases to The National Archives (TNA), what little we do know of the agencies after this period comes largely from their authorized histories. Christopher Andrew's The Defense of the Realm, published in 2009, builds on themes raised by former Director-General Stella Rimington's memoir Open Secret[15] while John Ferris' study of the Government Communications Headquarters (GCHQ) provides a useful history of women and British signals intelligence, and the policies that excluded the BAME and LGBT communities.[16]

Both books are an important step forward, even if the social history of SIS after 1949 is yet to be told, and significant gaps remain in the story of diversity and inclusion generally for the second half of the 20th Century.[17] The result is that the social study of UK intelligence remains lopsided, now heavily focused towards the era of the two world wars.[18] Such studies are useful in identifying important themes in the social history of British intelligence, but do little to tell us about the state of diversity and inclusion today or place the recent criticism that the UK's agencies are unrepresentative in contemporary historical context. It is also worth echoing the point made by Jim Beach that the social dimension is still dominated by studies of 'personalities' not of 'personnel' generally, a point also made by Shahan who rightly points out that the search for 'individual and exceptional women' has resulted in a 'patchwork of gender'.[19]

It is also worth mentioning that while Chiefs have gone on record in Black and LGBT History Month to apologize for past discrimination and point to the positives today, the detail of what they are apologizing for remains hidden. 'My ultimate goal is for more people to consider a career in MI6 and to get rid of the myth that it's all about having studied at Oxford or Cambridge or having advanced hand-to-hand combat skills', Alex Younger said in October 2017, adding: 'That stereotype really couldn't be further from the truth'.[20] Yet the stereotype remains strong as we lack the history. Unfortunately, those looking to complete a comprehensive sociological analysis of agency recruitment and staffing based on archival research will be disappointed for a long time, the gap in knowledge largely filled by anecdote, memoir, and popular stereotype.[21] The irony is that while UK-based historians are able to study the experience of women and black employees in the US Central Intelligence Agency (CIA) since 1947, helped by the release of official agency files in 2013, we cannot do the same for the UK in the post-war period.[22]

It also is much easier study change across the modern-day US agencies, thanks to reports from the Office of Director of National Intelligence (ODNI).[23] In 2015, the ODNI launched its 'Equal Opportunity and Diversity Enterprise Strategy', and in June 2016 released its first intelligence community-wide data on agency demographics – information that had been provided to congressional oversight bodies from 2005. In January 2017, ODNI's Equal Employment Opportunity and Diversity Office, set up in 2006 to support the Chief of Equal Employment Opportunity, released a further report drawing on community-wide data, suggesting there was much room for improvement in policy affecting leadership, organizational culture, recruitment, career advancement, flexible working and maternity, and disability. Although the report concluded much had changed, leadership of the US intelligence community still lacked minority representation, while the agencies struggled 'to provide the type of inclusive workplace culture' to develop talent pipelines for leadership.[24]

In the UK, access to historical records and detailed data on modern-day recruitment and progression remains patchy. Though Andrew and Ferris provide insights into the experiences of women especially, historians are mostly unable to access historical documents on the in-house policies of the UK's agencies. Moreover, it is also clear that SIS's newfound openness has clear limits, appearing to be restricted to selected briefings and succinct, if largely welcome, and statements on the past. While Richard Moore's sincere apology on the treatment of gay men and women in the service rightly received widespread press attention and plaudits, the experience of women in the service after 1949 remains largely hidden and their story largely untold, even if progress was generally positive and one of progressive (if slow) change. Of course, this differs with other parts of Whitehall; the Foreign, Commonwealth & Development Office Historians have written extensively on diversity and the slow evolution of attitudes to gay men, race and gender. James Southern correctly highlights that research in the field 'serves as a basis for the beginning of a long-overdue conversation aimed at building a more inclusive organization' – a salutary lesson for some of the UK's agencies.[25]

If the history is generally lacking, so is the data. The reports of the ISC, first established under the Intelligence Services Act 1994 and its powers expanded under the Justice and Security Act 2013, provide broad detail on gender, LGBT, BAME and disability groups.[26] Generally, the figures show increasing diversity across the agencies, yet it does not explain what roles are filled by the growing numbers of women in the agencies. The absence of regular figures, detailed data and information also places some limits on the researcher, even if agency public speeches, social media feeds and websites provide more on recruitment and supporting diversity externally. The latest annual report for 2018–19 published in July 2020 contains no data unlike several previous reports; under 'diversity and inclusion' the report noting that MI5 came fourth place in the Stonewall Top 100 LGBT employers list, with SIS also obtaining a Stonewall Top 100 listing, while GCHQ launched REACH, a new network for race, ethnicity and cultural affinity.[27] Even the data itself, as the ISC acknowledges, 'is not sufficiently robust'.[28] As a result, this article will not be the full story, but it at least starts the conversation and offers a substantial platform for others to build on.

Diversity and the ISC

In July 2018, the Intelligence and Security Committee reported on Diversity and Inclusion in the UK intelligence Community. For several years, the committee had collected data on the diversity of staff, hearing first-hand of the importance of a varied talent pool across the intelligence community. The subject was not entirely new; the ICS's 2011–12 annual report, issued in July 2012, stated bluntly that the leadership of SIS, GCHQ and MI5 remained 'largely white, male-dominated'. Analysis of the numbers of staff in Senior Civil Service (SCS) grades[29] provided stark reading; just 12% in SIS's leadership were women. Ten of the 47 SCS in GCHQ (21%) were female – compared to 35% of women in the agency generally. For MI5, though women made up 40% of the workforce, just 21% were SCS. The committee also criticized the poor statistics on BAME, reaching the conclusion that, despite MI5 making a 'real effort to create an inclusive working environment', high non-declaration rates and a general lack of progress were worrying.[30]

GCHQ had come in for particular criticism from the Cabinet Office for 'poor' delivery against targets, then Director Ian Lobban agreeing in March 2012 that performance was 'not good enough'.[31] The government's response to the ISC noted the agencies had been doing much to create an 'ethnically-diverse workforce' with the long-term aim to recruit a broad talent pool which would in time lead to diversity 'at higher grades'.[32] In their next annual report, the ISC acknowledged the cultural and security impediments to quick change, yet added it was vital that the agencies fix the issue, not only to provide 'competitive advantage (increasing innovation and creativity amongst employees, and improving staff motivation and efficiency)' but also to address the range of threats facing the UK and, from an analytical standpoint, guard against the dangers of 'unacknowledged biases' or groupthink.[33] In short, diversity was necessary in the wider drive for equality and inclusion across government, and for operational reasons in light of the changed contemporary threats. Many of the issues seen in the ISC's earlier papers were reflected in the March 2015 report, Women in the UK Intelligence Community. 'Logically, if all intelligence professionals are cut from the same cloth, then they are likely to share "unacknowledged bias"', wrote Labor MP Hazel Blears in the preface.

'Diversity should therefore be pursued not just on legal or ethical grounds – which are important in themselves–but because it will result in a better response to the range of threats that we face to our national security.'[34] Generally, the report argued that despite positive work already underway, there was still much to be done to improve the recruitment and retention of women, finding that just 38% of the agencies' staff were female. Worse still, just 19% of agency leadership were women.[35] Internally, the report found that the focus on female role models, use of focus groups by MI5 and SIS to shape future recruitment and advice from wider women's networks were positive factors, SIS even seeing a 'small' increase in new female recruits by 2014. Yet the recruitment of women into technical and specialist roles was a particular problem, even if the ISC praised GCHQ's educational outreach programmes on science and computing. GCHQ were encouraged 'to ensure these activities encourage girls to engage at an early age, in order to overcome damaging perceptions that these are not subjects they might be interested in'. By contrast, it was reported that MI5 had looked at a similar programmes, concluding that 'cover and security issues' made it near impossible.[36]

Other than new candidates, the ISC also pointed to difficulties with maternity and flexible working arrangements, often impacting on the retention and progression of women already in the agencies, becoming effectively a 'brain drain' of highly talented officers. The ISC also noted that in-house culture impacted heavily on diversity, but remained stubbornly resistant to new ways of working: 'there still appears to be a sense of "this is the way it has always been done". Whilst those at the top of the organization may be personally committed to encouraging diversity, it is by managing

71

and tackling the behaviour of those at middle management level that they can best demonstrate that commitment'. As one unnamed senior female GCHQ official said, 'Having entered a male-dominated workplace where there are very few female role models, women often feel intimidated or encounter unconscious bias'.[37]

Claims that diversity and inclusion were not a top priority could not be levelled at the heads of the agencies. In July 2017, National Security Advisor Mark Sedwell, in the forward to the publication Mission Critical: Why Inclusion is a National Security Issues and What You Can do To Help, explained 'we need a national security workforce of different backgrounds, perspectives and ways of thinking', the paper identifying five ways that diversity was key: performance, recruitment, innovation, public trust, and cultural insights.[38] It was a message embraced by agency leadership. In a rare interview to blackhistorymonth.org.uk, Alex Younger said SIS's success depended on 'getting the very best and brightest . . . regardless of their background', adding: 'I want MI6 to be as diverse as the country it represents, and to attract the best from all its communities, including BAME'.[39]Speaking to the Cyber UK conference in April 2018, GCHQ Director Jeremy Fleming also admitted 'we don't always do enough to make a career accessible to everyone who could contribute to our mission' and, even if things had started to change, GCHQ needed to 'do better'.[40]MI5's then Director General Andrew Parker had also told a meeting of the campaign group 30% Club, committed to gender diversity on boards and senior management teams, that MI5 needed the 'richest mix of talents'[41]

Such sentiments could only go so far, the ISC's July 2018 report presenting a mixed picture. The central charge was that the UK's agencies were still not gender balanced at senior levels and did not 'fully reflect the ethnic make-up of modern Britain'.[42] Certainly, the ISC's findings made unpleasant reading for the agencies if parallels were drawn with the rest of Whitehall. By 2018, over half (54%) of civil servants were women.[43]Of the civil servants who declared their ethnicity as of March 2017, 11.6% were from an ethnic minority background, up half a percent from the year before.[44] By contrast, based on data from 2017, the committee showed that gender representation across all grades in GCHQ stood at 35.2% (in 1995 it was 28%[45]), SIS 38.9% and MI5 42.2%. The report also showed stubbornly low representation of all groups at SCS grades. Although the ratio of women on the Boards of all three agencies compared favorably with FTSE 100 companies, they were in a minority at most senior levels; the 2017 data showing that 31% of MI5's leadership were women, GCHQ having 27% and SIS just 24%.[46] This was a modest increase on three years earlier; data given to the ISC in August 2014 had showed SCS numbers for women in MI5 at 26.5%, GCHQ with 17% (10% below 2017 figures) and SIS at 15% (9% lower than 2017).

Of course, the smaller number of SCS grades made the data prisoner to fortune; for instance, while the ISC had reported that 21% of GCHQ's senior leadership were women in based on figures for 2011,[47] data for March 2015 showed a small drop to 18%. Nonetheless, the data suggested a long-term growth in the number of female SCS grades.[48] The same could not be said of BAME representation, a situation the committee found 'lamentable'. Only GCHQ had any ethnic minority staff in a senior position (just 4.8% of SCS grades).[49] In their reply, the government recognized that despite the good work there was 'still a long way to go'.[50] The story was slightly more positive for BAME recruitment generally; 8.6% of MI5's workforce came from ethnic minority backgrounds, SIS's BAME staff at 7.7% (up from 6% in 2015). The percentage of GCHQ's staff from ethnic minority backgrounds remained much lower at just 3.1%.[51] Explaining their findings and suggesting the path forward, the committee pointed to nationality rules and vetting as having a disproportionate effect on BAME candidates.

In particular, the committee argued that the nationality and residency rules needed to obtain Developed Vetting (DV) failed to keep up with 'changes in British society' and often had a negative impact on those seeking to join, while many vetting officers conducting interviews were 'white, male and middle-aged' suggesting a diverse pool of officers and unconscious bias training was needed.[52] At the recruitment stage it was also suggested that the agencies generally should target talent from underrepresented groups, even adopting more widely SIS's return to a traditional 'tap-on-the-shoulder' approach. Also, new ways of engagement and outreach were needed. Internally, other than improve the datasets available on recruitment and the workforce, the identification of new talent across all underrepresented groups was a priority to help individuals 'think more strategically about their careers, raise their ambitions and ultimately fulfil their potential'. Leadership was another area for change; the committee identifying the lack of BAME role models and fully integrating diversity and inclusion into agency objectives with the correct resourcing and effort.

The Time Factor

If the UK intelligence agencies were not fully representative of society, such criticism needs to be placed in historical context. For one former senior MI5 officer, the ISC's criticism overlooked the fact that the agencies had come a long way, pointing out that the Security Service had 'senior female staff for a long time', notably having two female Director General's– Dame Stella Rimington (1992–1996) and Baroness Manningham-Buller (2002–2007).[53]Another former officer points to the significant 'time lag' between the agencies and Whitehall, a factor the ISC itself had recognised.[54] The collapse of the Berlin Wall in 1989 and subsequent fall of the Soviet Union marked an important turning point. Even before the end of the Cold War, MI5 had already arrived at the conclusion that public avowal and a new legal framework was necessary, ultimately leading to the Security Service Act (1989). Changing times and the drive for openness in government also led GCHQ and SIS to follow a similar path, becoming statutory bodies under the 1994 Intelligence Services Act, and formally announcing SIS Chief Sir Colin McColl and GCHQ Director Sir John Adye.[55] But there were limits to openness; through MI5 gradually built up its public profile, McColl, one SIS officer told journalist Mark Urban, concluded that 'mystery and secrecy' remained essential to recruitment.[56]

In effect, recruitment remained largely 'disguised'.[57]The impact was an uneven approach to transparency. McColl's successor, Sir David Spedding, was publicly announced, yet the recruitment of intelligence officers remained fairly traditional and still 'Cold War focused'.[58] Even if requirements were changing, the recruitment of intelligence officers still largely revolved around the right universities and the old tap on the shoulder cliché, resulting in the recruitment, one officer recalled, of more 'male white dudes' from a small talent pool dominated by 'white Oxbridge groups'.[59] In today's digital environment, it seems extraordinary that SIS only set up its website in October 2005, the site receiving 3.5 million hits in the first few hours after going live. It was 'pretty astronomical', one Foreign Office official responsible for SIS media enquiries admitted.[60] By April 2006, the service went a step further launching its first public recruitment campaign with a half-page advert in The Times careers supplement, calling for 'operational officers' and 'efficient administrators'.[61]

In contrast, MI5 had launched its first public campaign in May 1997, which exceeded expectations by generating 12,000 calls to the advertising agency Austin Knight on the first day, though just four new candidates joined as a result.[62] Yet the unbalanced approach to public facing activity, added to the fact that parts of the intelligence community were far behind the rest of Whitehall. In the civil service generally, public facing and open to candidates to apply, women had typically accounted for just under half of civil servants, even if, as Rodney Lowe and Hugh Pemberton write in the authorized history of the UK civil service, they were generally concentrated at the bottom. Slower progress was made on the recruitment of BAME officials, estimated to be just 2% of the overall civil service.[63] Towards the end of the 1990s gender was reaching a near 50/50 split, while those Civil Servants who chose to declare their ethnicity reached 5.7%–slightly ahead of the 5.3% of 1000 D. W. B. LOMAS such groups in the economically active population, though, as before, such groups remained underrepresented in middle and senior leadership.[64]

Gender

Women working in post-war intelligence community long suffered, as with professional women across British society, with the inability to break through the 'glass ceiling' placed upon their careers.[65] Historically, while women had performed important clerical and administrative work across Britain's agencies – roles that were vital in the development of modern-day intelligence bureaucracies, their experience was certainly far beneath middle and senior management, a situation lasting well into the 1990s. Whether agent running or cryptanalysis, the view generally – as summarized by a former MI5 officer quoted in the service's authorized history–was that women were 'good NCOs' not management.[66] As future Director-General Stella Rimington found when she joined MI5 in 1969, men were recruited as 'officers' while women had their own career pathways, despite the fact she was ahead of many of the men, having a degree and joining in her mid-thirties. For both SIS and MI5 there was a traditional view that women would not make good agent runners; as late as February 1973, a meeting chaired by MI5 Director General Sir Michael Hanley reached the unanimous decision (supported by SIS's experience) that the running of agents was 'a male preserve', even if Rimington made history later that year by becoming the first women to be selected for MI5's agent running course.[67]

The pattern was a familiar one in SIS; Daphne Park, who joined in 1948, was a rare exception and no women were made full officers until the 1960s when 'one or two were allowed in before the door was once again slammed shut until the late 1970s'.[68] For the Security Service, the 1970s was to see a gradual breaking down of the walls between men and women, witnessing Rimington and others being appointed as full, rather than assistant, officers, and the rules changed on who could finally run agents, though Rimington herself would still recall a 'male-dominated, old-fashioned organization, which was going to take years to change' even in the early 1980s.[69]' The Service was quite late coming to terms worth gender equality in the 1970s', recalled one MI5 official, 'and was generally quite insular and conservative on most issues at that period', yet, as another officer recalls, it was the 'younger generation in the Office' who were increasingly supportive of the need to overturn 'artificial barriers'.[70]

The situation was to change greatly, especially under Anthony Duff, appointed Director General in March 1985, who 'brought more modern attitudes to management and relations with staff'.[71] The service, as its authorized history observes, had been appointing ever increasing numbers of women to senior roles; having been made Deputy Director-General (A), Rimington recalls the fact 'I was a female ceased to be relevant to the progress of my career'.[72] SIS appears to have been much slower; in 1975 Daphne Park was appointed as Controller Western Hemisphere, the first women to ever reach the rank and a remarkable achievement, but few followed.[73] As in MI5, although SIS recruited a sizable number of female staff they were largely restricted to the clerical and administrative grades, the most powerful women often being personal assistants to the Directors, having risen slowly through the service, with few other women in leadership positions, and a pattern reflected elsewhere.[74] One female official explains, 'Progress was very slow indeed and it was hard to break out of the box you were in. Women in key roles were few and far between so there were few role models'. The small number of women breaking into leadership had, they recalled, 'almost without exception came up from admin roles and were atypical of the population (e.g. unmarried, perceived as tough or emulating male stereotypes'.[75]

Even if men and women worked side by side on administrative and clerical work, there was traditionally a divide on operational matters; men were the intelligence officers, dominating recruitment to the intelligence branch, and women, if posted abroad, providing the support, though the artificial barriers gradually broke down.[76] As SIS itself explains, 'secretaries often assumed real operational roles while employed overseas (often those with the least staff)'.[77] The career of Valerie Pettit is perhaps representative; having failed to join the FCO due to inadequate shorthand, Pettit joined SIS as a secretary serving in Poland, Jordan, Iraq and Mexico and in 1972 took an exam to become an officer, later becoming deputy to the head of SIS's Soviet operations section, devising the audacious escape plan of Oleg Gordievsky, a KGB officer recruited by SIS who defected to the west in July 1985.[78] As in other areas of British society at the time, the UK's intelligence agencies were also not immune from sexist behaviour, even if restrictions on what women could do largely stemmed from general stereotypes of male and female roles, and the generational differences between leadership and the new entrants. 'I was totally aware I was in a man's world', one female intelligence officer said, 'but that's the environment I was growing up in' and 'I was never going to have anyone telling me I couldn't do it if I was a girl'.[79] Former SIS officer Richard Tomlinson, recruited in 1991 into the service's intelligence branch, recalls in his memoirs 'it was striking how similar the new recruits were.

They were from nearly identical backgrounds, were white, male, and conventional and middle class. All of us were university graduates, mostly from Oxford or Cambridge. The homogeneity of the room reflected MI6. Roughly just 10% of the IB were female, he recalled.[80] Although for many women in clerical roles, often working predominantly in all-female teams, there was little feeling they were in a patriarchal organizational culture, those working as intelligence officers, even as late as the 1990s, were well aware they were in a minority, even if things were, one officer recalls, no 'different to my experience at university'. Nevertheless, there was a feeling amongst some that women in operational roles had to be 'twice as good as the men' and working in an environment where they were 'outside the club'.[81] The emphasis on male intelligence officers and selective recruitment into such roles also went against women reaching middle and senior management posts, having to complete a series of roles to get further up the ladder, and questions about career and family often led talented female officers to leave the service on unpaid maternity.

Even though they were often welcomed back, many women fell behind their male peers who had joined at the same time. Moreover, there seems to have been a lack of female role models, a reflection of the traditional male dominance of intelligence branch roles, a necessary step to progress into the small number of senior roles in the service. But internal policy may also have played a role; SIS itself admitted in 2019 that internal policy was far from 'enlightened' at times and followed Whitehall's 'more restrictive employment practices until their amendment in the 1970s', particularly for women SIS's adherence to 'Diplomatic Service Regulation No. 5', also known as the 'Marriage Bar', requiring women to leave the service having got married, a rule removed by the FCO in 1973.[82] The impact is impossible to determine; even into the 1990s, the few senior women in the service were unmarried, with SIS perhaps 'losing a very talented generation of women'.[83] The Foreign Office's example tells us that the bar had lasting effects.

It was not until 1987 that Veronica Sutherland became the first married ambassador, the bar and internal culture, as the department now acknowledges, ending 'the growth of a substantial cohort of talented pioneer women at the Foreign Office'.[84] The glass ceiling was smashed in 2021 with the appointment Menna Rawlings as the UK's first female ambassador to France, women now holding the ambassadorships to the G7 group of top industrialized nations.[85] Inside GCHQ experiences were mixed. 'When I joined the department [in the 1980s] as an analyst working against the Warsaw Pact in the intelligence factory that was J Division there was nothing unusual', one former GCHQ officer said, 'about women in the executive class heading analytic teams nor in those teams containing a mix of men and women from the clerical and executive classes'. The numbers decreased as grade increased, 'females running teams were common, running sections unremarkable, but beyond that – at the very top of the executive class and into the administrative class–they were rare'.

There was also a fair proportion of women across the linguist class, reflective of the proportion studying languages at university, though promotion was generally slow and the gender imbalance in management generally accepted at the time as the way things were.[86] 'We'll only have real equality', one female manager said, 'when incompetent women are promoted as easily as incompetent men'.[87] By 1995 women made up 28% of GCHQ's workforce, although the percentage does not tell the full story. GCHQ's 'support' divisions (HR, finance) tended to be female dominated at the lower levels, though men were more dominant in the higher grades.[88] It was only in July 2006 that GCHQ had its first female Superintending Director sitting on the Board, Judith Hodson, daughter of former Director Sir Arthur 'Bill' Bonsall.[89] Naturally, in light of university education and industry generally, STEM-related aspects of GCHQ's work were largely male. For several women, the imbalance on such work became clearer once GCHQ moved away from the small, compartmentalized office spaces and lab facilities at the Oakley and Benhall sites and into the open plan world of the 'Doughnut' in 2004.[90] The staffing of intercept sites was similarly dominated by men, largely shaped by the fact that the majority of intercept operators were former military or merchant marine.[91]

Race and Nationality

If the position of women in the intelligence agencies was a gradual process of evolution, the role of ethnic minority candidates was near non-existent even until relatively recently, the issue, columnist Hugh Muir once observed, 'weighted with historical baggage, burdened by context'.[92] As with growing gender representation following avowal, the gradual recruitment of BAME officials was a slow and uneven process across the agencies, few non-white candidates entering until the 1980s. GCHQ's authorized history acknowledges the issue remains 'painful and incomplete'.[93]Naturally, the traditional methods of recruitment and backgrounds of candidates in parts of the community discriminated against those from non-Oxbridge backgrounds, and the recruitment of BAME staff remained prisoner to past practices. With the exception of a smaller number of specialist linguists or clerical grades, the intelligence agencies even into the 1990s were largely white. One male GCHQ officer who joined in the 1980s recalls the organization 'was almost pure white – to the extent that anyone black in the place was assumed to be a visiting American'.[94]

This was partially a result of the nationality rules, partly 'a reflection of some of the recruiting pools (e.g., STEM graduates, the military), and partly bloody Cheltenham itself', a place described as 'pretty monocultural' with implications for recruitment ('most of the recruits to the clerical class and other entry level posts were from local school leavers, and they were white').[95] The adoption of a black candidate, John (later Lord) Taylor, as the Conservative Party's parliamentary candidate for Cheltenham – considered a safe Conservative seat–at the 1992 general election, led to claims of racism and even abuse from his own constituency party[96] It was only in the 1980s that MI5 started to recruit staff from ethnic minority backgrounds largely because, as one former officer recalls, 'targets (notably the Russians) did not believe that we employed such people and, in consequence, did not "see" them', drawn from the armed services. 'The consensus . . . was that this was a good thing'.[97] This was not an effort to promote diversity–'diversity was not a topic of conversation', another former MI5 officer recalls – but a pragmatic response to operational requirements at the time. Nonetheless, there were limits on targets with no or limited ethnic diversity, another officer nothing it was useless to employ a black surveillance officer against targets where there was no BAME representation.[98]

Another factor was the strict nationality rules. Although there was certainly some flexibility for candidates with dual nationality from Commonwealth or English-speaking countries (in SIS, the rule was that such candidates would need to drop their dual nationality at the request of the other government[99]), the recruitment of staff from ethnic minority backgrounds was complicated by rules governing who could enter secret work. Before 1940, anyone born in Great Britain or the self-governing Dominions, with at least one parent (or two in the case of the Foreign Office and service departments) could join the civil service, with discretion for departments to bend the rules in isolated cases. In wartime, departments had relaxed rules to recruit naturalized British subjects ('foreign' nationals granted British nationality), yet after 1945, the subject of race and nationality was increasingly complicated by the growing non-white migrant population of the UK, traditionally heralded by the Empire Windrush in 1948.[100] The British Nationality Act which came into force on 1 January 1949, allowed anyone formerly with the title 'British subject' to become a 'Commonwealth citizen' with the right to enter, settle and work in Britain, yet the growth of the 'wrong sort of British subject' led to curbs in security departments.

For SIS and MI5, controlling their own recruitment, migration meant very little, yet for GCHQ recruiting through the civil service channels, restrictions were put in place. In February 1956, GCHQ argued that nationality rules needed to be tightened, ruling out citizens from the Irish Republic, anyone married to an 'alien' or a 'coloured person', defined as 'one either or both of whose parents is not of Old Dominion white stock'. Although GCHQ argued the first two groups were 'quite straightforward' to identify, there would be cases, it was suggested, 'Anglo-Indians for example–where we can't be positive one way or the other on the basis of a visual inspection of the candidate . . . we cannot risk a candidate connecting G.C.H.Q.'s refusal to have him with his coloured ancestry'.[101]The clear implication of the ruling was that even 'coloured' individuals born in Britain would be ineligible to join, thanks to security concerns about their past.

Security departments in other areas of Whitehall such as the Ministry of Defence required individuals to have lived in the UK for a period of ten years before becoming eligible to apply, though there also seems to have been other reasons for the lack of non-white officials often wrapped up in language that would be unacceptable today. In May 1967, MI5 Director-General Martin Furnival Jones told the Official Committee on Security that concerns about the employment of 'coloured' candidates in security departments went far beyond time spent in the UK and 'stemmed simply from the colour of a man's skin, which gave him a chip on his shoulder', telling the committee 'It must be assumed that the Communist intelligence services were fully aware of the possibilities of recruiting agents from among disaffected coloured people in this country'.[102] The passage of the 1968 Race Relations Act, making it illegal to refuse housing, employment or public services on the grounds of race, gave the government the right to discriminate on national security grounds, departments having the mechanism to reject candidates if, having seen evidence, a Minister signed off an exemption from the terms of the Act.[103]

Nationality remained a significant factor. In October 1996, former soldier, Luigi Manelfi, challenged nationality rules in the High Court claiming they were 'irrational, wholly unreasonable and unlawful'. The son of a German mother and Italian father who had resided in the UK since 1959, Manelfi had been born in the UK but, in a case supported by human rights group Liberty, sought to overturn GCHQ's rules that the agency would not employ anyone with non-British parents save for rare exceptions.[104] Sources told journalists that under GCHQ rules, while spouses or partners of staff could be American or EU citizens, parents needed to come from a Commonwealth country.[105] Nationality rules became more of an issue in the 2000s as the UK's agencies moved away from traditional targets to 'international terrorism' in the post 9/11 world.

For the Security Service especially, the need to attract British Asian recruits was a reflection of the need to target Islamic groups themselves, and operational benefits of having officers able to run informants or penetrate such communities, and also having the necessary cultural awareness.[106] In June 2002, the ISC was 'concerned' the agencies had limited flexibility to cover the necessary languages they needed,[107] raising the issue a year later and citing 'nationality' rules and vetting as one reason for the failure to meet targets on the recruitment of staff with 'specialist languages'[108] Although having raised the subject of nationality rules being too restrictive, the ISC reported in April 2005 that 'individuals with key language skills, such as naturalized immigrants and the children of immigrants' were disproportionately affected by nationality restrictions: "Candidates must be British citizens, with one parent either also a British citizen or with substantial ties with the UK. British nationality can have been acquired by any lawful means, whether by birth, descent, registration or naturalization. The nationality rules also state that candidates must normally have been resident in the UK for 10 years prior to the date of application, although the Agencies told us that they were willing to consider a five-year minimum wherever possible".[109]

GCHQ had opened a specialist office where individuals with key language skills, but without the highest clearances, could still work on 'appropriate material', but the agencies failure to hit targets for ethnic minority recruitment targets was a matter of concern for Home Secretary David Blunkett and Foreign Secretary Jack Straw. Figures reported by the committee revealed that while 15% of applicants to SIS were from a BAME background just 9% of staff overall were from a minority group, and, despite concerns about operational impacts, had not applied for a nationality waiver – a rule that agencies could in rare cases employ candidates not usually eligible to work if the relevant Secretary of State had signed off – in 16 years. Over 17% of MI5's applicants were from BAME backgrounds in 2004–5, with 8% of the overall workforce from such backgrounds. The service had one nationality waiver during this period.[110] Interestingly, the number of BAME staff at all grades in SIS and MI5 reflected patterns in the civil service generally.[111]

By June 2006, the ISC had been told that Charles Clarke, who had succeeded Blunkett in the Home Office, had taken the decision to delegate nationality waivers to a 'senior official', a process also followed by the FCO, though vetting and nationality rules remained important.[112] In July 2006, security sources told The Guardian that several Al-Qaida sympathizers had tried to join MI5 but weeded out in the vetting process.[113]Perceptions of the agencies also mattered. Even in the late 1990s, having turned to a recruitment specialist for help, one MI5 officer noted the general view was that 'many people from ethnic minority communities would think "there were crocodiles in the corridors"' (specifically it was too frightening to think about working for MI5), although ethnic minority recruitment had significantly improved by the early 2000s.[114] 'There was certainly no organizational hostility to such recruitment', the officer recalls.[115] By 2004 an MI5 recruitment drive was targeting Britain's Asian community responding to the events of 9/11 and in the face of 'intense opposition from private companies and other government agencies for Arabic speakers'. It was reported that 9% of the service's recruitment were from ethnic minority backgrounds, although figures released to the BBC three years later revealed the number of ethnic minority staff overall was 6.5%.[116]

In 2006/7, SIS was also able to use targeted advertising to attract 10% of new entrants from ethnic minority groups.[117] 'I feel very, very strongly that if you are able to do something to make a difference, you should make that difference', an SIS officer only identified as 'Yasmin' told BBC News, in November 2007. SIS's head of recruitment told reporters, 'We want to be truly representative and reflective . . . we do need to have Muslims in our organization because of the insight and understanding they bring'.[118] Nonetheless, despite the positive steps forward, as with other parts of government and police, the perception the agencies were not a place for ethnic minorities took hold in some communities. In 2010, a review, leaked to The Sunday Times, admitted the number of BAME candidates in GCHQ was 'very small' with some feeling they were 'constantly challenged about my loyalty to Britain' or asked questions that were often 'culturally inappropriate, insensitive and offensive'.[119]

Two years later GCHQ made an out of court settlement with a former employee alleging racial harassment.[120] Views amongst some ethnic minority groups about what the agencies do and who joins them were limiting, tapping into a wider suspicion, as Steve Hewitt has written, that government policy was failing to win over the 'hearts and minds' of the communities terrorists and terrorist sympathizers came from, adding to long-held inherent suspicions of government generally.[121] 'I think if people found out that someone was working for the security services, people would be wary of that person', one interviewee told the BBC Asian Network in November 2016.[122] Even Nikesh Mehta, a Director at GCHQ, admitted there was the 'unspoken belief' that intelligence was a 'career for "them" and not for "us"'. He explained, 'There are so many falsehoods . . . These falsehoods may deter ethnic minorities from applying to join MI6, MI5 or GCHQ. Contrary to what some people think, recruits will not be asked to spy on their own community'.[123] A GCHQ spokesperson admitted in May 2020, 'It has historically been difficult for GCHQ to de-mystify and translate its mission and values, particularly to those communities from an ethnic minority background'.[124]

Sexuality

The position of LGBT officers was also problematic. Officially, there were no gay officers in the agencies, their sexuality hidden thanks to Positive Vetting (PV) rules banning gay officials dealing with secret information, though certainly there were many officers who had joined having hidden their sexuality for career purposes. Concerns about the security risks of employing homosexuals went back to 1951 and the fallout from the defection of Foreign Office officials Guy Burgess and Donald Maclean, leading to rules emanating from the Cadogan report on security in the department that sexuality was a mark of unreliability that would also undermine the ability of the department to manage Britain's diplomatic relations.[125] Here, the Foreign Office appears to have been ahead of the rest of Whitehall; generally, it seems, although homosexuality was illegal, the issue of sexuality as a security risk per se was never considered before the 1950s with several staff at Bletchley Park known to be gay.[126]

The report of a committee of Privy Counsellors in 1956 placed increasing emphasis on the so-called character defects and effectively brought the rest of government in line with the Foreign Office, suggesting that greater emphasis needed to be 'paid to character defects as factors tending to make a man unreliable or expose him to blackmail, or influence by foreign agents', especially 'serious failings such as drunkenness, addiction to drugs, homosexuality or any loose living that may seriously affect a man's reliability'. These rules applied to Whitehall departments and the intelligence agencies.[127] In 1951, MI5's Graham Mitchell noted that homosexuals were 'maladjusted to the social environment and may therefore be of an unstable character', often stuck together and were 'backward in giving information' and 'in so far as their activities are felonious they are at least in theory open to blackmail by a hostile intelligence agency'.[128]

For security officials the threat of the gay men was realized with the case of John Vassall, recruited by the KGB while serving as a clerical officer in the staff of the British naval attaché in Moscow, having been photographed at an orgy and blackmailed into spying. Vassall's career as a Soviet agent ended in 1962, yet fears of homosexuality continued even resulting in MI5 obtaining warrants for telephone checks on four gay civil servants which revealed conversations of a 'revolting nature' but little in the way of security related issues.[129] The passing of the Sexual Offences Act 1967 did little to change the situation. In December 1967, the Official Committee on Security ruled that, despite a change in the law, the 'risk of blackmail or pressure in homosexual cases' remained significant, while 'importuning in public' was still a criminal offence, and the 'social stigma' of homosexuality meant there were still significant reputational risks in coming out.[130] Moreover, while seen as a landmark piece of legislation, the 1967 Act still made homosexual activity with anyone under the age of 21 illegal and did not apply to Scotland or Northern Ireland. Additionally, although homosexuality was no longer a bar to employment in the home civil service, it continued to pose issues for the Foreign Office, armed forces and intelligence agencies.

Nonetheless, several homosexuals joined and ran the risk of dismissal. 'It could happen at any moment', one former officer said. 'Same sex relationships were impossible in the current understanding of the term forcing any attempt at relationships deeply into the shadows'.[131] Perhaps the most extraordinary example is that of Sir Maurice Oldfield, SIS Chief between 1973 to 1978, who lied about his sexuality, having told vetting officers in 1966 he had 'never felt any leanings or temptations' on the matter.[132] Oldfield had been appointed security coordinator in Northern Ireland in 1979, only to return to London a year later through ill health and adverse reports from Special Branch on his private life, resulting in a review of his vetting history. Remarkably, Oldfield was interviewed by MI5 thirteen times between April 1980 and January 1981, during which it emerged he took an 'undue interest' in young male clerks employed by

SIS, disclosing that, although he had never slept with SIS officers or agents, he had been 'introduced to homosexuality at university' and 'engaged in homosexual practices intermittently' until 1979.

Oldfield admitted his relationships were, for the most part, with 'restaurant waiters and the like'.[133] A final summary of the case by MI5 Director General Sir Howard Smith, noted: 'It is clear that he was not very discreet in his homosexual relations and that he laid himself dangerously open to compromise, notably through his admitted homosexual relations with hotel stewards in the Far East during the 1950s'. Though he had never been targeted by a hostile agency, Oldfield was, Smith wrote, 'indiscreet and vulnerable' and had been 'less than frank'.[134] Others were less fortunate. In 2016, GCHQ Director Robert Hannigan apologized to 'Ian', who had transferred to GCHQ from the RAF in 1961 who, after several years of exemplary service, was found to be gay and dismissed. Although finding a new role in the civil service, 'Ian' had no help from GCHQ and his 'health suffered and the psychological effects of that humiliation were long-lasting'.[135]

In April 1981, having reviewed security concerns about homosexuals, MI5 ruled that restrictions for PV posts would stay, citing fears of blackmail by hostile intelligence agencies.[136] Later that year the report of the Security Commission ruled that 'homosexuality, even if acknowledged, should continue to be a bar to employment in any PV post', though the rule was not binding on GCHQ a reflection, perhaps, that the agency had started to recognize the total bar was counterproductive for candidates with specialist skills.[137] However, as the Security Commission later noted, there was a 'rigorous' adherence to vetting standards across the agencies.[138] In April 1983 MI5 reported that transsexuals and transvestites were 'in general treated by the public with humorous derision or aversion' and ineligible for PV posts meaning they were effectively excluded from the agencies.[139] Only one declared homosexual was granted a PV status in the second half of the 1980s, even if across the agencies and Foreign Office there was pressure for a change in the rules despite cultural, political and organizational pressures for a maintenance of the status quo.[140] Within MI5 there were differences over policy and, as one former officer recalled, many discreet gay officers slipped under the radar.[141]

By 1990, Foreign Office Permanent Under-Secretary Sir Patrick Wright had already started to push for a change in the rules, nothing in his diary that even SIS was now 'positive' to change.[142] In July 1991, Prime Minister John Major announced that 'no posts involving access to highly classified information for which homosexuality represents an automatic bar to security clearance', except the military where such acts continued to be subject to the service disciplinary Acts.[143] By 1997, following MI5's first ever newspaper advert in The Guardian, Security Service sources told journalists at the Pink Paper that homosexuals were not to be 'discouraged' from applying, while GCHQ told staff that being gay was 'not of itself a security worry'.[144] Yet limits on gay men and women in the intelligence agencies remained and the effects of the bar 'lingered'. One SIS officer recalled, 'There were three communities – those who embraced the change, those who opposed it openly or in the background by their actions, and those in the middle who drifted in the wind according to events'.[145] 'John', a member of SIS's LGBT+ Affinity Group who joined in the early 2000s, recalled it was not 'terribly safe to start with . . . In those early years I was quite reticent [about being out at work], both for personal reasons and also wondering, 'Will there be an impact on my career?'.[146] As with women and BAME officials, change was slow and it took a generational change for a new culture of inclusivity and diversity to emerge, possibly even accounting for the lower than usual declaration rates across the agencies in ISC data.[147]

Although there is still much to learn about historical inclusion and diversity across the UK's intelligence agencies, the picture now emerging suggests that – despite starting relatively late in Whitehall – the agencies have come a long way. The ISC's criticism that parts of the community are still behind Whitehall figures generally, and the data on senior leadership, suggests that there is still much work to be done, yet the general criticism that the agencies are unrepresentative in some areas generally overlooks the point that late avowal, recruitment, nationality and the legacy of past policy, mean it will take a significant period of time for SIS, MI5 and GCHQ to catch-up with the rest of government. Nonetheless, as even the ISC's report acknowledged, the latest data suggests that recruitment is becoming increasingly representative, though still behind comparisons with the civil service and UK demographics. In 2018 about 13.8% of the population came from ethnic minority backgrounds,[148] women making up 51%.[149] Within the agencies, on gender, 46.8% of MI5's recruitment and 45.2% of SIS new entrants were women (a significant increase from just 34% in 2006/7[150]), even if GCHQ remained far behind at 30.1%.[151]

Internally, things have changed 'beyond recognition'–a point made by several officials across the agencies.[152] The government response to the ISC's July 2018 report also suggested there had been further progress in leadership with '38%, 35% and 27% of staff at Senior Civil Service level in

MI5, GCHQ and SIS respectively being female (increases of nearly 7%, 8% and 3%)', though there were no new statistics on BAME leadership. 'Across the Intelligence Community', the response went on, 'departments and agencies continue to innovate through working with external partners and sharing best practice'.[153] These figures are also affected by the small numbers of senior officials involved; one individual moving in or out of leadership is going to have a significant impact on the percentage figures, compared to the civil service. There are also limits; SIS's gender pay gap reports actually show there has been a slight drop in the number of women from the ISC's July 2018 report, with the service's workforce headcount made up of 37% of women in 2019,[154] and 38% in 2020,[155] down from 38.9% in 2018.[156] There were slight increases in the proportion of female staff in GCHQ and MI5.

The reports also highlighted the ongoing issue of women being concentrated in lower pay quartiles.[157] Analysis of the civil service also suggests that besides diversity as set out in this article, the socio-economic background of candidates might in future be another benchmark to examine, though access to recruitment data and policy for the agencies remains an issue.[158] Moreover, while more women and minority groups are entering the agencies, it remains to be seen whether they are doing similar jobs as before or whether there is a growing proportion now breaking into frontline intelligence roles. Public speeches, news articles and ISC data provide overall percentages of groups in the workforce and at SCS grades, yet, to fully understand diversity and inclusion, the question that needs to be looked at in future is what roles are women, BAME, LGBT and disability groups doing now? Today, change is certainly needed. For HUMINT agencies, agent recruitment is no longer – as one former officer says – the realm of 'hard driving, hard drinking blokes'.[159] Speaking to The Times as part of an SIS recruitment campaign in March 2014, 'Lisa', a serving officer, said that women make 'bloody good spies', adding: 'We are quite good at multi-tasking. We are quite good at tapping into different emotional resources. You can get into a lot of places'.[160]

Other former officers would agree; though both men and women make excellent agent runners, each can bring important skills and run agents differently.[161] In April 2018, it was reported that Alex Younger had 'made sure' that one of three candidates vying to succeeded him as 'C' was a women. Sources told journalists the officer had run agents across the world and had 'strong operational capabilities', even being honored by The Queen for her services, though Younger was succeeded by Richard Moore, first announced in July 2020.[162] Yet even though positive change is being made, there are internal and external factors that mitigate against quicker shift. History is certainly one factor, another is that organizational culture and career pathways take time to change. Traditionally, as one former officer said, 'your entrée to more outward-facing work . . . was looking and sounding middle class'. Although change was the buzzword, living up to a 'middle-class stereotype' was prized while female role models in management were 'white and middle class'.[163] In effect, diversity would result in more women, but 'more women just acting like the men'. Also, even if change is happening across the board, a 'macho culture' will undoubtedly remain in places.[164]

There have been significant efforts to change internal culture and promote change, all three agencies having well established networks for women – SIS (DEUCE) and MI5 (GENIE) – and BAME groups – SIS (EMBRACE), MI5 (My5), GCHQ (REACH). LGBT and disability networks have also been formed.[165] For GCHQ, the REACH network has 'led to increased engagement across the organization, a change in approach to recruitment and traction with BAME communities across the country'.[166] Thanks to internal work the Security Service was named best employer of the year by Stonewall in 2016,[167] remaining in the organization's top 100 LGBT list of employers. Both SIS and MI5 were also listed in The Times top fifty employers for women in 2018.[168] There are also factors outside agency control. GCHQ's difficulties can be explained by a general shortage of women in STEM subjects; according to UCAS and HESA data just 35% of STEM students were women. Representation in 'Computer Science' and 'Engineering and Technology' was just 19% and GCHQ has been forced to reach out and promote women in STEM subjects to develop a talent pipeline.[169] Equally, the collapse of languages in UK higher education is worrying; according to a January 2020 report in the Financial Times, 19 university language departments were downsized or cut entirely thanks to a significant drop in student numbers.

The report also warned that just 32% of 16–30 year olds can read and write in another language. 'We are looking for people with top end language skills', 'Chris', a GCHQ linguist told the BBC in 2011, adding: 'we are not finding as many as we were finding at the beginning of the 2000s'.[170] Though speakers of French, German and other European languages with language aptitude still form a core of GCHQ's intake, speakers of Arabic, Mandarin Chinese, Mirpuri, Russian, Urdu and other sought after languages are still hard, placing a growing focus on candidates that may not pass nationality rules.[171] Another factor against GCHQ has been location; the ISC's July

2018 report said Cheltenham was 'less diverse'–a conclusion others would agree with.[172] One BAME Whitehall official once remarked he avoided oversight stays because Cheltenham was 'not my sort of town'.[173] Nikesh Mehta has also pointed out, 'Unlike most civil service departments, our main office is not in a diverse urban metropolis like London . . . This might put some people off'.[174] The opening of GCHQ's new Northern or Manchester hub, first announced in October 2019, at the heart of a thriving tech sector and one of the most culturally diverse cities in the UK has the potential to challenge such views.[175]

One solution to the problem of perception and the conscious decision by some groups to self-select a career in intelligence has been wider engagement, though these efforts are not entirely new. The successful launch of SIS's website in 2005 'significantly increased the number of applications' to the service, followed by a national media campaign'.[176] In the same year, MI5 ran adverts for 'older, wiser women' to join the service.[177] GCHQ reached out in new ways; a campaign in 2007 to place in game advertising in two Ubisoft titles, 'Splinter Cell: Double Agent' and 'Rainbow Six: Vegas', led to a 500% increase in visits to the agency's dedicated recruitment site. One GCHQ official said, 'There is no doubt that the gaming idea and subsequent media publicity has significantly increased awareness of GCHQ as a potential employer'.[178] GCHQ officials told the ISC in early 2009 they were considering the use of video boards on the London Underground and mass marketing on commuter routes into the capital as well as dedicated websites to attract 'internet specialists, those with particular language skills, and technologists'.[179] Though such campaigns and speeches by heads of agencies were not new, what is different now is the visibility and growing occurrence of recruitment and outreach work. Initiatives such as GCHQ's 'Cyber first'–alongside wider engagement work such as Code Club, language programmes and summer schools–have challenged women to join areas traditionally dominated by men. In addition, initiatives such as 'GCHQ-Decoded' have been used to ensure 'that many more applicants from an ethnic minority background are maintained throughout the recruitment pipeline and increased their success rate at interview', leading, to 'further tailored engagement with applicants from across a number of different backgrounds'.[180]

GCHQ has also tried to expand knowledge of the organization by joining the social networking site Twitter in May 2016, reaching over 133,000 followers by May 2021.[181] They are not alone; MI5 joined Instagram in April 2021, Director-General Ken McCallum writing in The Telegraph (ironically behind a paywall) that his service needed to become 'more open' and 'tap into the diversity and creativity of UK life.[182] SIS also reached out in new ways; the service launched its first cinema advert in spring 2017. The advert, titled 'But She Can', aimed to attract applications from 'all backgrounds' and featured a young, mixed-race women handling everyday situations before concluding she had the right emotional intelligence and people skills to join the service.[183] A year later, the service launched a new 'Secretly We're Just Like You (#SecretlyWereJustLikeYou) campaign. The first advert, aired during the Channel 4 evening news, featured a young mother comforting her child, the aim being to challenge the popular perception of Bond.[184] A follow-up 'Barbershop Advert' was released on YouTube and Google Display in January 2019.[185]

The intelligence agencies have certainly come a long way, even if much still needs to be done around BAME recruitment and progression, the development of female leadership role models and in demystifying the work of the UK's agencies whilst maintaining the necessary secrecy to continue to function effectively. Judgements of current issues regarding diversity and inclusivity need to be taken in historical context, though it remains difficult to research the social history of intelligence for much of the post-war period thanks to a lack of documents and secrecy. Even so, the picture that does emerge is that even into the 1990s, the UK's agencies were far behind Whitehall generally and were relatively slow to grasp that change was necessary. While women had always played an important role historically in the UK's intelligence agencies, their role was often in clerical and support roles, few breaking the artificial 'glass ceilings' put in place.

Recruitment practices, organizational cultures and the closed nature of British intelligence often meant that the agencies were divorced from experiences elsewhere in government, and even into the 1990s were effectively running on a pre-avowal outlook that effectively maintained the status quo, a legacy still left today. Although change in some areas remains frustratingly slow, today's intelligence agencies have, it seems, come a long way in representing an increasingly diverse Britain, drawing on new talents and expertise for pragmatic and image reasons falling increasingly in line with the rest of Whitehall. There remains much work to be done by future researchers; agency heads have gone on record to discuss disability, particularly GCHQ, which has talked about the positives of 'neurodiversity'. In future, it is hoped that researchers will look at such issues, as well as the areas identified in this article. Nevertheless, it should be pointed out that, though the ISC's criticisms are certainly valid and a catalyst for continued change, placing these criticisms in context shows how far the UK intelligence community has come.

Acknowledgements

The author would like to thank Prof. Rory Cormac and Drs. Andrew Defty, Claire Hubbard-Hall, Christopher Moran, Christopher Murphy and Samantha Newbery for help with the article. I would like to thank the anonymous sources for their powerful insights into the world of diversity and inclusion in the past – you know who you are. Particular thanks goes to Dr. Jessica Shahan for permission to cite her thesis, 'Spying Gender: Women in British intelligence, 1969–1994'. Thanks also go to the Institute for Historical Research's Scouloudi Foundation for their generous grant supporting research on this subject. Disclosure statement: No potential conflict of interest was reported by the author(s). Notes on contributor: Dan Lomas is author of Intelligence, Security and the Attlee Governments, 1945 – 1951, published by Manchester University Press (2016), teaching on intelligence and security issues at the University of Salford. He is currently writing a forthcoming book for Bloomsbury on the history of security vetting, and a documentary reader on reviews of the UK intelligence community for Edinburgh University Press. ORCID: Daniel W. B. Lomas http://orcid.org/0000-0002-4254-2225. References: *The National Archives (TNA) CSC 5 CAB 21 CAB 134 PREM 19. The premier journal of intelligence studies" Eliot A. Cohen, Foreign Affairs. Intelligence has never played a more prominent role in international politics than it does now in the early years of the twenty-first century. National intelligence services are larger than ever, and they are more transparent in their activities in the policy making of democratic nations. Intelligence and National Security is widely regarded as the world's leading scholarly journal focused on the role of intelligence and secretive agencies in international relations. It examines this aspect of national security from a variety of perspectives and academic disciplines, with insightful articles research and written by leading experts based around the globe. Among the topics covered in the journal are: The historical development of intelligence agencies representations of intelligence in popular culture, public understandings and expectations related to intelligence, intelligence and ethics. Intelligence collection and analysis. Covert action and counterintelligence. Privacy and intelligence accountability. The outsourcing of intelligence operations. The role of politics in intelligence activities. International intelligence cooperation and burden-sharing. The relationships among intelligence agencies, military organizations, and civilian police departments. Authors for Intelligence and National Security come from a range of disciplines, including international affairs, history, sociology, political science, law, anthropology, philosophy, medicine, statistics, psychology, bio-sciences, and mathematics. These perspectives are regularly augmented by research submitted from current and former intelligence practitioners in several different nations. Each issue features a rich menu of articles about the uses (and occasional misuses) of intelligence, supplemented from time to time with special forums on current intelligence issues and interviews with leading intelligence officials. Journal information: Print ISSN: 0268-4527 Online ISSN: 1743-9019, 7 issues per year. Intelligence and*

ForgetJamesBond: diversity, inclusion and the UK's intelligence agencies. Daniel W. B. Lomas. To cite this article: Daniel W. B. Lomas (2021) #ForgetJamesBond: diversity, inclusion and the UK's intelligence agencies, Intelligence and National Security, 36:7, 995-1017, DOI: 10.1080/02684527.2021.1938370. To link to this article: https://doi. org/10.1080/02684527.2021.1938370. © 2021 The Author(s). Published by Informa, UK Limited, trading as Taylor & Francis Group. Published online: 02 Jul 2021.

Chapter 5

Executive Accountability and National Security

Lorna Woods OBE, Lawrence McNamara, Judith Townend

Abstract

The protection of national security has traditionally been an exception to general norms of public accountability, based on prerogative powers. The last three decades have seen efforts to bring national security closer to the normal constitutional control mechanisms of parliament and the courts. The design of and changes to mechanisms of accountability have, however, been accepted without discussion of the often narrower purposes for which they were first established (most notably for oversight of surveillance), the extent of their departure from constitutional principles, or their impact in embedding new forms of exceptionalism in the constitutional framework. This article critically assesses these developments, prompted for example, by the Law Commission's recommendations to reform official secrets laws, which adopted trusted intermediary and indirect accountability models without full consideration of historical and contemporary concerns or the exceptionalism on which they were based. Though focused on the UK, our account provides a cautionary tale for national security law reform in any modern democracy.

Introduction

The British constitution is based on the accountability of the executive to parliament with an independent judiciary ensuring compliance with the law. Traditionally an exception to these general norms of public accountability, the protection of national security constitutes an area where information flows are tightly controlled and the executive can act without approval of the legislature and where judicial intervention will be rare and limited. Secrecy has been demanded to protect the national interest, though this and national security are terms which can cover a range of interests and arise in many different contexts. From the late 1980s there have been moves to bring national security matters closer to the normal constitutional control mechanisms of parliament and the courts, changes vital and valuable for a modern democracy in which the executive is accountable for its actions. Nevertheless, by no means did the underpinning of the security and intelligence agencies (SIAs) by statute and the introduction of external oversight constitute a golden age of transparency and responsibility.[1]

Given the sensitive nature of national security, the shift towards ordinary standards and processes has inevitably been incomplete. Indeed, concerns about the need to counter terrorism have given rise to state calls for further powers, especially in the light of technological developments, and a reassertion of the need to keep these capabilities and their deployment secret in the service of national security. This process has seen measures and models put in place seeking to balance the competing imperatives. These are different from, if not inconsistent with, the usual mechanisms to ensure governmental accountability, which ordinarily require considerable openness and transparency.[2] Many of these measures, as they have emerged, have been subject to criticism.[3] What is lacking in the existing scholarship is a focus on the ways that, as the law has been reformed, changes in the mechanisms of accountability on the basis of the exceptional nature of national security have been accepted and replicated, the circumstances in which they are used expanded, and, taken together, the consequences for the constitutional settlement. It is only as time has passed that the full extent of this has become apparent.

This article argues that there has been an increase in oversight and transparency measures that rely on 'trusted intermediaries' in the area of national security, establishing a model that is repeatedly redeployed and normalised. While re-using existing approaches may seem uncontroversial, even sensible, our concerns arise because those developments become treated as unproblematic once adopted and then used as a model going forward in wider contexts. The focus on the benefits of using an intermediary has over-shadowed the design constraints within which those intermediaries operate, and the limited extent to which there is either accountability or transparency. The deployment of the trusted intermediary model has had significant consequences, most notably a lack of accountability to parliament, a limitation of transparency in the courts

94

(open justice) and a troubling re-shaping of the judicial role and function under the constitution.

This discussion might have been prompted by any number of developments in recent years. For example, the Snowden disclosures paved the way for a new tranche of cases dealing with mass surveillance before both the European Court of Human Rights (ECtHR) and the Court of Justice of the EU (CJEU) and which resulted in the enactment of the Investigatory Powers Act 2016 (IPA 2016).[4] These cases build on earlier jurisprudence on covert surveillance which themselves may have affected the approach to SIAs.[5] While not expressly linked to Snowden, we also note the consultation paper published by the Law Commission of England and Wales in 2017 which reviewed the law relating to official secrets.[6] It was striking because it was expressly premised on earlier developments in the area of national security. Crucially, those developments primarily related to the oversight of surveillance, but the Law Commission applied them to the wider management and protection of national security, both in the consultation paper and in the subsequent much-delayed 2020 report.[7]

While the consultation process led to a report that acknowledged some of the problems with the original proposals, and had the effect of mitigating some of the more deleterious possibilities, the Commission did not ultimately engage with the deeper concerns we raise here. The issues and challenges are not purely historic; Brexit, the pandemic, concerns about foreign electoral interference and advances in facial recognition technology have demonstrated that major challenges will continue to arise with the consequent temptation to deploy these models again. We approach our inquiry by examining oversight in different institutions: parliamentary oversight, including through the Intelligence and Security Committee (the second part of this article); judicial oversight through the courts (the third part); and oversight by judicial commissioners, which has blurred the boundaries between regulatory and judicial oversight (the fourth part). This approach recognises that there is no single chronological, institutional or substantive starting point, and that each is distinct but inter-connects with the others. In each part, we demonstrate how a model has been developed and re-used even though these mechanisms might be flawed, and the implications of these changes for executive accountability. The conclusion draws these threads together and presents some of the most significant implications that follow from them.

Paying attention to these developments reveals how uncritical re-use of special measures and models undermines the modern constitutional imperative of executive accountability – the public interest in knowing that the government is acting legally, ethically and consistently with the will and authority of parliament, in national security as in any other area. We show that a degree of accountability can be achieved without general transparency, at least in specific instances, but a systemic absence of transparency cannot foster public confidence and poses risks that inadequate processes will persist and flaws remain hidden. Ultimately, we argue that the incremental and inter-related exceptionalism is suggestive not merely of flawed and limited accountability mechanisms but also of unacknowledged distinctions between transparency and accountability, and a deeper, unspoken re-shaping of contemporary constitutional functions and powers.

Parliamentary Oversight

A core function of parliament is to hold the government to account;8 ministers are responsible to parliament for their departments' actions.[9] An essential element of this accountability is the flow of information, underpinned by the obligation on ministers to be truthful and as open as possible towards parliament (and the public).[10] Yet, while the SIAs were put on a statutory footing by the Intelligence Services Act 1994 (ISA 1994) in an attempt to increase openness and institute 'proper arrangements for accountability',[11] substantial exceptionalism to the usual principles of parliamentary accountability in national security remains. A particular concern is the information advantage ministers (and sometimes the Prime Minister) have over the rest of the legislature as these 'arrangements for accountability' often give the executive the right to control the release of information about the SIAs' activities. Where oversight powers are positioned within the executive, and oversight findings are closely held by it, there is a risk that state failures will not be adequately revealed or addressed. This weakness may undermine the ability of the legislature to assess or report on the working of the system itself, in essence undermining the ability of parliament to hold the executive to account.

Starting with section 94 of the Telecommunications Act 1984 and moving on to the reporting mechanisms in the Interception of Communications Act 1985 (IoCA 1985), ISA 1994, the Regulation of Investigatory Powers Act 2000 (RIPA 2000), and IPA 2016, we demonstrate both the executive control over information made available to parliament and the risks of executive self-oversight mechanisms subverting and limiting the effectiveness of parliamentary control. Consideration of the reporting mechanism's effectiveness, and the extent to which problems in its operation have been recognised and addressed, is needed, yet debate has been sparse and for many years key information has not been forthcoming. We begin with section 94, even though now repealed, because concerns arising from its operation–and specifically the impact of unrestricted executive control over information – have not been sufficiently considered. The exceptions in the reporting mechanism can be seen now as problematic yet a similar executive power over information flows arises in the models found in subsequent statutes. In successive reforms, including the IPA 2016, information asymmetry remains. When future proposals suggest reliance on oversight provisions where the executive has control over what is reported to parliament these deficiencies and especially the lessons of section 94 should be addressed.

Intertwined with this is the development since the Telecommunications Act of a particular model for balancing national security secrecy interests with accountability–the indirect accountability model –on which there is increasing reliance. Rather than permit parliament direct access to information about SIAs' activities, this model permits a trusted intermediary some access to operating information and the intermediary then reports to parliament. This indirect form of accountability substitutes the principle of general transparency with a principle of transparency to the trusted few. Transparency is in issue at two stages: between the executive (including SIAs) and trusted intermediaries; and between trusted intermediaries and parliament (or the general public). There are constraints on both steps, but those at the second step in particular have tended to be overlooked, and the consequent impact upon parliament's ability to hold the executive to account has not been fully considered.

Reporting by the Secretary of State

Section 94 of the Telecommunications Act 1984 needs some explanation because the provision and its workings have been somewhat obscure. Section 94 empowered the Secretary of State to make 'directions of a general character' to any person in the interests of national security or international relations, which could include a requirement that the person not disclose the existence or content of those directions.[12] Although section 94 was amended in 2003 by the introduction of a test of necessity and proportionality, it remained a broadly drafted power.[13] Moreover, while the Secretary of State was required to 'lay before Parliament a copy of every direction given', under section 94(4) the Secretary of State was excused from so doing if he was 'of the opinion that disclosure of the direction is against the interests of national security or relations with the government

97

of a country or territory outside the United Kingdom, the commercial interests of any person'.

Arguably, section 94 was a product of its time, enacted when national security was generally still seen as a matter of prerogative power or a category of information that government was simply entitled to keep secret;[14] the jurisprudence from the ECtHR on surveillance was in its infancy.[15] Nonetheless, concerns were expressed. One MP observed: 'the Secretary of State decides in secret to give secret instructions to the Director-General, who ... is not allowed to reveal those directions. This is a massive power to the Secretary of State and ... will be operating in total secrecy without any accountability to the House of Commons. That is totally and utterly wrong in any sort of democracy.'[16]

The deployment of this exception eviscerated parliamentary oversight. Its use depended on the individual understanding of the Secretary of State, and the Act did not require the opinion to be reasonable or proportionate or take into account any particular factors; seemingly, it could be used even beyond national security.[17] Moreover, this evisceration was persistently hidden. When the statute was amended in 2003 (in light of the Human Rights Act 1998), the extent and nature of the use of section 94 directions was not mentioned by ministers. In 2012 the Joint Committee on the Draft Communications Data Bill could find no information about section 94 directions, even though it sought it.[18] In 2014, the Home Affairs Select Committee noted that 'there is no public disclosure of how this is used ....'[19]Similarly, although there was a potential overlap with the RIPA 2000 regime, the use of section 94 directions for bulk data collection does not appear to have been disclosed by ministers until March 2015.[20]No section 94 directions were ever laid before parliament, which suggests that the section 94(4) exception was used in all instances.

With scrutiny limited,[21] oversight of the executive was for many years carried out by the executive itself. As the Interception of Communications Commissioner (IoCC) subsequently noted, effectively the whole process was secret.[22] The lack of oversight and the fact that decisions were in practice unlikely to be challenged facilitated the broad interpretation the executive gave the powers in section 94. An expansion in quantity and type of surveillance techniques was thus enabled without the executive needing to disclose that expansion to parliament. This is an important lesson about the dangers of giving unbounded control over information flows to the Executive, but a lesson that has not been learned as the constraints imposed on the oversight Commissioners illustrate.

Reporting by a Commissioner

The year after section 94 was enacted, the UK, in response to the Malone case, legislated to put surveillance by means of interception of communications on a statutory footing; the issue of accountability was debated but extension beyond the traditional techniques of ministerial accountability rejected.[23] The Interception of Communications Act 1985 did, however, introduce an oversight body: the Interception of Communications Commissioner (IoCC) whose role was 'to keep under review the carrying out by the Secretary of State of the functions' under the IoCA 1985.[24] The IoCC was granted powers to request information, though he had no powers to compel change. Though the effectiveness of those information gathering powers was questioned,[25] by 2016 it was said that the IoCC's office was 'given access without reservation not only to all the material they requested but to the Agencies' own systems and to the processes of the warrant granting department'.[26]

Significantly for transparency and consequently also accountability, IoCA 1985 required the IoCC to publish a report on his activities, though the impact of the reports depended on the scrutiny given to them. The Security Service Act 1989 (SSA 1989) and ISA 1994 each instituted another commissioner, with similar roles in relation to the operations of SIAs in general.[27] At this stage the effectiveness of this mechanism was questioned but dismissed on the basis that there was no evidence it did not work.[28] The surveillance regime was updated again by RIPA 2000, including the provisions related to the commissioners. When some sort of oversight regime following Snowden was brought in for section 94 directions, it was these regimes that were co-opted.[29] In each instance, the model was one of indirect accountability based on a trusted intermediary with oversight obligations, a model which originated in IoCA 1985, was replicated in the SSA 1989 and ISA 1994, and retained in RIPA 2000.

Although an improvement in oversight in relation to section 94, weakness existed. The commissioners' reports did not necessarily constitute full disclosure. First, since none of the section 94 directions were public it was difficult to discuss them publicly.[30] Secondly, and more generally, the commissioners had to report annually to the Prime Minister, who was to lay the report before parliament.[31] However, the commissioners could limit what was to be disclosed to parliament.[32] Additionally, showing information flow controls similar to section 94(4), the Prime Minister could exclude from the report certain content. Given the temporal proximity of section 94 and IoCA 1985, it may be that the ideas behind the one influenced thinking about the other. By the time RIPA 2000 was enacted the list of grounds on which content could be excluded comprised not just the types of content mentioned in the foregoing statutes (notably national security, detection or prevention of serious crime, and the economic well-being of the United Kingdom) but also 'the continued discharge of the functions of any public authority whose activities include activities that are subject to review by the Commissioner'.[33]

Given the large number of public authorities which would fall within IoCC's purview, this was a broad exception not necessarily connected to national security. Some of the other objectives were phrased equally broadly but transplanted from earlier statutes into RIPA 2000. As with section 94(4), there is no requirement of reasonableness or proportionality. Moreover, while the commissioners were to be consulted on any redaction from the report and parliament had to be told if information had been redacted (admittedly a crucial difference from the position under section 94(4)), the final decision on content lay with the Prime Minister. There was no timescale for tabling the report, and no requirement that the Prime Minister justify or explain any decision to delay or exclude material.

The de facto deference to the executive under section 94(4) had, in a retrograde step, become a de jure deference under first IoCA 1985 and then its successors, including RIPA 2000. The lessons from section 94 – particularly regarding the breadth of the exception and the questions of who made the relevant determinations and on what basis–were not considered at RIPA 2000's enactment, nor since. It may be that section 94 was seen not to be relevant given that these were more general reporting obligations, taking place against a warrant-based system and relying on the effectiveness of indirect accountability. Alternatively, it could be that the use of section 94(4) and lack of oversight of section 94 were not recognised by the parliament precisely because of the secrecy and obscurity surrounding the provision, and they were not disclosed by the executive because section 94(4) provided the executive with total control over information flow.

This model has been replicated in other contexts, including policing and even beyond. In the Protection of Freedoms Act 2012 (PoFA 2012), two commissioners the Biometrics Commissioner (BC) and the Surveillance Camera Commissioner (SCC) were introduced to deal with retention of DNA by the police[34] and the over-use of CCTV[35] respectively. Accountability was achieved through the provision of reports to the Secretary of State and thence to parliament. Material could be redacted in the reports of the BC on broad grounds (including but not limited to national security),[36]raising the usual concerns about information flows. By contrast, the SCC appears as an aberration because there is not (as yet) an equivalent restriction in respect of the SCC's reports, but the terrain covered by the SCC is much broader than that of the oversight commissioners, covering not just public bodies but also the use of surveillance cameras by private actors. Currently the Government is seeking to consolidate the two commissioners into one appointment.[37]

The model of indirect accountability developed from IoCA 1985 through to RIPA 2000 was again re-deployed when the surveillance regime was reconstructed through the IPA 2016. The UK government claimed that the IPA 2016 introduced a 'world leading oversight regime'[38]but, while it may well have introduced some significant safeguards controlling the use of surveillance powers, the extent to which it ensures executive accountability to parliament is questionable. As before, a key mechanism for such accountability is the annual report of the Investigatory Powers Commissioner (the replacement for all commissioners under previous acts) under section 234 of IPA 2016 on the carrying out of the functions of the Judicial Commissioners, who review executive decisions to issue warrants. Despite the concerns about its predecessors,[39]the IPA 2016 still allows for self-censorship and reports are still subject to executive control. The IPC reports to the Prime Minister alone (despite attempts in Public Bill Committee to change the reporting obligation to parliament). The Prime Minister must publish the report and lay it before parliament, but can exclude matter on the same broad grounds as under RIPA 2000.[40] The Minister of State for Defence stated that any redaction would be made only on national security grounds.[41] If this is the case, then the other grounds should be repealed.

The IPC's first report provided coverage and scrutiny of numerous matters, including errors made in the exercise of powers.[42] It was, however, opaque about the reasoning and standards for decisions about whether errors were serious enough to require a person to be notified and when national security would preclude notification. In its 2018 Report, the perceived need to suppress information is evident; the IPC, for example, reports being unable to supply how many times the Consolidated Guidance to Intelligence Officers and Service Personnel on the Detention and Interviewing of Detainees Overseas, and on the Passing and Receipt of Intelligence Relating to Detainees was followed because of the 'sensitivity' of the topic.[43] Control of information apparently stays within the hold of the executive. In sum, the replication of earlier flaws of RIPA 2000 is apparent. Despite Anderson's praise for the IoCC's reports there are still, as he also noted, constraints on transparency.[44] It might be argued that the worst excesses of section 94(4) secrecy have been avoided as the fact of redaction is visible, but this still leaves parliament at an information disadvantage vis-a-vis the executive.

The Law Commission in its consultation paper viewed the IPA 2016 as a good model, referring to the IPC as a template for a statutory commissioner to receive concerns and complaints from members of the security services about the way those services are operating.[45] The Commission observed that the annual reporting obligation 'would potentially include details of any investigation'[46] but did not consider the fact that historically these reports have not gone into details of particular operations. In its subsequent report, the Commission maintained its view that a statutory commissioner should be used and that the IPCO framework was an appropriate model.[47] It acknowledged however concerns about whistle blowers and freedom of expression (which it had not addressed in its consultation paper).[48] Rightly, the Commission saw as problematic the options of reporting on whistleblower complaints to the Prime Minister or to the Intelligence and Security Committee (discussed below) because that could lead to a public perception that the process is 'internal' not 'external'[49] However, the Commission does not identify core problems that underpin the oversight system as a whole as regards executive control over information flows. Moreover, there was no critical consideration of whether a model designed to back up a warrant system is suitable for co-opting to a broader context and different purposes (criticisms seemingly being more practically focussed), though the BC and SCC may in any event be precedent for this.[50]

Reporting by the Intelligence and Security Committee of Parliament

A further avenue of parliamentary oversight of the SIAs was introduced through the ISC, established under the ISA 1994. This was a development from the existing regimes then in place under the IOCA 1985 and the SSA 1989 and seemingly arose from a concern expressed in parliament about the effectiveness of a model based on reporting to a minister. Despite this, we question the degree to which the ISC counters executive control over information. It is another example of the model of indirect accountability that relies on a trusted intermediary with the weaknesses in transparency and accountability outlined above. The introduction of the ISC probably reflected a more general attitude that the SIAs–now creatures of statute– should be more open and accountable within the underlying constitutional framework. The ISC was established to 'examine or otherwise oversee the expenditure, administration, policy and operations' of MI5, MI6 and GCHQ.[51]

In this, the ISC is a form of trusted intermediary. Yet, regardless of the ISC's views about the way powers have been exercised in any given circumstance and any political effect it may have through embarrassment to or pressure on the government following a report, executive power cannot be limited or controlled by the ISC. There has been significant criticism of the ISC, specifically as regards its independence. It remains a sui generis committee rather than a standard parliamentary select committee and, under the statute, subject to a degree of Prime Ministerial control.[52] Moreover, its members often have held roles in the bodies they now oversee (for example ministers and, via appointment to the House of Lords, former senior officers in the agencies themselves) leading to concerns that the oversight body in practice becomes deferential to those agencies' assessments of legality, necessity and proportionality.[53] The Home Affairs Committee saw the system as weak, and ineffective, and that had 'an impact upon the credibility of the [SIAs'] accountability, and ... the credibility of Parliament itself.'[54] That the ISC is unique in Parliament is, yet again, suggestive that exceptionalism should be acceptable where national security is concerned.

Nonetheless, the ISC has at times appeared willing to hold the executive and its agencies to account in a way that suggests the membership risks outlined above have been mitigated: its 2018 inquiry into extraordinary rendition was a landmark of scrutiny.[55] However, it is information that is key–both the ISC's access to information and its ability to make this information available through its reports –and in these regards the ISC faces significant hurdles both as regards access to information and in its ability to make its report public.

There are severe limitations on the ISC's ability to make agencies fully comply with the obligation to share information in a timely manner[56] and the Secretary of State can deny the committee access to sensitive material (comparable to the original limitations in section 94 and RIPA 2000).[57] It is noteworthy that the ISC seemingly only became aware of the use of section 94 as a result of the Snowden disclosures[58] and from its report on surveillance in the run up to the IPA,[59] it is unclear how much, if anything, the ISC was told about the use of section 94 directions. Since the ISC is already a limited, pre-approved group this limitation seems unnecessary and hobbles its effectiveness as a trusted intermediary. Although the ISC reports are now made to parliament – an improvement on the original position – they are supplied in advance to the Prime Minister.[60]The Prime Minister can require material to be excluded from any ISC report if, after consultation with the ISC, he is of the opinion it would be prejudicial to the ability of the SIAs to discharge their functions.[61] For example, in Privacy and Security: A modern and transparent legal framework, redaction occurred in the part of the report dealing with section 94.[62]

Further, there are no requirements on when reports must be published.[63] The risk that a publication could be delayed occurred in 2019 when the Prime Minister's office refused to publish an ISC report on Russian interference in UK elections; no reason was given despite its salience given the impending General Election.[64] It would be ten months until publication; with the legislation setting no deadline for the ISC to be established in a new parliament, the government – by not making ISC appointments – was effectively able to delay the publication of the Russia report and any new scrutiny.[65]Where the ISC makes reports other than its annual report there is no requirement that the ISC lay those reports before parliament. It is not clear whether the ISC needs to disclose the fact it has conducted any such inquiry or made any report to the Prime Minister. The 2013 JSA reforms made some improvements but it was a lost opportunity to strengthen oversight. Concerns raised at the time of reform were seemingly overridden by traditional concerns about the need for secrecy, just as they were at the time the ISC was introduced.[66]

The ISC gained a power in the IPA: it can request an investigation by the IPC.[67]This power is, however, of limited effect because, again, an investigation would only become public if included in ISC or IPC reports to parliament. There was no recognition of the fact that executive control over information that will be provided to the ISC could adversely affect the ability of parliament to hold the executive to account.

The effectiveness and limits of parliamentary oversight

Overall we see a picture of national security oversight where traditional prerogative exceptionalism has been replaced by a model of statutory exceptionalism that uses indirect or even private approaches to accountability with its reliance on a trusted intermediary (whether in the form of a commissioner's report or that of the ISC). It entrenches executive control over information flows. Parliamentary reporting requirements are weakened so substantially that their ability to achieve the accountability and oversight for which they were designed must be called into question, particularly in times of crisis. The models have become embedded, and largely taken for granted. The weaknesses of this model–demonstrated over time–are overlooked all too easily, or evidence is not available to support concerns.

While the IPA 2016 overcame some weaknesses in the oversight regime for SIAs, it did not address those that have long been evident in the mechanisms that should provide for executive accountability to parliament; the position of the ISC has not been revisited. The fact that the Law Commission, while it accepts the importance of some form of disclosure in relation to whistleblowing investigations (and even accepts a public interest defence to criminal liability), does not engage with these weaknesses and underlying executive control illustrates the point. When existing structures have been adopted, as for example with regards to PoFA 2012, it also risks a repetition of these weaknesses and their expansion into areas not inherently connected with surveillance. This acceptance may be understandable, but not justifiable, given that similar special treatment characterises other institutions that hold the executive to account. Exceptionalism is also found in the courts, where oversight mechanisms are taken forward even though past experience should call for caution.

Oversight in the Courts

The courts, with an independent judiciary, ensure the executive is acting lawfully and is accountable.[68] They provide redress where action has been unlawful and, through exposure during proceedings, shed light on acts of the state.[69] Even in the national security sphere, they provide oversight of executive power, even if this is not complete.[70] Yet pressure on open justice remains given the perceived need for secrecy in the field of national security. When national security issues arise, two main mechanisms have emerged to manage them. One was the establishment of specialist tribunals, for example the Proscribed Organisations Appeal Commission (POAC),[71] the Special Immigration Appeals Commission (SIAC), and the Investigatory Powers Tribunal (IPT).[72] The other was reliance on special procedures, not just in the specialist tribunals but also in the ordinary courts. The impact each of these approaches has on individuals' rights, open justice and the flow of information varies, and their cumulative impact has not been considered.

The existence of specialist tribunals has, in providing a venue to decide issues that could not be dealt with by the ordinary courts, to some extent improved individuals' ability to scrutinise and challenge executive decisions. The IPT has been seen as part of the oversight mechanisms for the SIAs and therefore a step forward in accountability. Moreover, the establishment of SIAC allowed some individuals to seek judicial review of a Home Secretary's decision to deport them, albeit only in that specialist tribunal. Similarly, POAC hears challenges (under judicial review principles) to the refusal by the Secretary of State to remove an organisation from the list of proscribed organisations. From some tribunals (for example, POAC), appeal through the ordinary appellate courts is possible.[73] While RIPA 2000 originally sought to limit individuals' rights of access to the general courts,[74] the IPA introduced the possibility of appeal against the IPT's decisions.[75] Nonetheless, the existence of these tribunals still institutionalises the special treatment of executive action.

More worrying are special procedure mechanisms, which may be relied on in the ordinary courts as well as in specialist tribunals. Although possibly limiting the extent or effectiveness of judicial oversight, some special procedure mechanisms respect the constitutional benchmarks of equality of arms and open justice. Public interest immunity (PII), for example, allows the executive to withhold evidence in a dispute, but the executive cannot rely on that evidence and so equality of arms is not compromised; this may incentivise acceptance of open justice. Courts can hold hearings in camera or impose reporting restrictions, which may limit open justice, but only where necessary for the administration of justice or, sometimes, to protect national security. Recent changes, however, go to the heart of what constitutes a fair and open trial. We examine two instances: in civil proceedings (including administrative) through the use of closed material procedures; and in criminal proceedings through new approaches to limiting access to hearings. These show how a procedure developed in one context is re-deployed elsewhere. Moreover, as we detail below, the Law Commission proposals in relation to official secrets adopt these models for use in a new context without consideration of the extent to which retreats from fair trials and open justice have consequences for executive accountability.

Civil and administrative proceedings: the rise of closed material procedures

Closed material procedures (CMPs) have emerged from processes designed to manage deportation on security grounds[76] which were found to be incompatible with the ECHR.[77] While developed for use in SIAC, CMPs are also available in POAC[78] and the IPT has procedures in place that parallel them.[79] Under CMPs, security sensitive information cannot be disclosed to applicants or their lawyers. Instead, a 'special advocate' is appointed to represent the applicant in a closed hearing. The special advocate sees all the information on which the state relies, but after seeing that information may not communicate with the applicant or the applicant's lawyers about the case.[80] This introduction of a 'trusted intermediary' into the process parallels that seen in the reporting mechanisms under ISA 1994, RIPA 2000 and IPA. CMPs were established to enhance rights protection; those subject to deportation were no longer vulnerable to executive control alone but would have an independent tribunal and informed legal representation, albeit representation with whom they had a different relationship.

The government has attempted to use CMPs in relation to security sensitive material in broader circumstances: to defend civil actions brought by returning Guantanamo Bay detainees alleging UK complicity in torture and rendition. The Supreme Court, however, held that the courts had no general power to permit CMPs. They were at odds with natural justice and open justice.[81] CMPs would only be available if statute permitted.[82] The government subsequently proposed legislation extending the use of CMPs to civil proceedings generally,[83] even though the deficiencies of CMPs as they operated in SIAC were on record. A special advocate commented that, 'the public should be left in absolutely no doubt that what is happening ... has absolutely nothing to do with the traditions of adversarial justice as we have come to understand them in the British legal system'[84] However well motivated, representation in CMPs cannot be as effective as representation in ordinary proceedings. Controversially, the effect of CMPs under the JSA proposals was not to safeguard rights but to diminish them. Nevertheless, the JSA was enacted, albeit with some safeguarding amendments. Its procedures were quickly deployed beyond the narrow range of cases for which it was ostensibly intended.[85] It seems that where a mechanism exists, it will be used (as was section 94(4) of the Telecommunications Act); a point which should be taken into account when considering amendments to the mechanism or its further redeployment.

The consequence of CMPs for accountability is complex. CMPs limit the extent to which the executive is accountable through the courts as far as equality of arms and openness are concerned. Conversely, judges may see material from the executive that might not otherwise come before judicial eyes. There is a conflict between accountability that is public and accountability that is not public, which has parallels with concerns about executive control over information flows. Both require extraordinary degrees of trust in the executive and judicial branches but the latter – non-public accountability – even if it could be effective, is difficult to assess because of the secrecy that shrouds it.

The contraction of open justice in criminal proceedings

Developments in the past few years are eroding commitments to open justice in criminal matters. Guardian News and Media Ltd & Ors v R & Incedal[86] (Incedal case), which concerns terrorism-related offences, represents a significant change in the acceptable management of criminal trials in the national security context. It offers further evidence of diminished state accountability, with insufficient regard to the public interest in open justice and an individual's right to a fair trial and is a dangerous precedent for case management more generally. The trial judge had imposed what was effectively total secrecy. This was overturned on appeal, but restrictive conditions were imposed: the only public proceedings would be the swearing in of the jury, the reading of charges, parts of the introductory remarks to the jury, parts of the prosecution's opening address, the verdicts, and perhaps some of the sentencing remarks. Everything else would be closed. In a novel arrangement, ten 'accredited journalists' were to be permitted to attend 'the bulk of the trial' and to take notes, which were not to be removed from the court. Reporting restrictions were imposed.[87] While not formalised in the way that the oversight mechanisms in ISA 1994, RIPA 2000 and IPA 2016 were, there is a similar preference for relying on a small group of trusted intermediaries who can only access and disseminate approved information, reducing transparency. At the end of the case the media unsuccessfully applied for permission to report some detail from the closed part of the trial.[88] In the absence of accountability through open courts, the Court of Appeal suggested that 'public accountability' could be achieved by the ISC, but did not consider the limits on the ISC.[89]

The judgments reveal an ill-defined, sui generis approach with no statutory basis. The trial judge relied on 'ministerial certificates' from the Secretaries of State. Although not disclosed, the certificates were apparently similar to those used in PII but, from the way the Court of Appeal refers to the certificates underlying the in camera order, the mechanism is not the same as PII.[90] Under PII, if a fair trial requires disclosure of evidence the executive must choose between disclosure or withdrawing charges. This new process means that the prosecution would not have to choose between keeping material secret or bringing a prosecution; it will be able to do both.[91] There is no monitoring of when or how this new process has been used,[92] bringing to mind the total secrecy of section[93] and its consequences, nor is there any indication that media or civil society organisations will be notified if such arrangements are sought in future. This is particularly worrying given that the Incedal case reportedly came to public attention by chance. Admittedly, in Incedal the complete blanket of secrecy was removed, but the substantive result and the procedure used to reach it are worrying. There is a new but opaque model for departing from open justice that, with the Court of Appeal's imprimatur, risks diminishing the transparent scrutiny of executive actions, has not been subject to parliamentary scrutiny, and has now emerged as the basis for law reforms.

The creeping influence of Incedal and CMPs

The Law Commission consultation paper treated the Incedal decision as an unproblematic precedent that provided an acceptable way of excluding the public from criminal proceedings; that view underpinned the Commission's proposals about the way that Official Secrets Act (OSA) offences should be tried. The Commission suggested reforming section 8(4) of the OSA 1920, which empowers a court to hear a case entirely in private except for passing of sentence, removing that draconian power but retaining the option of complete secrecy that, given Incedal, it clearly saw as an entirely tenable option. It proposed excluding the public only if it is 'necessary to ensure national safety ... is not prejudiced'.[94] The report subsequently put a gloss on that, recommending exclusion only if it 'must be necessary for the administration of justice having regard to the risk to national safety'.[95]

While a necessity test would be an improvement on the existing model, the proposed change would still fall well short of what is required to ensure scrutiny of the executive. In particular, 'national safety' was undefined, rendering the provision vulnerable to broad interpretation, if not abuse, as demonstrated by the interpretation of a similar phrase in section 94(4) of the Telecommunications Act. Crucially, the Commission did not in its consultation paper or report consider the absence of a statutory basis for the Incedal approach. Significantly, the Commission did not step back from its consultation view that accepted unquestioningly the Court of Appeal's position that the ISC provides an adequate path for executive accountability; as we have argued above, that position is unconvincing.

In both the consultation and report the Commission observed the contrast between the development of approaches in criminal and civil proceedings, noting that the JSA provides for CMPs in the latter. The Commission stated that its 'aim is not to suggest that the procedure that is applicable in the civil context ought to be imported wholesale into the criminal'.[96] However, it added that reviewing criminal procedure in this area 'would provide the opportunity to tailor these powers' to the criminal context.[97]The Commission's consultation proposals indicated that it regarded CMPs as now an established fact and form of procedure and, more importantly, suggest it saw no need to consider reasons why they might not be appropriate and adaptable to a broader range of circumstances. The report maintains this position, observing that CMPs may be used in SIAC and under Terrorism Prevention and Investigation Measures (TPIMs) proceedings, but does not engage with those developments as either problematic or as expansions of secrecy.[98]

The consultation proposals exemplified the way that approaches from one area of national security could be extended to another without full consideration of the implications. In the report, the treatment of the responses regarding adapting civil law to criminal needs is cursory; the report recites competing strands of evidence for and against need for a review to consider adaptation but engages with neither. The recommendation for a review is ultimately an assertion made regardless of evidence rather than because of it.[99] It is not an answer to say the matter is 'not strictly within our terms of reference'; if a recommendation is made– and it was – then that should oblige the Commission to engage with the critiques in the evidence.[100] In failing to do so it neglects the conflation of the ways in which secrecy is managed in Incedal and CMPs. It places them on a single scale for managing secrecy and security, with the result that exceptionalism in criminal and civil law are uncritically combined on a single legal landscape. This is problematic because they are fundamentally different.

In Incedal the criminal defendant could hear the evidence relied on by the state, but in CMPs the non-state party may be denied access to evidence relied on by the state. This has consequences for transparency and accountability because taking the civil provisions and principles into criminal cases will further and systematically diminish the ability to scrutinise executive behaviour. The Commission viewed one of the factors in the balance as being upholding the principle of open justice but this is misguided; the JSA is not concerned with open justice, it dispenses with it.[101] The legislature rejected the 'open' administration of justice as a criterion and the JSA refers instead to the 'effective' administration of justice.[102] In the Incedal approach, open justice is severely contracted but equality of arms remains insofar as the defendant is able to hear the evidence relied on by the prosecution, and the possibility of some media scrutiny is retained.[103] CMPs, however, have stronger limits on open justice and equality of arms. Even if one accepts that the Commission was cautious in taking no substantive view about adapting the civil provisions for criminal cases, the very fact that this appeared an untroubling option in the consultation stage suggests a disturbing sanguinity to undermining rights and protections in the criminal process.

That speaks to the lack of consideration given to the wider national security legal framework, which is characterised by concessions to executive control and systemic weaknesses in accountability mechanisms, and the failure to identify persistent exceptionalism as the context in which its reform proposals are made and which they would bolster. The changes in criminal and civil proceedings plainly raise concerns for accountability. They take place against a backdrop in which national security exceptionalism facilitates the transposition of rules dealing with a specific issue to a broader range of applications. The judicial role has not been exempt from these trends and warrants particular attention.

Judicial Commissioners: The Blurred Boundary of Regulatory and Judicial Oversight

Executive accountability has long been viewed in terms of the relationships between the three branches of government but with the passage of the IPA 2016–and arguably a partial attempt to respond to the oversight failures surrounding the use of section 94 directions –there has been a blurring of executive and judicial boundaries in the creation of 'judicial commissioners' to provide oversight of the SIAs. The absence of bright lines of judicial power is not always problematic. On the contrary, a flexible deployment of judges may increase public confidence in scrutiny of matters and might even be 'incontestably to the benefit of good government'.[104] However, attention to the nature of and rationales for judicial roles –more sharply separated from other branches of government since the Constitutional Reform Act 2005 –helps illuminate the constitutional framework and the ways in which integrity and accountability are ensured. With national security exceptionalism pervading institutions and mechanisms so as to limit accountability to parliament, the blurring of judicial and executive boundaries is troubling and significant.

The Judicial Function

In the UK there is no circumscription of judicial power that is found in other common law jurisdictions.[105] Nevertheless, the archetypal function of judges is to interpret and apply the law in the resolution of disputes. Judges are valued for their skills in analysing evidence, managing parties' interests and making determinations, but also because judicial independence gives rise to confidence that conclusions will be based on evidence, rather than political or other needs.[106] Institutional and individual independence ensures that decisions will be made without influence and visible independence from other branches of government safeguards confidence in the legal system. There are, however, well established departures from that view of the judicial role, some of which arise and function effectively precisely because the judiciary is independent, and because that independence is respected and valued by the executive and legislature.

Among these departures is the appointment of judges to conduct inquiries into issues of public importance. There has long been concern that such appointments do not sit well with the judicial role, but it is now well-established practice.[107] While the view has traditionally been that appointments of judges to inquiries are not an exercise of the judicial function, one former Lord Chief Justice considered 'the provision of a suitably qualified judge to conduct an inquiry [is] an important part of the duties of the judiciary … [and] an important part of our constitutional framework.'[108] A corollary of this is that 'general constitutional principles concerning judicial independence must apply.'[109] This has practical consequences; for example, the Lord Chief Justice must consent to a judge chairing and a judge cannot be questioned by parliament.[110]

At what point, however, do judges cease to exercise an adjudicatory (or where relevant, independent inquiry) function and become closer to the role of systemic reviewer or even decision-maker within the administrative state?[111] While inquiries might be seen as part of public administration their ad hoc nature means they do not form part of a regulatory structure.[112] The independence of regulators and judges is quite different: regulators derive their independence from statute, whereas judicial independence is constitutional. The nature of judicial commissioners' independence under the IPA 2016 is unclear and, as a consequence, the extent to which they are distinct from the executive and can hold the executive to account requires consideration.

The Investigatory Powers Act: a changing judicial role?

The patchwork of commissioners overseeing aspects of surveillance each uses an oversight model that is regulatory (in the sense described above) but which is reliant on judicial independence.[113] The established nature of these positions distinguishes them from the ad hoc posts created for inquiries, making them more like independent regulatory authorities. These commissioners reviewed, but did not approve, the work of the SIAs and the exercise of surveillance powers. Unlike many regulators, however, the Commissioners were not selected for technocratic expertise but instead because of their independence, with appointments typically being retired senior judges. Arguably, their incorporation into the service of the executive had little impact on judicial independence as they no longer carried out judicial roles.

Building on these models, the IPA 2016 further obfuscates the boundaries of the judicial role by creating 'judicial commissioners' to provide oversight of the exercise of investigatory powers, and specifically to participate in the approval of warrants.[114] The IPA 2016 established the Investigatory Powers Commissioner (IPC) and the Investigatory Powers Commissioner's Office (IPCO), replacing the existing commissioners and their offices. The IPA 2016 continues the established Commissioner model, as the IPC must be a person who 'holds or has held a high judicial office', as must any other commissioners supporting the IPC.[115] However, the IPA 2016 creation of judicial commissioners marks a new and very important part of the judicial role for two reasons. The first builds on traditional features, but the second is a radical departure.

First, the model aspires to be more significantly underpinned by judicial independence than its predecessors. This is evident in three ways: from the process for appointment and removal, the standing of the office's inaugural occupant, and the scale of the operation. This underpinning is valuable and largely consistent with traditional conceptions of the judicial role and independence. The Prime Minister appoints the IPC and Commissioners for three-year renewable terms but they must be jointly recommended by the heads of the judiciary of England and Wales, Scotland and Northern Ireland, and by the Lord Chancellor.[116] Removal requires a resolution of both Houses of Parliament.[117] While the Prime Minister's powers are limited and the process suggests a robust respect for judicial independence, concerns were raised while the Bill was in draft.[118] Even if the Prime Minister in reality has little to do with the appointment,[119]

it is questionable whether, as required by Convention jurisprudence,[120] a Judicial Commissioner is perceived as independent. Turning to the scale of the operation, resources will inevitably be at issue because a key element of independence is adequate funding. As the outgoing IoCC observed, 'The appearance of independence is undermined if one has to go through the minister whose work one is supervising.'[121] Very substantial resources have, however, been committed to IPCO, with over 50 staff and 15 commissioners. Thus, in form, substance and scale, the establishment of the IPC and IPCO constitutes a significant and new departure from the established conceptualisation of the judicial role in a way that earlier Commissioner Models did not. It relies on core components of institutional and individual independence, most notably where warrants do not require judicial approval but are subjected to a so-called 'double lock' that for its legitimacy and effectiveness relies on judicial independence more than judicial power.

That independence is weaker with three-year terms, but there is a measure of protection insofar as a judicial commissioner is unlikely to be removed for political reasons. Most importantly, the extent to which judicial commissioners have the independence of judges is necessary (though not of itself sufficient) for effective oversight of executive action. In constitutional terms, the regime has the hallmarks Lord Thomas saw in the judicial chairing of public inquiries: 'the provision of a suitably qualified judge ... [is] an important part of the duties of the judiciary ... and an important part of our constitutional framework.'[122] That is a strength, but it is one that simultaneously carries risks because of the positioning and limits of commissioners' powers in an oversight model with constraints on public reporting Secondly, and radically, the role of judicial commissioners under the IPA 2016 is extensive in scope, which puts more stress on the established conceptions of judicial independence and separation of powers than would occur if it was narrow in scope, and thus makes the blurred boundary particularly significant. Commissioners' responsibilities are wide, wider than those of the commissioners under RIPA 2000, covering numerous aspects of surveillance approval and oversight.[123]

In deciding whether or not to approve a warrant, a commissioner must review the executive conclusions about whether it is necessary on relevant grounds, and whether the conduct the warrant authorises is proportionate to the objective of the warrant. The Commissioner is to 'apply the same principles as would be applied by a court on an application for judicial review.'[124] There is also a general limitation that judicial commissioners should have regard to privacy rights.[125] However, these processes are not the same as those that ordinarily characterise judicial review or even proceedings that use CMPs. There are limits to how effective the judicial commissioner model can be as a regime that holds the executive to account. Commissioners are exercising an oversight function from within the Executive. This is apparent in several ways. The model is quite different from that envisioned in the original recommendations of the Independent Reviewer of Terrorism Legislation, which were that in most instances the Secretary of State should apply for a warrant and a judge should decide whether to authorise it.[126] Commissioners must always have regard to national security as the prime consideration.[127]

Other matters–including privacy, necessity and proportionality–must also be considered[128] but executive views about national security and the particular context will inevitably carry exceptional weight and demand deference. In its wider oversight functions of audit, inspection and investigation the IPC is expressly limited by section 229(6) under which he 'must not act in a way [he considers to be] contrary to the public interest or prejudicial to (a) national security, (b) the prevention or detection of serious crime, or (c) the economic well-being of the United Kingdom'.[129] Moreover, Judicial Commissioners will not hear interparty arguments.[130] Without adversarial challenge or at least a special advocate (however problematic the latter may be), the Commissioner must both identify the arguments that a person affected might put, and judge those arguments.

The IPA 2016 has resulted in a comprehensive, centralised system that takes the judicial role–and sitting judges–if not into the executive, then beyond and outside the traditional conceptions of the judiciary. This move relies on an independent judiciary and a clear separation of powers, yet simultaneously risks compromising them. The IPC has stated that 'Judicial Commissioners will act totally independently of government,'[131] but the IPA 2016 limits the powers of review and requires deference to ministerial judgment on national security decision-making. While individual and institutional independence of Commissioners approaches what might be expected of the constitutional protections for the judiciary, the limits of oversight powers and the approval of executive actions (rather than judicial authorisation on application) seem to align more closely with oversight positioned within the executive. There are other, fundamental ways Judicial Commissioners do not act as the judiciary.

They are not conducting a judicial review of executive action (and so appear to be acting as a part of the executive, albeit with an oversight function) and cannot keep under review the exercise of any function by a judicial authority[132] (and such a limit would also be characteristic of an executive function). The shift from a sitting judge being IPC to a retired judge (as with the earlier commissioners) is also significant: it reduces the constitutional and institutional conflict but the power and independence of a sitting judge may make for more effective accountability. It is too soon

115

to tell whether this is a harbinger of more permanent change. In the end, the constitutional location of Judicial Commissioners is ambiguous. There is much to be said for the role of Judicial Commissioners being set out explicitly in statute, and for an oversight mechanism respecting judicial independence. However, the development of Judicial Commissioners with a broad and expanding[133] range of responsibilities in relatively short time represents a fixture on the constitutional landscape that affects the institutional role of the judiciary and blurs the boundary between executive and judicial functions. There is a stark contrast with the role of judges conducting inquiries: whereas that was viewed as a departure for at least a century prior to Lord Thomas' position that it is a part of the judicial role, the role of judges as commissioners has occurred in far quicker time and with far less controversy. Against this background, the Law Commission proposals can be seen clearly as an acceptance, without remark, of this new system.

Building on the IPA 2016 foundations: the Law Commission proposals

The Law Commission adopted the IPA 2016 judicial commissioner model as a cure for all ills. It proposed and then recommended a new statutory commissioner to address serious concerns of current or former SIA staff. It did so without considering the specific purpose for which the IPA 2016 was brought into being, nor the many debates and concerns at the time, or the fact that much of European jurisprudence expresses a preference for judicial oversight of surveillance through the courts. The Commission is, however, at its best where the report recommends a public interest disclosure defence for whistleblowers to 'fortify' the statutory commissioner role.[134] Engaging with the evidence it notes that the aim is not merely Article 10 compliance, but 'a fair law that takes seriously the public interests in national security and in accountable Government'.[135] Our concern nonetheless remains that adopting the judicial commissioner model in new circumstances recognises neither the difficulties with the model nor the way it shifts still further from the now well-accepted role of judges conducting inquiries. These unexamined structural matters are not remedied by a public interest disclosure defence.

What can be seen in the emergence of the judicial commissioner model as established by the IPA 2016 is an expansion of the judicial role, with judges exercising power over the executive, but not clearly from outside the executive branch of government. This is not necessarily an insurmountable problem, especially as the model–at least in the IPA 2016 framework–

substantially respects judicial independence both in form and substance. What is a problem, however, is that this shift has occurred without a discussion or acknowledgment of the changed constitutional role, especially if this changed role covers wider ground. Judicial commissioners have become actors with a general and ever-expanding remit, yet an ill-defined place in the constitution. The Law Commission proposals are an indicator of the extent to which the new judicial commissioner role is viewed as a go-to panacea for the executive's security needs. That trend is worrying. An examination of the practical and constitutional concerns would alleviate the risk of such a rush to simplistic adaptation. The constitutional scope and limits of the judicial role in this area need to be articulated; uncertainty and ambiguity here are undesirable because of the risk of retreat from modern accountability benchmarks.

Conclusion

The context for this article is the constitutional tensions between executive accountability for actions done for national security reasons, the transparency and information flow required to facilitate executive accountability, and the public interest in protecting national security, which may require some secrecy. We have noted a series of statutes – particularly those putting the SIAs on a statutory footing – which have constrained the scope and exercise of prerogative power. The move towards some parliamentary control in this area is to be welcomed. The result of the changes, however, is not the normal application of constitutional principles but instead sees the use of special frameworks and approaches that privilege executive control and secrecy, with a lack of transparency. This exceptionalism occurs across the institutions of the state. It is apparent in the national security exception in section 94, in the executive controls over reporting to parliament and in its influence over the ISC. The principles of open justice have been diluted in both civil and criminal cases and 'extra-statutory' regimes have been developed and expanded.

While the IPC as a quasi-regulator (the status of which in itself raises constitutional questions) oversees the SIAs, the actions of those overseen are never fully brought into the light. The IPC and judicial commissioner roles were established in response to a lack of effective controls over surveillance but are at risk of being treated as the solution for all national security challenges without consideration of the implications of taking that path. Whether or not each of the examples considered constitutes an appropriate balance between the needs of national security and principles of control and accountability is an important question, but our concern is different. It relates to the use of existing compromises and exceptions in new situations and the way that exceptional solutions are then applied in contexts broader than originally envisaged or for which they were designed, especially in the light of new technologies or new threats. Such application is not automatically wrong; indeed, we accept that the consideration of existing models for balancing competing interests is a practical starting point for the resolution of conflicting imperatives.

Nonetheless, we consider that the tendency (as we have demonstrated) has been simply to adopt the model, sometimes in new contexts, without consideration of the systemic consequences. While that may have been forgivable in individual instances, the scale and scope of deployment means that is no longer the case. The fact of acceptance and the subsequent re-use of a model is a process through which the exceptions become entrenched. This risks the normalisation of particular models that are premised on indirect accountability and thus the persistence of exceptionalism, executive control and limited accountability, but utilising parliamentary and judicial mechanisms rather than prerogative powers. Against this background we suggest that when considering existing models as reference points for further reform, both the weakness and the strengths of these models should be considered, as well as the context in which they have operated.

Individual compromises should not be seen in isolation. The acceptability of exceptionalism in one area is informed by its acceptability in others. Taken together, they may have a significant impact on our understanding of the constitution, effectively re-asserting the specialness of national security generally, rather than in specific, identified and justified contexts. The individual instances we discuss may be the tip of the iceberg representing a more fundamental change, most notably as regards the mechanisms to ensure executive accountability. The contribution of this article, at least in part, has been to demonstrate the extent to which techniques to address concerns in one context have been redeployed despite significant concerns about their operation which have not been resolved.

Viewed through that prism, a key issue is the need to distinguish between oversight, accountability and transparency. It becomes apparent that in national security matters accountability is not based on transparency with information open to all (in principle), but instead relies on oversight regimes where what might be called a 'trusted intermediary' is provided with some information, but is constrained on how it may use or disclose that information. Oversight operates on the basis that someone sees, but that is a form of accountability which is more limited and in which the ability to sanction (in many respects generally weak) is weaker still; these limitations tend not to be discussed. Our concern is that executive accountability becomes diluted in ways that give the misleading appearance of accountability. Moreover the danger of disregarding the cumulative effect of these changes is that there will be a temptation – when faced with new challenges whether within the security field or not – to replicate these models without reflection and that with that replication comes the risk of an irreversible shift in the constitutional balance.

© 2021 The Authors. The Modern Law Review published by John Wiley & Sons Ltd on behalf of Modern Law Review Limited.(2021) 84(3) MLR 553–580This is an open access article under the terms of the Creative Commons Attribution-Non Commercial-No Derivs License, which permits use and distribution in any medium, provided the original work is properly cited, the use is non-commercial and no modifications or adaptations are made. Respectively, Professor of Internet Law, University of Essex; Reader in Law, University of York; Senior Lecturer in Media & Information Law, University of Sussex. The authors are grateful to numerous people for the comments we received on drafts at various stages, including Simon Halliday,Jenny Steele,Pablo Iglesias-Rodriguez and the three anonymous reviewers for this journal. We would also like to thank our colleagues at the Information Law & Policy Centre at IALS, which provided the forum for our early discussions of the ideas in this article. Executive Accountability and National Security. Lorna Woods OBE, Lawrence McNamara, Judith Townend. 22 February,2021https://doi. org/10.1111/1468-2230.12624.https://onlinelibrary.wiley.com/doi/10.1111/1468-2230.12624

The Modern Law Review was established in 1937 as a charity devoted to the promotion of legal education, the study of law and all other arts and sciences which may be of interest to those involved in the study or practice of law. The Review promotes these objectives by the publication of the law review and also by the organisation of lectures, seminars, scholarships and prizes that support legal education and scholarship. The activities of the Review are undertaken by an Editorial Committee. The work of the Committee is overseen and supported by an Advisory Board. The Scope and Purpose of the MLR: The Modern Law Review is a generalist legal journal founded to 'deal with the law as it functions in society'. We encourage submissions from all legal and regulatory fields and all approaches to legal scholarship. The objective of the journal is quite simply to publish the best and most innovative, significant and insightful legal scholarship from whatever area of law or whatever approach to the study of law from which such scholarship heralds. The History of the MLR: The Modern Law Review was first published in June 1937. More than eighty years on, it is one of the leading academic law reviews in the world, continuing to uphold the founding editors' aim of publishing scholarship which 'deals with the law as it functions in society'.[1] As well as publishing six issues of the law review each year, the MLR organises lectures and *supports seminars, scholarships and prizes in order to promote legal education and the study of law. The MLR was founded by a group of like-minded legal scholars from LSE and across the University of London, though under its first general editor, Lord Chorley (General Editor between 1937 and 1970) it became increasingly associated with LSE.[2] In an essay published in the MLR celebrating fifty years of the journal, Cyril Glasser vividly portrays the early twentieth century context against which the journal was founded.[3] In this period, legal scholarship, for the large part, lacked in critical engagement with contemporary issues and focused on 'technical aspects of the law treated from such varying points of view as the historical, analytical and descriptive';[4] legal education predominantly sought to serve the profession; and the idea of law as a modern social science was seen as radical and potentially subversive. By the mid-1930s, however, a more progressive approach to legal teaching and scholarship was emerging, which was greatly catalysed by the arrival of Jewish scholars fleeing the Nazi regime. This group included Otto Kahn-Freund, who was a founding member of the MLR. These two groups, respectively, make up the 'Radicals' and 'Refugees' in the title of Glasser's 1987 essay.[5] From the beginning, the MLR sought to 'usefully supplement'[6] other legal academic periodicals, by taking a 'modern' and unconventional approach to legal thinking. Accordingly, the Review sought, as it still continues to seek, to publish the highest quality scholarship covering diverse legal topics in a way which reflects the social conditions in which law operates. The impact of the extraordinary scholarship which has been published by the MLR over the last eighty years can be usefully traced in four virtual issues of the MLR on labour law legal scholarship, international legal scholarship, and in tribute to the ground-breaking scholarship of Professor Simon Roberts. Alongside all of the MLR content from 1937-1997, these four virtual issues are freely available online. The first virtual issue of the MLR fittingly addresses the labour law legacy of Otto Kahn-Freund. Kahn-Freund had been a labour law judge in the Weimar republic, and he fled Germany in response to persecution by the Nazis after his judgment regarding claims for unfair dismissal in the 'radio case'. The issue opens with the first English translation of that pivotal judgment in the Berlin labour court in 1933, followed by an expert commentary provided by Professor Mückenberger. The subsequent contributions are devoted to the modern contextual approach to the study of labour law which Kahn-Freund introduced, and which he nurtured in the pages of the MLR. Today, the MLR goes from strength to strength. It is published six times a year, with sections devoted to articles, reviews, book reviews, cases and legislation. It has recently added an online Forum to facilitate the discussion of MLR content past and present. The present Editorial Committee is made up of legal scholars from six different universities, though a majority are still from LSE. A distinguished Advisory Board provides support to the Committee. There have been eight General Editors of the MLR in its eighty year history. Following Lord Chorley were Lord Wedderburn, Professors Simon Roberts, Tim Murphy, Martin Loughlin, Hugh Collins, and Julia Black. The current General Editor is Professor David Kershaw.*

Chapter 6

Scottish Independence after Brexit

Eve Hepburn, Michael Keating and Nicola McEwen

On 18 September 2014, people in Scotland participated in a referendum that asked them to vote Yes or No to the question 'Should Scotland be an independent country?' With a record turnout of 84.6%, a majority (55.3%) voted No while 44.7% voted Yes. How did the 2014 referendum come about? After the SNP won a majority in the 2011 Scottish Parliament elections, it asked the UK Government to empower the Scottish Parliament to hold a referendum. After lengthy negotiations, the two governments reached an accord in 2012, known as the Edinburgh Agreement. This included a commitment to (temporarily) transfer powers to the Scottish Parliament to pass legislation for a referendum on Scotland's constitutional future (UK Government, 2012). The Agreement set out some of the terms of the referendum, including that: there be one question only; the franchise would be similar to that used for Scottish Parliament and local elections; and it would be guided by the rules on campaign spending, the conduct of the referendum and oversight by the Electoral Commission that are set out in the Political Parties, Elections and Referendums Act 2000 (PPERA). But, otherwise, the final say on key issues, including the wording of the question and extending the right to vote to 16 and 17 year olds, was given with the Scottish Parliament.

Crucially, the Edinburgh Agreement committed both governments to respect the outcome of the referendum, whatever the result. This meant that, in contrast to other independence debates, for example in Quebec or Catalonia, few people challenged the right of Scots to decide their constitutional future. Instead, the focus was on the merits of independence against maintaining the Union with the rest of the United Kingdom. The question posed in the 2014 referendum was disarmingly simple: Should Scotland be an independent country? Yes or No? Beneath the clarity of the question, however, lay considerable uncertainty about what it meant to be independent and what the consequences of Scottish independence would be. Campaign groups debated the virtues of being a small independent country versus part of a larger one. There were sharp disagreements over the Scottish Government's proposal to share the Pound Sterling. Protagonists lobbed claim and counterclaim about the value of North Sea Oil and the economic prospects of an independent Scotland, and what independence would mean for public finances, personal wealth and wellbeing.

Both the Yes and No sides claimed ownership of the welfare state and promised that it would be more secure in their hands. Both sides were committed to remaining in the European Union, but the No side suggested that an independent Scotland would find it difficult, if not impossible, to join the EU. Issues of security and defense policy were raised, including whether Scotland could join NATO while removing nuclear weapons from the Clyde (Keating and McEwen, 2017). These often-heated debates provoked intense public interest, and a hunger for information from impartial sources. In Scotland's Decision: 16 Questions, academic experts evaluated the claims made by the Yes and No camps and provided their own assessment of what was at stake. That e-book represented a valuable contribution to wider debates and citizen engagement evident across the country as a record number of voters prepared to cast their vote.

One of the legacies of the 2014 referendum was a public that had educated itself on the issues involved in determining Scotland's future. Of course, then as now, many voters already had a strong conviction that independence represented the right path for Scotland, while many held the opposite view. Others came to a view after hearing the issues debated in the 2014 referendum, and they may have held fast to that position today. Yet there are many who remain uncertain about Scotland's future, and uncertain about how the choice they might face in a future referendum is affected by the changes that have taken place since 2014.

Brexit Perhaps the biggest change of all is that the UK, including Scotland, is no longer a member of the European Union. The UK withdrew from the EU on 31 January 2020 and in December 2020, at the end of an 11-month transition period, the UK and EU finalized negotiations on a Trade and Cooperation Agreement (TCA). The UK-EU trade deal amounts to a 'hard Brexit'. It ensures tariff- and quota-free trade in goods, but does not represent a comprehensive free trade agreement, nor does it include the wider provisions of the single market. It does little to facilitate trade in services or create a wider partnership framework around justice and home affairs cooperation, security and defence. The UK has also opted to leave some EU programmes, including Erasmus, the student exchange and mobility scheme. The UK Government has agreed not to relax environmental and labour laws. This is not legally enforceable but could trigger retaliatory action, after arbitration. Nor does the trade deal require the UK to keep in line with any EU enhanced rights and standards in the future. Instead, it allows either side to take 'rebalancing' action if they consider that divergent rules affecting employment, social and environmental standards or sustainable development have a detrimental impact on trade and investment. This might discourage UK governments from drifting too far from EU rules. Nevertheless, the 'thin' deal means that trade between the UK and the EU is now more complicated, will take longer, involve more bureaucracy and more costs. Some of the disruptions that we have seen since January may ease once traders and hauliers get accustomed to the new rules.

And the rules themselves may change if there are further negotiations in the future. But the UKEU deal points to a much weaker economic and political relationship between the UK and the EU in the years to come. These changes alter the context of in which the Scottish independence debate is taking place. The new challenges it presents for the prospects of independence movement will be explored in the chapters that follow. The Brexit process has also affected the politics of independence and union. The 2016 Brexit referendum saw 52% of people across the UK vote for the UK to Leave the European Union, while 48% voted Remain. That narrow majority for Leave provided the mandate for the UK Government, first, to negotiate the terms of exit from the EU then seek agreement on the future UK-EU relationship. In Scotland, the picture was very different:

62 percent of Scottish voters supported remaining in the EU, while 38% voted Leave. This led First Minister, Nicola Sturgeon, to claim that Scotland was being taken out of the EU 'against our will', arguing that this represented 'a significant and a material change of the circumstances in which Scotland voted against independence in 2014' (Sturgeon, 2016). In the months that followed the Brexit referendum, the Scottish Government stressed the importance of remaining in the EU single market. If that prospect were ruled out by the UK Government for the UK as a whole, it looked for ways in which Scotland could retain single market membership or a special status within the EU even as the pro-Leave parts of the UK

severed ties. These proposals were rejected by the UK Government for Scotland, although the influence of the Irish Government and the shared desire to avoid a hard border on the island of Ireland resulted in Northern Ireland remaining within the EU single market for goods, albeit at a cost of hardening the sea border between it and the rest of the UK.

The Brexit process has also brought new challenges to the way the UK is governed, creating uncertainties about the future of devolution. Until now, EU laws and regulations have limited the opportunities for the UK and devolved governments to follow different paths, for example, in rules around food safety, environmental standards or animal health. In that sense, the EU single market rules have helped shape the internal market within the UK. In the context of Brexit, the UK Government has been seeking ways to ensure that removing EU regulations does not create new barriers to trade among the four territories of the UK. It has worked together with the devolved governments to develop UK 'common frameworks' to replace EU legal frameworks. The UK Parliament also passed new legislation to support the UK's internal market.

The UK Internal Market Act (2020) does not prevent the devolved legislatures from passing their own laws in pursuit of social, health or environmental goals by, for example, requiring manufacturers and service providers to meet certain standards. But the Act means that these rules would no longer apply to traders that were based in, and subject to different regulations, in another part of the UK. As a result, it weakens the authority of the devolved institutions. In contrast to the 'common frameworks' programme, the Internal Market Act was passed without the consent of the devolved parliaments, and despite their vehement protests, contributing to a deteriorating relationship between the UK and devolved governments.

Covid-19

The Covid-19 pandemic has also altered the economic and political landscape. The public health and economic crises it has generated might have been expected to reduce support for independence. In the early months of the pandemic, the Union of England, Scotland, Wales and Northern Ireland appeared to be working more efficiently and collaboratively than it had done for many years. Although responsibility for public health is devolved, other parts of the response are reserved. Ministers from the devolved governments worked closely with their UK counterparts in the early months of the pandemic to forge common policies in pursuit of a 'four-nation strategy', including in scientific collaboration, approaches to lockdown, and procurement of personal protective equipment. The UK Government has been able to mobilize massive resources through borrowing, a power not available to the devolved administrations. The largest expenditures–including the Job Retention (furlough) scheme to underpin wages, temporary increases in Universal Credit and working tax credits, and initiatives such as 'Eat out to help out'–relied on the powers, responsibilities and resources of the UK Government. In a reprise of the arguments from 2014, unionist politicians argued that only the broad shoulders of the United Kingdom could bear this burden. There was also an effort to mobilize sentiments of national unity and a wartime spirit.

However, cracks have also appeared. As emergency Whitehall committees were disbanded in favour of a smaller decision-making circle, the devolved governments were left out of the loop and increasingly pursued their own Covid strategies, adopting a more cautious approach to easing the lockdown. The Scottish First Minister (supported by a circle of ministerial colleagues and clinicians) assumed ownership of the response policy in Scotland. The Scottish Government's Covid-19 strategy, and the First Minister's handling of the crisis, has largely won the support of people living in Scotland, while the UK Government and Prime Minister have been found wanting. These perceptions held irrespective of whether those polled had voted Yes or No in 2014, or Remain or Leave in 2016 (Curtice, 2020).

Although it is not possible to prove a causal link, views regarding the respective governments' handling of the Covid-19 crisis may help to explain the increase in public support for independence in Scotland over the course of 2020. There had already been a rise in support for independence over the course of 2019 as the UK negotiated its exit from the EU, with polls suggesting, on average, that 49% would vote Yes were an independence referendum held then. This increase in support for Yes was driven primarily by those who had voted No to independence in 2014 but Remain in the 2016 EU referendum (Curtice, 2019). But from June 2020 until the end of the year, 16 opinion polls carried out by six different polling firms, all suggested majority support for independence, ranging from 51% to 59%. This represents the most sustained majority support for independence ever seen in Scotland.

Yet, like Brexit, Covid-19 has created new challenges to the case for independence, especially with respect to the economy. The massive increases in Covid-related spending have been financed by increased UK borrowing and increased UK debt. Economic recovery is expected to be slow, with declining tax revenues (amid increased unemployment) at least in the short term, and some measures to pare down the mounting debt. These economic challenges are expected to have a detrimental impact on devolution finances (Scottish Fiscal Commission, 2020), but bring added risks to the economic case for independence as well.

Politics

When the 2014 independence referendum was held, the SNP had a parliamentary majority in Holyrood, but 41 of the 59 MPs that represented Scotland in the UK Parliament were from the Labour Party. In the previous General Election in 2010, Labour had secured 42% of the vote in Scotland. While the Conservatives were in the ascendency south of the border, leading the UK coalition government with the Liberal Democrats, in Scotland they had just one MP. The independence referendum was to have a dramatic impact on the political landscape in Scotland. Three trends have been evident. First is the increased dominance of the SNP in every election since 2014 and in every electoral arena. In the most recent contest–the General Election in December 2019–the SNP secured a 45% vote share and won 48 of the 59 Scottish seats. Despite thirteen years in power, the SNP's support appears to have increased in voting intentions for the Scottish Parliament. This puts the party in a strong position to secure a comfortable victory in the forthcoming 2021 elections, although the proportional representation system makes it difficult for any single party to secure an overall majority. That the SNP achieved this feat in 2011 does not guarantee a similar outcome in 2021.

The second trend has been the sudden and prolonged collapse of the Labour Party. Just eight months after the 2014 independence referendum, the 2015 General Election saw the Labour Party reduced to just one MP while 40 of his colleagues lost their seats to the SNP. The party has struggled to recover its electoral fortunes since then. Since Nicola Sturgeon became SNP leader in the aftermath of the 2014 independence referendum, Scottish Labour has had four leaders and four acting leaders, all of whom have struggled to make an impact. Part of the explanation for Labour's travails has been a partial recovery for the Scottish Conservatives, especially in the 2016-17 period under the leadership of Ruth Davidson. The Conservatives both nurtured and benefited from the prevalence of the constitutional issue. Far from settling the independence question, the 2014 referendum resulted in issues of independence and union becoming the defining feature of Scottish politics. However, the UK Conservatives' difficulties with both Brexit and Covid have rebounded on the party's support in Scotland more recently.

The polarization of Scottish politics between the pro-independence, pro-Remain SNP and the pro-Union and now pro-Brexit Conservatives (the Scottish Conservatives were overwhelmingly pro-Remain in the 2016 referendum) has contributed to deep strains in the relationship between the Scottish and UK governments, although the two governments were hardly the best of friends in 2014. The period leading to the first independence referendum was marked by mutual distrust, but there was cooperation as well. The Edinburgh Agreement reflected the UK Government's acceptance that the SNP had secured an electoral mandate to pursue an independence referendum, and that the Scottish Parliament and Government should be given the responsibility to oversee the process. No such recognition has been given in response to the SNP Government's plans to hold a new independence referendum. Repeated requests to secure the transfer of power to hold a referendum on a similar basis to the one in 2014 have been refused by the Prime Minister, on the basis that the referendum held in 2014 was supposed to be a 'once in a generation' opportunity. In contrast to 2014, the legitimacy of an independence referendum is now hotly contested, and looks likely to be a dominant issue in the forthcoming Scottish Parliament elections.

Scotland's new choice Independence after Brexit. Edited by Eve Hepburn, Michael Keating and Nicola McEwen, Centre on Constitutional Change. Copyright © of individual chapters is held by the named authors 2021. The moral right of Eve Hepburn, Michael Keating and Nicola McEwen to be identified as the editors of this work has been asserted by them in accordance with the Copyright, Designs and Patents Act 1988. Provided it is in its original form, complete and unedited, this publication may be reproduced, stored or transmitted without the express written permission of the publisher. Illustrations by lushik via Getty Images. This edition (PDF format) ISBN 978-1-8384433-1-3. British Library Cataloguing-in-Publication data: a catalogue record for this book is available from the British Library. The Centre on Constitutional Change has provided strategic and logistical support for the development of this book, and Mobo Media have designed and digitized the e-book. Our thanks to them. The authors have sought to present our analysis in an impartial way that is accessible to readers; any views expressed are their own. This collection begins to fill that space. It builds upon the success of a previous e-book produced in advance of the 2014 independence referendum. Then, as now, we do not take a stand on the question of whether or not Scotland should be an independent country. Instead, we have drawn together leading experts to examine the key issues, opportunities and challenges surrounding the prospect of independence. Much has changed since the 2014 referendum – most notably, the UK's decision to leave the European Union. By providing factual information and impartial analysis, we hope that the book can support citizens to engage in debates and make up their own minds about Scotland's future. The Centre on Constitutional

Change applies the best of social scientific scholarship to the questions raised by the UK's evolving territorial relationships. The Centre on Constitutional Change (CCC) is a leading centre for the study of constitutional change and territorial politics in the United Kingdom and beyond. It was established in August 2013 to research the UK's changing constitutional relationships. Based at the University of Edinburgh, its current fellows include academics from the Universities of Aberdeen, Cambridge, Cardiff, Stirling, and University College Cork. The Centre also acts as a hub for a much wider network of scholars across the UK and beyond engaged in analysis of contemporary constitutional issues. It is one of the leaders of the Islands and Unions Network, linking academics and practitioners across the United Kingdom and Ireland. The Co-Directors for 2021/2022 are Meryl Kenny (The University of Edinburgh) and Karlo Basta (The University of Edinburgh). Our research is multidisciplinary, with the team spanning the fields of political science, economics, constitutional law, and public policy. The University of Edinburgh is a charitable body, registered in Scotland, with registration number SC005336, VAT Registration Number GB 592 9507 00, and is acknowledged by the UK authorities as "Recognised body" which has been granted degree awarding powers. Centre on Constitutional Change 3rd Floor, St John's Land the University of Edinburgh Edinburgh EH8 8AQ. www.centreonconstitutionalchange.ac.uk Introduction copyright © Eve Hepburn, Michael Keating and Nicola McEwen 2021, Copyright © of individual chapters is held by the named authors 2021.

Chapter 7

Contesting Sovereignty and Borders: Northern Ireland, Devolution and the Union

Mary C. Murphy & Jonathan Evershed

Abstract

Supported by UK and Irish membership of the European Union (EU), the 1998 Belfast/Good Friday Agreement's post-sovereignist compromise helped to diminish the contested politics of the border in Ireland. However, by altering the status of the border, Brexit aroused and fomented politically charged divisions in Northern Ireland. We explore the confluence of four consequences of Brexit for Northern Ireland. Firstly, we detail how Brexit highlights the inadequacies and dysfunction of the UK's territorial architecture. Second, we examine the specific structural, institutional and relational weaknesses of Northern Ireland's devolved system. Third, we explain how Brexit further weakened the scaffolding that supports Northern Ireland's devolved settlement. And fourth, we explore why Brexit has prompted profound reconsideration of the UK's existing territorial set-up. Brexit's challenge to the status quo in Northern Ireland, and by extension the UK's constitutional and territorial integrity, is linked not just too internal political dynamics in Northern Ireland, but also to the ambiguity of the existing asymmetrical UK devolution settlement, its lack of embeddedness within the UK constitutional order and the absence of binding cultural narratives. Finally, we extend this analysis to posit that Brexit has revived the 'Irish question' and stirred a potentially destabilizing debate about Irish unity.

Keywords: Northern Ireland; devolution; Belfast/Good Friday Agreement; Brexit; Irish unity

Introduction

In 1920s' Northern Ireland, the establishment of the devolved Stormont regime, and the 'Orange State' (Farrell,1980) over which it came to preside, entrenched patterns of power and (sectarian) discrimination which, in the mid to late 1960s, catalysed a prolonged period of political violence. As Cramer (2006, p. 63) suggests, 'the euphemism "the Troubles", for the conflict in Northern Ireland from 1968 to 1998, captures some of the definitional ambiguity of that conflict,'which hinged on a number of overlapping issues, including political economy, culture and ethnonational identity. Ultimately, however, the conflict was (and is) about the zero-sum question of sovereignty and of Northern Ireland's constitutional status. As Woodwell (2005, p.167) asserts,'[w]hat started as civil rights based rioting was able to develop into a much larger conflict because of the fundamental political difference regarding the legitimacy of the Ireland–Northern Ireland border' (see also O'Callaghan, 2006).

After decades of conflict, the signing of the Belfast/Good Friday Agreement in 1998 signalled some prospect for peace by creating a post-sovereignist context for managing contested relationships and competing political aspirations. The roll-out of devolved power in Northern Ireland after 1998 was part of a broader constitutional reform programme which included the devolution of powers to Scotland and Wales. This process of advanced and asymmetric decentralization happened against the backdrop of shared UK and Irish membership of the European Union (EU). For Northern Ireland in particular, the joint EU framework and context judiciously lowered the stakes over matters of sovereignty while the European Union single market (SEM) complemented the terms of the Agreement (Hayward&Murphy, 2018).

Although the border between Northern Ireland and the Republic of Ireland was retained, it was transformed and virtually disappeared as a physical barrier. Cross-border relationships and cooperation were buttressed by all-island institutions, and all-Ireland markets were encouraged. Social and political tensions were lowered. Despite this, Northern Ireland's devolution settlement has not been stable. A combination of residual conflict issues and structural weaknesses has interrupted the evolution of its devolved system of governance. Brexit's challenge to the status quo in Northern Ireland, however, is not just linked to internal political dynamics. These potent domestic forces also interplay with a tradition of ambivalence and ambiguity about the UK's constitutional arrangements. The shock of Brexit (further) exposed the limits of the UK's existing territorial arrangements, challenged the solidity of Northern Ireland's place within that territorial governance architecture, and heightened constitutional anxieties and agitation across the devolved territories.

In what follows, we start by providing a contextual overview of Northern Ireland's governance arrangements. We then explore the confluence of four consequences of Brexit for Northern Ireland. First, we detail how Brexit highlights the inadequacies and dysfunction of the UK's territorial architecture. Second, we examine the particular structural, institutional and relational weaknesses of Northern Ireland's devolved system. Third, we explain how Brexit has further weakened elements of the scaffolding which support Northern Ireland's devolved peace settlement. And fourth, we explore why Brexit has prompted profound reconsideration of the UK's existing constitutional and territorial set-up. We argue that Brexit's challenge to the constitutional status quo in Northern Ireland is linked to more than internal political dynamics. It is also connected to the ambiguity of the existing asymmetrical devolution settlement, its lack of embeddedness within the UK constitutional order and the absence of binding cultural narratives. Finally, we extend this analysis to posit that the resurgence of the 'Irish question' and the developing debate about Irish unity in the wake of Brexit may prove to be part of the undoing of the Union.

The Genealogy of Devolution in Northern Ireland

That Northern Ireland was founded as a 'Protestant state for a Protestant people' is a claim attributed to its first Prime Minister, James Craig. While this is something of a misquoting of Craig, it nonetheless captures the essential nature of Northern Ireland's early experiment in devolution from 1921 to 1972, which was predicated on forms of state- and nation-building which sought to institutionalize forms of Protestant and Unionist privilege, and effectively marginalized the Catholic and Nationalist minority (Farrell, 1980; Whyte, 1983). This reflects something of the way in which 'Unionism' in Northern Ireland has been, and remains, more 'ethnic' than 'civic': conceived of as a form of ethno-communal designation as much as an expression of constitutional preference (McAuley, 2010; Todd, 1987, 2020). Northern Ireland's first period of devolved government ended abruptly as peaceful civil rights protests against Unionist (mis)rule became entangled with and gave way to violent constitutional conflict. The outbreak of violence and serious civil unrest heralded the end of the devolved Stormont regime and the introduction of direct rule from London.

The years that followed were scarred by a violent and intractable conflict based on differing Unionist versus Nationalist interpretations of the Northern Irish state and its legitimacy. The calling of paramilitary ceasefires in 1994, however, marked a historic breakthrough and paved the way for negotiations which led to the signing of the Belfast/Good Friday Agreement in April 1998. The agreement represented an attempt to de-escalate, deterritorialize and, crucially, remove the gun from this conflict (Morrow, 2012, 2017), and move it from the streets to the debating chamber. From 1972, devolution remained at the forefront of ongoing attempts to address the Northern Ireland conflict. The ill-fated Sunningdale Agreement (1973) introduced a new form of devolved government based on power-sharing between 'constitutional' nationalism, moderate unionism and the nascent cross-community Alliance Party (Eggins, 2015), as well as new cross-border institutions. It was opposed by Republicans (who had been excluded from its negotiation) and ultimately crushed by strong Unionist opposition to its cross-border provisions and a general strike underpinned by loyalist paramilitary muscle (McCann & McGrattan, 2017).

The Northern Ireland Constitutional Convention of 1976 unsuccessfully sought to revive the prospect of devolved power-sharing, with Nationalists having refused to participate because the initiative lacked an 'Irish dimension' (Byrne, 2001). The British government again attempted to devolve power on a partial and rolling basis to a Northern Ireland Assembly following elections in 1982. Although Unionists supported the creation of this Assembly, Nationalist political parties boycotted it. Despite these unsuccessful attempts to restore devolution in Northern Ireland, 'the idea of devolved power sharing, located within a wider political framework, had not gone away' (Tonge, 2000, p. 46).

Following extensive political negotiations, a new devolution formula materialized in 1998 with the signing of the Belfast/Good Friday Agreement. Parity of esteem, power-sharing and the principle of consent sought to protect the group identities and interests of both communities in Northern Ireland. The consent principle requires that constitutional change in Northern Ireland is (1) a matter of democratic consent and (2) a matter for the people of Ireland alone to decide upon. It is the responsibility of the Secretary of State for Northern Ireland to trigger a border poll (or referendum on Irish unity) in Northern Ireland if s/he is persuaded that there is majority support for constitutional change. Historically, demographic trends, election results and opinion polling have pointed to ongoing majority support for the constitutional status quo. In this context, the inclusion of an Irish dimension in the Belfast/Good Friday Agreement was particularly significant for Nationalists as it explicitly recognized and gave expression to their political identity and aspirations.

New East–West provisions sought to offset Unionist concerns about the institutionalization of North–South relations. Whereas Sunningdale had sought to build a new form of devolved power-sharing around a moderate centre through the exclusion of both Unionist and Nationalist 'extremes', the negotiations that led to the signing of the Belfast/Good Friday Agreement deliberately sought to bring these extremes into the fold. From the outset, the devolved institutions have actively involved both the Democratic Unionist Party (DUP) (Tonge et al., 2014) and Sinn Féin (Whiting, 2017) in the governance of Northern Ireland. In ways discussed further below, this has, in the end, been to the electoral detriment of the more 'moderate' Ulster Unionist Party (UUP) (Tonge et al.2019) and Social Democratic and Labour Party (SDLP) (Farren, 2010; McLoughlin, 2010). The 1998 Agreement includes territorial, cross-territorial and non-territorial elements. The non-territorial dimension contains provisions in relation to human rights, policing, prisoners, security and equality. The territorial dimensions, based on three separate strands, created a set of interlocking institutions: the power-sharing Northern Ireland Assembly and Executive, the North–South Ministerial Council (NSMC) and British–Irish Council (BIC) (Table 1).

Table 1. The Belfast/Good Friday Agreement (1998): Key Strands.

	Strand Characteristic	Institutions
1	Internal	A directly elected 108-membera Northern Ireland Assembly operates on a cross community basis with full legislative and executive control over 'transferred matters' (and some reserved matters)
3.	East-West	The British–Irish Council (BIC) comprises representatives from the UK and Irish governments; representatives of the devolved administrations in Scotland, Northern Ireland and Wales; and representatives from the Isle of Man and Channel Islands. It was established 'to promote the harmonious and mutually beneficial development of the totality of relationships among the peoples of these islands' (Strand 3, para. 1). It aims to reach agreement on cooperation on matters of mutual interest and does so through discussion, consultation and the exchange of information. In addition, the Agreement creates the British–Irish Intergovernmental Conference (BIIGC), which brings together the British and Irish governments to promote bilateral cooperation at all levels on all matters of mutual interest within the competence of both governments.
2.	North-South	The North–South Ministerial Council (NSMC) comprises representatives from the Irish government and the devolved Northern Ireland administration. It meets in sectoral and plenary format 'to develop consultation, co-operation and action within the island of Ireland – including through implementation on an all-island and cross-border basis – on matters of mutual interest within the competence of the Administrations, North and South' (Strand 2, para. 1)b

Notes: [a] the size of the Northern Ireland Assembly was reduced to 90 members in 2016.

[b] The Belfast Agreement stipulates a range of areas for North–South cooperation and implementation: agriculture; education; transport: environment; waterways; social security/social welfare; relevant EU programmes; inland fisheries; aquaculture and marine matters; health; and urban and rural development. The work of the NSMC is supported by a series of all island implementation bodies – one such body is the Special EU Programmes Body (SEUPB), which oversees cross-border EU funding programmes.

[c] the Belfast Agreement is less prescriptive in relation to areas of BIC cooperation, when compared with the NSMC. However, the Agreement does suggest that suitable areas for early discussion may include transport links, agricultural issues, environmental issues, cultural issues, health issues, education issues and approaches to EU issues. The work of the BIC has since expanded to 12 work-streams. Source: Adapted from Murphy (2018, p. 5).

Devolution in the UK: Ambivalence and Ambiguities

The signing of the 1998 Agreement was part of a wider process of constitutional reform, which included the asymmetrical devolution of powers to constituent parts of the UK. This ambitious process of state restructuring and rescaling is viewed by Jeffery (2009, p.92) as 'partial disintegration' of the UK into different territorial communities with new and increasingly distinct forms of territorial politics. The process was based on a piecemeal approach that failed to identify 'an overall conception of the impact of devolution on the UK state' (p. 92). Sandford and Gormley-Heenan (2020) note that 'constructive ambiguity' has been the hallmark of the UK's territorial constitutional arrangements, and Wincott et al. (2020, p. 2) similarly demonstrate that ambiguities attached to devolution are in fact 'a long term feature of the UK's territorial constitution'. This ultimately reflects what Welsh First Minister Mark Drakeford (2019) has referred to as 'deep and profound ambivalence to devolution' at the centre.

The sum of these ambiguities makes for what Gaskell et al. (2020, p. 3) categorize as 'an especially complex hybrid of…two multilevel governance models, with a strong emphasis on functional division combined with territorial autonomy granted in different forms to Scotland, Wales and Northern Ireland'. The devolved territories differ markedly in terms of the powers they enjoy. In practice, this has meant that when policy issues cut across devolved and reserved functions, difficulties and often failure can result. Moreover, following the onset of the global financial crisis in

2007, McKinnion (2015, p. 51) notes how episodes of policy disagreement and divergence were linked to ideological and party differences between the British government and devolved administrations. The functionality of the system was also hampered by the inability of informal and ad hoc intergovernmental structures to adequately moderate and manage this challenging policy landscape (Gallagher, 2012).

The 2016 UK vote in favour of leaving the EU (and more recently the coronavirus pandemic) has revealed these inherent tensions within the devolution settlement, and radically disrupted the process of 'devolve and forget' which had defined the politics of the UK's territorial constitution since 1998 (Wincott, 2018). The result of the referendum was determined by English voters (Henderson et al., 2017) and it conflicted with the majority support for Remain recorded in Scotland and Northern Ireland. In the aftermath of the vote, the character of devolution arrangements, coupled with an absence of effective intergovernmental mechanisms (McEwen et al., 2020), limited the extent to which the UK's approach to the Brexit challenge could be managed collectively and concordantly by the British and devolved governments. In its totality, therefore, the UK's devolved system's inbuilt structural inadequacies militated against the emergence of shared or binding narratives about what Brexit should mean, prevented joined-up thinking and compounded the problem of managing cross-territorial tensions. In this way, Brexit served as a catalyst for bringing questions about the scope and limits of devolution to the surface (Wincott et al., 2020). This has perhaps been nowhere more apparent, or of greater consequence, than in Northern Ireland, where devolution has not only been characterized, but also been largely defined by sustained political contestation, structural weakness and systemic fragility.

As outlined above, set against the other of the UK's constitutional arrangements, Northern Ireland's devolution settlement emerges as particularly complicated and delicate. All its interlocking parts are vulnerable to disruptive shocks (Cochrane, 2020). And before Brexit, Northern Ireland had already long been an unstable part of a more widely inconstant and fluctuating territorial constitution.

Devolution in Northern Ireland: Fits and Stats

The devolution 'settlement' in Northern Ireland has consistently proven itself to be anything but settled. Since 1998, the Assembly and Executive have been suspended or gone into abeyance five times, for a cumulative total of some eight years: around one-third of the more than 20 years since its first meeting. The latest hiatus, in the wake of the 'Cash for Ash' scandal (McBride, 2019), endured between January 2017 and January 2020. Even when devolution has functioned, Assembly and Executive business has often been stalled by brinkmanship, boycotts and walk-outs. A pattern of political crisis, (near) collapse, (re)negotiation and renewed agreement (often underpinned by a new injection of cash from the British exchequer) has been a (and perhaps the) defining feature of devolution in Northern Ireland since 1998 (Birrell & Heenan, 2017). A cycle of crisis-talks–crisis has produced five further agreements since the Belfast/Good Friday Agreement was signed: St Andrews (2006), Hillsborough Castle (2010), Stormont House (2014), Fresh Start (2015) and New Decade, New Approach (2020), each of which has tweaked the devolution settlement in an attempt to put it on a more sustainable footing, with (self-evidently) Somewhat mixed results.

This tinkering with devolution in Northern Ireland has sought to refine, rather than radically alter or undermine, the consociational model of governance enshrined in the Belfast/Good Friday Agreement. However, it is this model – with its mandatory coalitions, communal designation and bloc voting, mutual vetoes, and other measures to promote 'parity of esteem' between unionism and nationalism – that is arguably at the root of instability in Northern Ireland's devolved institutions. While its proponents have argued that consociationalism is simply a realist response to, and means of managing, violent and deep division in Northern Ireland's body politic (McGarry & O'Leary, 2004), critics have identified the role that consociation has played in sustaining and even deepening this division (Guelke, 2003; Hall, 2018; Taylor, 2008). Crucially, far from addressing the root cause of Northern Ireland's Troubles, that is, the fundamental conflict between divergent Nationalist and Unionist constitutional interpretations and aspirations, the Belfast/Good Friday Agreement has instead reinscribed this conflict as an organizing logic of governance in Northern Ireland.

As Nagle (2018, p. 401) argues, 'rather than resolve the question of self-determination, the Belfast/Good Friday Agreement incentivized those who could successfully frame themselves as the best parties to either deliver' Irish unity or secure the long-term future of the Union'. Those best able to represent themselves as either the staunchest defenders of the constitutional status quo or most likely to upend it, namely, the DUP and Sinn Féin, have benefited, to the detriment of their (allegedly) more moderate or conciliatory rivals. Recent shifts in patterns of identity and electoral trends (Hayward &McManus, 2019; Tonge, 2020) have not (yet) manifestly changed Northern Ireland's essentially zero-sum politics. This politics finds its expression in forms of cultural conflict which have often destabilized Northern Ireland's peace and political processes (Nagle, 2014; Nolan et al., 2014). But it also bleeds into other areas of social policy, which, on the face of it, have little or nothing to do with the constitutional question, including abortion and marriage equality, and 'bread and butter' issues such as welfare reform.

The 'culture war' that has defined post-conflict Northern Irish politics has thus seen almost all policy positions come to be identified as necessarily either 'Orange' or 'Green'. This has tended to marginalize the voices of the 'others'–the increasing number of Northern Ireland voters whose politics are not determined primarily by their constitutional preference (Hayward & McManus, 2019). Somewhat paradoxically, this culture war has also provided cover for a considerable degree of convergence between Northern Ireland's parties, in general, and the DUP and Sinn Féin, in particular, in the realm of political economy (Murtagh & Shirlow, 2012; Nagle, 2009). Redistribution of the dividends of economic development (such as they have been) have tended to be subject to an ethno-sectarian carve-up: a quid pro quo politics of the 'pork-barrel' whereby resources are divvied up between the DUP and Sinn Féin at the centre and then conveyed back to their respective 'communities' through patronage networks (DeYoung, 2018). Thus, and as Barry (2017) argues:

"increasingly Northern Ireland looks like it's heading towards a One party Janus faced system, where each ethnic champion publicly appeals to its sectarian base for electoral power by blaming the 'Other' for all the Assembly's faults while privately collaborating with the very same 'Other' to ensure they remain the dominant power in the political process".

Building on long-running fatalistic trends in Unionist political culture (Farrington 2001; Finlay, 2001), the framing of contemporary Northern Irish politics in terms of a zero-sum 'war by other means' (Curtis, 2014) has been a particular and defining feature of post-conflict Unionist discourse and praxis (Evershed, 2018; McAuley, 2010). As Nagle (2018, p. 401) argues, the Belfast/ Good Friday Agreement was framed by Nationalists as a victory, as representing 'the institutional expression of the "equality agenda", a positive process of redressing the historical experience of inequality and exclusion'. These Nationalist gains have been read by Unionists as necessarily implying Unionist losses, such that support for the Agreement has been weaker among Unionists than among Nationalists from the outset, and has declined steadily since 1998. Crucially, the

Agreement's post-sovereignist recasting of Northern Ireland's politics has been viewed by Unionists as an intrinsic and existential threat to Northern Ireland's long-term position in the Union.

Although the NSMC has no executive powers and the cross-border bodies have only a modest remit, there is Unionist antipathy to the institutionalization of the North–South relationship (Tonge et al., 2014, pp. 56–61; see also Hayes et al., 2006, pp. 155–156; Tannam, 2018). This is linked to the symbolic significance of institutionalized North–South cooperation as opposed to its practical outworking. The upshot has been that, like Strand 1 –which has arguably done as much to entrench as it has to overcome Northern Ireland's deep political division – the North–South dimension of the Agreement has never fully functioned as initially envisaged.

Tannam (2018) has examined how the promises of Strand 3 have likewise been incompletely fulfilled. As argued by Todd (2015), although the Belfast/Good Friday Agreement sought to deepen the institutionalization of the British–Irish relationship, this relationship has remained informal and somewhat ad hoc: reliant as much on the personalities and priorities of relevant government ministers in both London and Dublin as on the institutions established by the Agreement. In this respect, the British–Irish relationship since 1998 has mirrored many of the weaknesses of intergovernmental relations within the UK since devolution (McEwen et al., 2020). As Todd (2015, p. 64) notes, above all, the 'informal British–Irish mode of implementing the Agreement and of adjudicating on its principles was…dependent on the states' prioritization of Northern Ireland', which, in the face of the global financial and sovereign debt crises, the ascendance of the Scottish independence movement and the debate about the UK's future membership of the EU, has diminished steadily since 1998.

With both states distracted by other matters, and given the apparent success of devolution in Northern Ireland after St Andrews, Northern Ireland slipped off the political agenda. The British– Irish Intergovernmental Conference was allowed to go into abeyance, while the work of the BIC was largely 'tangential' (Tannam, 2018, p. 249) and garnered little interest or buy-in, particularly from the government in Westminster. The Brexit referendum, in general, and the surprise 'Leave' result, in particular, put severe and immediate strain on an East–West relationship that had been allowed to slacken, with knock-on implications for the other strands of the Belfast/ Good Friday Agreement (Murphy, 2018). Indeed, Brexit has more generally served to further destabilize Northern Ireland's already unstable governance arrangements.

Brexit and Borders

Enduring internal tensions in Northern Ireland's devolution settlement were complicated further by the British government's decision to hold a referendum on UK membership of the EU in 2016. In particular, the referendum and its aftermath served to refocus Northern Irish politics on the border. A key success of the 1998 Agreement had been the way in which it had diminished the salience of conflict about this border per se in day-to-day politics (albeit that, as noted above, the Agreement failed to finally resolve the constitutional question, and this conflict has found new expression in the 'culture war'). First, the 1998 Agreement guaranteed that constitutional change could only happen by peaceful means and with the consent of the majority. This responded directly to Nationalist ambitions for a united Ireland, whilst providing a guarantee for the Unionist majority that the prospect of such a change was unlikely in the context of existing demographic realities (where Unionists were in a majority) and a functioning devolved arrangement capable of quelling Nationalist dissatisfaction. Second, the Agreement provided for the expansion of cross-border cooperation, and the creation of North–South institutions. This was an especially vital component of the settlement for Irish Nationalists because such institutions gave expression to Nationalist identification with the rest of Ireland.

This effectively de-dramatized the contested questions of identity and political self-determination by allowing people living in Northern Ireland to identify as British or Irish, or both. It also accommodates opposing political ambitions allowing Unionists and Nationalists to legitimately (and peacefully) aspire to different constitutional futures. Membership of the SEM organically supported both the cross-border elements of the 1998 Agreement and the post-sovereignist compromise on which it was based. The SEM's four 'freedoms of movement' permitted the virtual disappearance of not just the physical, but also the metaphorical, border between North and South. Gormley-Heenan and Aughey (2017) note how EU membership helped 'to contextualise being either British or Irish or both, mainly for Nationalists but not only for them. In other words, it was yet another way of not talking about the border' (p. 502). Crucially, the UK decision to leave the EU in general, and the SEM in particular, represented a change in the status of the border between Northern Ireland and the Republic of Ireland (Hayward, 2018). Brexit, therefore, aroused and fomented the politically charged contestedness of the border in Irish politics and created conditions which provoked political division and constitutional agitation in Northern Ireland.

Significantly, any acknowledgement of the contested politics of the border in Ireland was absent from the British referendum campaign narrative. Little, if any, consideration was given by the British political establishment to the potentially risky impact of a Brexit referendum, or its outcome, on Northern Ireland, the border with the Republic of Ireland or the Belfast/ Good Friday Agreement (Cochrane, 2020; Murphy, 2018). The British campaign narrative was heavily focused on the supposed burden of EU migration and on the notion of 'taking back control'. These issues differed markedly from the more localized economic and political concerns of the Northern Ireland electorate, for whom political identity was a decisive factor in determining positions on the Leave/Remain referendum question.

Where Nationalists were wholeheartedly opposed to a UK exit from the EU, Unionists tended, by a factor of 2:1, to favour it (Garry & Coakley, 2016). Northern Ireland's 56% vote in favour of remaining in the EU did not facilitate any coalescing of Unionist and Nationalist positions. Instead, it precipitated the sharpening and hardening of ethno-national dividing lines (Murphy, 2018). Unionists of all shades moved to support the Leave position, while Nationalist opposition to Brexit crystallized around calls for 'Special Status' for Northern Ireland. As with other issues in Northern Ireland politics, Brexit quickly became starkly 'Orange' versus 'Green'.

The full implications of Brexit for Northern Ireland became increasingly apparent in the period after the referendum. Independent analyses highlighted the severity of Brexit's economic consequences for Northern Ireland (Budd, 2015; Oxford Economics, 2016; Springford, 2015) and concerns about the politically destabilizing impact of Brexit became more pronounced (Connolly & Doyle, 2019; Gormley-Heenan & Aughey, 2017; Teague, 2019). The latter centred on concerns, voiced predominantly by Irish Nationalists, but also shared by the Irish government, business and sectoral interests, and security services in Northern Ireland, about the damaging impact of a hard border between North and South on both the spirit and the practical operation of the provisions and institutions of the Belfast/Good Friday Agreement. In August 2016, the First Minister and Deputy First Minister reflected some of these concerns in a joint letter to Prime Minister Theresa May.

Shared concerns around Brexit's potentially damaging consequences for Northern Ireland, however, did not override existing political tensions. Sinn Féin's focus on the achievement of 'Special Status' as a formula for protecting (as far as possible) the political–legal status quo in Northern Ireland after Brexit was interpreted by the DUP and its political fellow-travellers as an affront to the constitutional integrity of the UK and as an attempt to institute Irish unity by the backdoor (Murphy & Evershed, 2020). Brexit was thus layered over, and arguably consolidated, existing divisions in Northern Ireland by becoming entangled in the elementals of the constitutional question.

By early 2017, these Brexit tensions were intermingling with existing and unresolved 'culture war' pressure points and eventually culminated in the 'Cash for Ash' scandal which precipitated the resignation of Sinn Féin Deputy First Minister Martin McGuinness in January 2017. This move collapsed the Northern Ireland Assembly, triggered an Assembly election and resulted in a prolonged hiatus for Northern Ireland's devolved government. Just over one week after the collapse of the devolved settlement, May's Lancaster House Speech committed the UK to leaving the SEM and customs union. This stoked further divisions in Northern Ireland because it jarred with concomitant assurances that there would be no return to 'the borders of the past' on the island of Ireland. Reconciling the objective of combining a seamless Northern Ireland–Ireland border with UK exclusion from the SEM and customs union was to remain a problem throughout May's period as Prime Minister. Her ability to overcome this problem, and deliver her preferred form of Brexit, was negatively impacted by her decision to call a general election in May 2017.

The election failed to return a Conservative Party majority and handed the DUP an unprecedented political opportunity in the form of a confidence-and-supply deal with the Conservatives. The arrangement included a generous financial package for Northern Ireland, and some policy gains for the DUP (Tonge & Evans, 2018), but an expectation of British neutrality on the 'Irish question' was shattered (Tannam, 2018, p. 86) and this served to further antagonize already precarious political relations. Brexit already represented the overriding of the express wishes of the majority in Northern Ireland, and seemed to fly in the face of the spirit, if not the letter, of the 'principle of consent'. May's tryst with the DUP served to entrench perceptions that Brexit was a functional reassertion of British sovereignty in and over Northern Ireland. It called into question the UK government's commitment to key pillars of its devolution settlement (Evershed, 2021).

This perception of a renewed and more muscularly Unionist interpretation of Northern Ireland's place in the Union (Kenny & Sheldon, 2020) came into sharp focus – but also into question – from December 2017 when negotiations between the UK and the EU were derailed by DUP objections to a proposed formulation for accommodating Northern Ireland's unique circumstances (Connelly, 2018). Prime Minister May's draft deal involved a limited degree of regulatory divergence between Northern Ireland and Great Britain, but within the context of a wider UK–EU customs partnership. Nationalists were largely supportive of the proposal, but the DUP were staunchly opposed, arguing that the deal diminished the constitutional link between Northern Ireland and the rest of the UK. Viewed through this prism, May's proposal was seen to facilitate a united Ireland by degrees. Tweaking of the withdrawal deal and what became known as the Irish border backstop did not assuage DUP objections. The party's pledge to support the government's Brexit policy was abandoned. On three occasions, the DUP failed to lend parliamentary support in the House of Commons to May's Withdrawal Agreement.

The party's anti-backstop stance was bolstered by Brexit hardliners in the Conservatives who alleged not to support the proposed differential treatment of a part of the UK, and who also voted to reject May's Brexit withdrawal formulation. The relationship between the DUP and Tory Brexiteers, however, ultimately proved highly contingent. When faced with the prospect of a withdrawal deal not passing through Parliament, formerly supportive Conservative MPs broke with the DUP. This followed a change of UK political leadership and a December 2019 general election which altered the political mood music in favour of finalizing the UK's exit from the EU. Prime Minister Boris Johnson's self-proclaimed commitment to the Unionist cause was short-lived and nominal (Kenny & Sheldon, 2020, p. 15). His support for the so-called 'front stop' broke the Brexit stalemate and provided a means for the UK to agree a withdrawal deal and formally leave the EU on 31 January 2020. The Protocol on Ireland/ Northern Ireland attached to the deal allows Northern Ireland to remain part of the UK customs territory. However, to ensure there is no return to a hard border in Ireland, Northern Ireland will de facto remain part of the SEM. This creates a necessity for some customs and regulatory checks between Northern Ireland and the rest of the UK.

The arrangement is utterly opposed by Unionists for its supposed impact on the constitutional integrity of the UK (Wilson, 2020). British government positioning on Brexit and its management of the negotiations did little to quell political division in Northern Ireland. Additionally, Brexit also sullied (already weakly institutionalized) North–South and East–West relations. The Irish government's persistent opposition to Brexit, and support for the EU negotiating position, led to a souring of relations with unionism in general, and the pro-Brexit DUP in particular (Murphy & Evershed, 2020). The collapse of Stormont in January 2017 precipitated the suspension of Strand 2 institutions, a move which eliminated opportunities for any form of structured dialogue – including on Brexit and its implications – between representatives of the Northern Ireland Executive and Irish government. The only functioning institutional strand of the Belfast/Good Friday Agreement during the withdrawal negotiation period was the BIC, but this had no substantive ability to confront the challenges thrown up by Brexit and was hamstrung by operational issues including irregular meetings and limited British government buy-in. In effect, the council did not materialize as a constructive space for dialogue or consultation on issues related to Brexit. Its evident impotence diminished a basis for bilateral cooperation at a critical turning point in the British–Irish relationship.

Existential Challenges

The Belfast/Good Friday Agreement created a post-sovereignist context for managing contested relationships and political aspirations while simultaneously removing the disputed Irish border from the political frontline. The Brexit referendum and the process of the UK's withdrawal from the EU placed enormous strain on all these dimensions of the Agreement. According to the House of Lords European Union Committee (HL EC) (2020, p. 86) in its June 2020 report on the Protocol on Ireland/Northern Ireland: The process of the UK withdrawal from the EU, and the negotiations leading to the agreement of the revised protocol on Ireland/Northern Ireland have regrettably placed [British–Irish] relations and [Northern Ireland's] stability under considerable strain, with a concomitant diminution of trust on all sides. In its final iteration, the Brexit Withdrawal Agreement, in general, and its Protocol on Ireland/Northern Ireland, in particular, is replete with new burdens for Northern Ireland's devolution settlement. The redrafted Brexit deal concluded between UK and EU negotiators in October 2019 replaced the all-UK 'backstop' negotiated by May with a new set of measures which will mark Northern Ireland as all-the-more enduringly distinct from the rest of the UK. As Hay ard et al. (2020, p. 20) have argued, this 'front stop' requires dynamic alignment between Northern Ireland and the EU, and is:

"no mere tokenism; the relationship [between Northern Ireland and the EU] will be substantive, with Northern Ireland set to follow EU regulations on goods and the Union Customs Code...the Protocol can be expected to determine the conditions of Northern Ireland's economic, regulatory, rights, etc. environment for the foreseeable future. Particularly with Johnson seeking as distant a future relationship with the EU as possible – and although the Withdrawal Agreement also emphasizes Northern Ireland's place in the UK's internal market–in practice, this necessarily implies new economic barriers (both tariff and non-tariff) between Great Britain and Northern Ireland. The conclusion of the Withdrawal Agreement and the redrafting of the Protocol on Ireland/ Northern Ireland was followed by uncertainty about its practical implications, and concerns about whether and how it will be fully implemented (Connelly, 2020; Rice, 2020). This stemmed in large part from confusing and contradictory messaging from the British government about implementation of the provisions of the Protocol, which alarmed its EU interlocutors and, at times, come close to suggesting an intention to resile from the legal commitments enshrined within it (Connelly, 2020; Rice, 2020).

The net result was a diminution in trust in Brussels of the UK government and its intentions. Critically, UK government equivocation, vagueness and ambiguity vis-à-vis the Protocol created a climate of grave uncertainty for government, businesses and civil society actors in Northern Ireland. Although final agreement between the UK government and the EU on implementation of the Protocol was reached, it is significant that this was ultimately without the express consent of the Northern Ireland Assembly, which voted to withhold its consent for the Withdrawal Agreement Bill passed by the UK Parliament in January 2020. Indeed, as Hayward et al. (2020) have noted, under the terms of the Withdrawal Agreement, scope for Northern Irish input into the mechanisms that will govern post-Brexit UK–EU relations is severely constrained, despite that Northern Ireland is arguably the region of the UK with the most at stake in the functioning of this relationship. 'In a real way', as Hayward et al. (2020, p. 20) argue (see also HL EC, 2020, p. 83):

Northern Ireland is at risk of being subject to legislation coming from both Brussels and London without Full sight or scrutiny of it...there is no automatic means by which Northern Ireland's devolved institutions will either be able to effectively scrutinise and shape EU law they need to download or be able to upload views to the EU. This democratic deficit is juxtaposed to the consent mechanism included in the Protocol, which gives the Northern Ireland Assembly the power to vote on its renewal every four (or, in the case that such a vote passes with cross-community consent, every eight) years. Given the politicization of the issue of Northern Ireland's relationship with the EU, and the manner in which this has been mapped on to the constitutional question at the heart of the political conflict in and about Northern Ireland, this too has the potential to be fractious and divisive. As noted by the HL EU (2020, p. 79):

"The democratic consent mechanism could exacerbate political division in Northern Ireland in the lead-up to each vote. It guarantees that the Assembly will be required repeatedly to debate the arrangements for trade within the UK and across the island of Ireland. The mechanism also creates the potential for significant economic instability and dislocation every four or eight years.

The form that Brexit has taken in Northern Ireland means that the question of its relationship with the EU – which, viewed through the lens of the constitutional conflict which defines Northern Ireland politics, is necessarily zero-sum–is now undivorcable from its territorial politics, and will remain so in perpetuity. The ultimate effect of this, and the other severe strains, that Brexit has placed on Northern Ireland's political settlement has been to raise, in stark terms, the question as to whether this settlement remains viable. In other words, it has stoked dissatisfaction with the functionality of devolved governance, re-enlivened the debate about the constitutional future of the island of Ireland, and imbued the question of Irish unity with an urgency it has not had since the height of the Troubles.

The Undoing of the Union

In the same way that devolution 'was not a one-time enactment of constitutional change, but rather a dynamic whose trajectory was open and whose endpoint was unclear' (Jeffery, 2009, p. 291), the Belfast/Good Friday Agreement has not provided a stable or final constitutional settlement for Northern Ireland. Instead, it has functioned 'a first, although as yet unclear, step toward a range of future constitutional changes' (Shirlow, 2001, p. 743). Until 2016, it was assumed that constitutional reform or transformation would take place in the context of UK membership of the EU. The removal of EU scaffolding has produced adverse consequences for devolution and for the UK's territorial stability, and this is felt profoundly in Northern Ireland.

Sandford and Gormley-Heenan (2020, p. 108) note that 'the technical requirements of Brexit will mandate the need for exact decisions where "constructive ambiguity" has existed up to now'. Nowhere has this been more apparent than when it has come to questions about borders and bordering on the island of Ireland, which Brexit has mandated can no longer be 'fudged' in the way they have been since 1998. Irish and UK membership of the EU accommodated and reinforced the Belfast/Good Friday Agreement's conception of the border as fluid. This blurring of identities and sovereignty is what makes the border acceptable to the two traditions in Northern Ireland. In altering the status of the border between Northern Ireland and the Republic of Ireland, Brexit has undermined the extent to which critically important characteristics like fluidity and 'fuzziness', as applied to both the practical and symbolic meaning and operation of the border, can be maintained.

The process of moderating Brexit's impact on the Northern Ireland border was complicated and restricted by UK governance arrangements which failed to adequately foster political and cross-territorial inclusivity. When Brexit collided with the UK's ambiguous and ambivalent constitutional arrangements, in general, and the idiosyncrasies of Northern Ireland's particular post-1998 governmental architecture, in particular, it produced conditions capable of fatally challenging the resilience and durability of this infrastructure. The referendum result and the ensuing UK–EU negotiations revealed opposing interpretative differences about the nature of parliamentary sovereignty (prioritized by the centre) versus popular sovereignty (variously relied upon by the peripheries) (Wincott et al., 2020). Vulnerable to suspension, collapse and stalemate on select policy issues, Northern Ireland's devolved system was unable to engage effectively with the wider UK Brexit conversation. The absence of a functioning devolved administration in Northern Ireland between January 2017 and January 2020 was a consequence of both bitter political infighting and the internal structural weaknesses of the power-sharing arrangement. Notably however, even where devolved government was operational (as in Scotland and Wales), an ability to substantially shape and influence UK Brexit policy was subject to constraints and limits (McEwen, 2020).

This lack of embeddedness of facilities to engage, include and accommodate devolved interests in the wider UK constitutional order has been exposed by Brexit and has revealed the extent of division, disagreement and divergence between the UK centre and the periphery. This scenario of dysfunction is further fuelled by the absence of binding cultural narratives across the UK. The UK referendum on membership of the EU was in fact an amalgamation of different territorial referendum campaigns. The Northern Ireland campaign generated territorially specific concerns about the border, EU Structural Fund support, the agriculture industry, among others. These differed markedly from those issues which dominated the wider British referendum campaign and exposed a gulf of misunderstanding between the periphery and the centre. This pattern of misunderstanding continued and intensified during the Brexit negotiation phase when, as a consequence of electoral arithmetic, Northern Ireland concerns were (at least initially) filtered through the DUP. Wincott et al. (2020, p.2) succinctly note that in relation to May's premiership: 'Little here suggested a willingness to address the competing demands from the DGs [devolved governments] directly; their positions had been seen, not fully heard.'

A Conservative victory in December 2019 meant that the British government could dispense with the confidence and supply arrangement. As Kenny and Sheldon (2020, p.15) note: 'Tory MPs were compelled to choose between the competing priorities of achieving a negotiated Brexit and treating Northern Ireland as an integral part of the UK.' In the event, they chose Brexit and a withdrawal deal, which was not supported by a single political party in Northern Ireland. This absence of a binding and unifying cultural narrative around Brexit, grounded in an understanding of competing territorial priorities, undermines the merits of the devolved system and has spurred support for alternative constitutional futures.

In Northern Ireland, this is characterized by increased agitation for advancing the achievement of a united Ireland. The Irish unity agenda is most closely identified with Sinn Féin, a party which after the 2017 Assembly election was only one seat short of becoming the single biggest party in the Northern Ireland Assembly, and in 2020 was the most popular electorally in the Republic of Ireland. In the aftermath of the Brexit vote, Sinn Féin has spearheaded a renascent debate on Irish unity. This is premised on an increase in support for a border poll and for Irish reunification in the short to medium term among voters on both sides of the Irish border (though this increase has not been steady or consistent) (Donaghy, 2019, 2020). The SDLP has also moved to strengthen its united Ireland credentials by proposing the creation of a New Ireland Commission (Irish Times, 2020). Other parties, including Fine Gael and Fianna Fáil – whose coming together in a 'grand' coalition in June 2020 itself marks significant shifts in Ireland's post-Brexit politics – have also now begun to take an interest in the concept of a 'shared island' (Tannam, 2020).

The prospects for constitutional change, however, are based on the principle of consent as set out in the Belfast/Good Friday Agreement. The Unionist community's resolute opposition to constitutional change is supported by those who identify as neither Unionist nor Nationalist. The so-called 'neithers' is the largest single segment of the Northern Ireland population and a majority of this group consistently favour the constitutional option 'devolution within the UK' (Hayward & McManus, 2019). This suggests that overall support for the constitutional status quo persists (for now). This is despite unionism having lost its inbuilt electoral majority, failing to win a majority of either votes cast or seats available in any election in Northern Ireland since March 2017. To some extent, the Unionist (and 'neithers') position is supported by successive Irish governments who are not persuaded by a simple majoritarian calculation in favour of a border poll and have tempered and nuanced their position: initially favouring the status quo, and latterly committing to 'build on the foundations laid in the Belfast/Good Friday Agreement to deepen peace and prosperity in Northern Ireland' (Irish Government, 2020, p. 104).

In contrast, the British government's Brexit strategy is perceived to have 'sold out' Unionists and side-lined the Unionist plea for Northern Ireland to leave the EU on the same terms as the rest of the UK. Unionist anxiety is further fuelled by concerns that Conservative Unionist discourse does not include 'an authentic commitment to Northern Ireland' (Kenny & Sheldon, 2020, p. 15) and is aggravated by a British public which only flimsily supports Northern Ireland remaining in the UK (YouGov, 2019, 2020). The appetite for constitutional change is also influenced by the growing number of non-aligned voters in Northern Ireland who tend to be more inclined to 'don't know' in terms of having a constitutional preference (Hayward & McManus, 2019). Because the underlying dynamics that impact on Northern Ireland's constitutional future are less settled and more mutable in the aftermath of the UK decision to leave the EU, this adds to the layered tension felt by a perennially insecure Ulster unionism in its mission to maintain the constitutional status quo.

Northern Ireland's constitutional future lies at the intersection of dynamic, complex and clashing forces. Brexit's challenge to the status quo in Northern Ireland, and by extension the UK's constitutional and territorial integrity, is linked not just to internal political dynamics in Northern Ireland, but also to the ambiguity of the existing asymmetrical UK devolution settlement, its lack of embeddedness within the UK constitutional order, and the absence of binding cultural narratives. Insofar as it illuminates the underlying ambiguities of the UK's system of devolved powers, Matthews (2017, p. 608) characterizes the Brexit crisis as 'a "perfect storm", dramatically exposing the hollowing-out of the constitution'. The sum of these developments has produced tension, instability, and some contemplation of new constitutional ideals and opportunities on the island of Ireland. This is consequential for the future of the UK's devolution settlement, and for the future of the Union. It has the potential to portend the end of Northern Ireland's devolved political settlement, as part of a wider possible disintegration of the UK.

Disclosure Statement: No potential conflict of interest was reported by the authors. Funding: This research was supported by the Economic and Social Research Council (ESRC) project 'Between Two Unions: The Constitutional Future of the Islands after Brexit' [grant number ES/P009441/1]. Orcid: Mary C. Murphy http://orcid.org/0000-0003-4099-7792. *Jonathan Evershed* http://orcid.org/0000-0003-4714-141X. *Territory, Politics, Governance. Contesting sovereignty and borders: Northern Ireland, devolution and the Union. Mary C. Murphy & Jonathan Evershed. To cite this article: Mary C. Murphy & Jonathan Evershed (2021): Contesting sovereignty and borders: Northern Ireland, devolution and the Union, Territory, Politics, Governance, DOI: 10.1080/21622671.2021.1892518. To link to this article:* https://doi.org/10.1080/21622671.2021.1892518. *Aims and scope: Territory, Politics, Governance is an interdisciplinary journal from the Regional Studies Association. It is committed to the development of theory and research in territorial politics and the governance of space. This journal creates a platform on which to explore the interface between territory, politics, economy, identity and the organisation of political space. It confronts topical and emergent issues of world economic and political concern. The journal publishes original, high quality international scholarship from this growing, international and increasingly vibrant field directed at a worldwide academic audience and at policy makers, activists and other communities of practice. The journal is indexed in Clarivate Analytics' Social Sciences Citation Index and Scopus and has a significant circulation footprint as it is distributed with its sister journals, Regional Studies, Spatial Economic Analysis and Area Development and Policy. It is essential reading for academics and practitioners alike. With the advantages of being a relatively new journal with shorter average turnaround from submission to review to decision the journal publishes five issues annually. To be accepted, a paper must adhere to a high standard of scholarship and make an important contribution to this emerging field. Original paper submissions are sought from political scientists, geographers, sociologists, planners, lawyers, humanists and others working on territorial politics and the governance of space. We encourage contributions that develop the field and promote communication across spatial and disciplinary borders. The following examples illustrate some of the subjects of interest: • Links between territories and politics across time and space, • Globalization and geopolitical imaginations • Territorial identities and politics • Theories of socio-spatial relations such as territories, places, scales, and networks • Territory, planning, and development • Multi-level governance, federalism, and supranational organizations*

• *Territories of resistance* • *Spaces of postcolonial governance. Journal information Print ISSN: 2162-2671 Online ISSN: 2162-268X. 6 issues per year. Now Indexed in Clarivate Analytics' Social Sciences Citation Index ® . Indexed in Scopus Regional Studies Association and our publisher Taylor & Francis make every effort to ensure the accuracy of all the information (the "Content") contained in our publications. However, Regional Studies Association and our publisher Taylor & Francis, our agents (including the editor, any member of the editorial team or editorial board, and any guest editors), and our licensors make no representations or warranties whatsoever as to the accuracy, completeness, or suitability for any purpose of the Content. Any opinions and views expressed in this publication are the opinions and views of the authors, and are not the views of or endorsed by Regional Studies Association and our publisher Taylor & Francis. The accuracy of the Content should not be relied upon and should be independently verified with primary sources of information. Regional Studies Association and our publisher Taylor & Francis shall not be liable for any losses, actions, claims, proceedings, demands, costs, expenses, damages, and other liabilities whatsoever or howsoever caused arising directly or indirectly in connection with, in relation to, or arising out of the use of the Content. Terms & Conditions of access and use can be found at http://www.tandfonline.com/ page/terms-and-conditions.*

Chapter 8

Governing 'Levelling-Up' in the UK: Challenges and Prospects

John Connolly, Robert Pyper & Arno van der Zwet

Abstract

Following the Conservative Party's victory in the 2019 UK General Election, and its success in achieving significant electoral gains across traditional Labour Party 'red' areas in the north of England, Prime Minister Boris Johnson vowed not to let down the new Conservative voters and pledged that his government would address long standing regional inequalities in the UK. Consequently, 'levelling up' became part of the public policy lexicon, and, in March 2021, the government published its Levelling up Fund prospectus. The concept of levelling up enjoys widespread political support, has featured in important policy initiatives beyond the UK, and has been the subject of considerable theorising. This article considers how social scientists might evaluate the success or otherwise of the UK government's levelling-up agenda. The article suggests that any evaluation of this agenda requires the need to take into account aspects of network complexity, the resource allocation arrangements attached to the policy, and what the policy signifies in terms of governance leadership in the context of delivering public value. The article concludes that the UK government's plans risk falling short of delivering a sustained reform programme to reduce area-based inequalities.

Keywords: levelling-up; inequalities; public policy; evaluation; public value

Introduction

The UK is Europe's most regionally unequal major economy (Forth, 2021); therefore, the general idea of addressing inequalities enjoys widespread support. The basic idea of levelling up and addressing territorial inequalities is not new. Research shows that the UK has seen numerous regeneration initiatives which can be traced back decades (Tomaney & Pike, 2020) – in short, recognition of the problem of levelling-up and a focus on forgotten places, towns, and cities is far from new and remains a 'daunting task' to address (Davenport & Zaranko, 2020). The UK government's levelling up agenda under Prime Minister Boris Johnson has to be seen in the context of the fact that community development initiatives have continually tried, and often failed, to address social disadvantage (Loney, 1983; Scott, 2017; Institute for Community Studies, 2021). The 2019 UK General Election was a critical juncture in political terms because the result revealed a strain in the relationship between working-class voters and the Labour Party (Wager, Bale, Cowley, & Menon, 2021, p. 6). The Conservatives benefited from a favourable vote swing in those areas of Britain which had voted 'leave' in the 2016 Brexit referendum.

Labour saw dramatic losses in the North of England and the Midlands, with many areas being represented by a Conservative MP for their first time in history (examples include Ashfield, Bishop Auckland, and Workington) (Curtice, 2019). The victory by the Conservative Party led to the replacement of the pre-Brexit 'red wall' by a post-Brexit 'blue wall'. The Levelling Up Fund (LUF) was created by the UK government as a way to build on the electoral gains in the north of England (i.e. the 'red wall') and this was considered to be the Shared Prosperity Fund (also billed as the replacement for EU structural funds) (Brien,2020). The phrase 'levelling up' became part of the Conservative government's policy language and, as has been the case with other phrases associated with populist politics, has resonance to other well-known political sound bites such as 'take back control' (Baldini, Bressanelli, & Gianfreda, 2020).

The main focus of the fund is to invest in infrastructure projects to reduce inequalities across areas in the UK. The LUF is not just one pot but comprises a number of schemes as part of a multi-faceted approach to investment in 'left behind' places. The schemes include the UK Community Renewal Fund, the UK Community Ownership Fund, and the Plan for Jobs, the Freeport's programme, the UK Infrastructure Bank and the Towns Fund (HM Treasury, 2021). The Levelling up Prospectus provided details of the funding (HM Treasury, 2021). This article considers the importance of the levelling up agenda for the social sciences and examines the implications of the levelling-up fund prospectus and its implications for the wider post-Brexit political agenda. The article considers the complex governance arrangements of the levelling-up policy, the degree of politicisation surrounding the funding, and the wider public policy issues concerning the need for robust evaluation in the context of public value leadership.

The levelling up agenda and the importance of the social sciences

Will Hutton, appointed President of the UK Academy of Social Sciences in April 2021, and made the case that social science research is crucial for understanding how to recover from the Covid-19 pandemic. He argued that: geographers, social epidemiologists and economists have expertise to examine why Covid-19 is proving more stubborn to eradicate in some parts of the country. Those areas within towns that are poorer, with multi-occupied housing, with lower levels of educational attainment, patchy access to broadband and whose members have to travel to work on... public transport have emerged as Covid hotspots (Hutton, 2021).

There is clearly a need for social scientists and the learned societies which represent them to cultivate and coordinate social researchers from across disciplines to make meaningful contributions to understanding how recovery from Covid-19 can complement (or otherwise) attempt to 'level-up' the country. The policy space around levelling up and post-pandemic recovery are vast and, consequently, it is possible that government can manoeuvre, obfuscate and avoid blame due to ambiguities and lack of clarity. Jennings, McKay, and Stoker (2021, pp. 6–8) highlighted five ambiguities and contradictions, which should influence the direction of social science research:

1. Equalising regional imbalances may address aspects of geographical inequalities, but there are significant differences within regions and between areas.

2. Is the primary objective of levelling up to focus on lagging places with centres of growth, or to make local economies more self-sufficient and resilient?

3. Does levelling-up relate to investment in physical capital (via the LUF), or is it about Human capital (such as skills and education)?

154

4. The idea of levelling up links to the devolution of political power relating to constitutional concerns to protect the union, yet the levelling up has been managed centrally.

5. Levelling up implies a redistributive programme based on expanded public spending with the state becoming more interventionist, yet the impacts of this could be challenged, or even off-set, by the long shadow of austerity over the past decade which has cut funding for public services.

The contractions and challenges highlighted by Jennings et al. (2021) provide avenues for social science research in terms of unpacking the issues. Yet, there are further areas that need to be considered by social scientists, including the extent to which the UK government's levelling up agenda interplays with visions of levelling up and inclusivity across the UK. The Scottish Government's approach is based on social justice, inclusive growth and wellbeing (Scottish Government, 2021). Its vision resonates with the Welsh Government's commitments to the 'wellbeing of future generations' and the foundational economy (Welsh Government, 2021), and the most recent Northern Ireland Programme for Government (Northern Ireland Executive, 2021). These different approaches raise questions about inter-governmental narratives of shared prosperity and the relationship between policy elites (governing actors and interest groups) and citizens (individual voters and civil society).

Considering the wider role of social sciences in relation to the levelling up agenda, it is also valuable to look across borders. If we view levelling up as the reduction of territorial disparities, then almost every country faces such challenges. The terminology used is variable. The EU employs the concept of territorial cohesion. France refers to La France peripherique (peripheral France), in the Netherlands Krimpgebieden (Shrinking regions), abgehängte Regionen (suspended regions) in Germany, Area Interne (inner areas) in Italy, and the rustbelt in the US (MacKinnon, Tomaney, & Pike, 2021). These terms all refer to 'left behind' regions that require targeted policy interventions. However, they differ in terms of the territorial scope, which in some cases is quite clearly defined, like the Netherlands and Germany, using a statistical index, whereas, in others like the UK and US, the territorial scope is more malleable and can apply to a variety of territories that can differ quite considerably in terms of their characteristics. The key issue is that the experiences from these countries offer valuable benchmarks in terms of implementation, governance and evaluation. They can point towards a variety of coordination mechanisms

155

and different trends in terms of centralisation and decentralisation (Ferry, 2021). Given the priorities, concerns and foci within the social sciences, and the variations in international approaches to the challenges of levelling up, what are the key issues and debates in the UK context, in view of the government's 2021 initiatives in this sphere? We begin by examining the basic framework for the new policy.

The Policy Framework for Levelling up in the UK

In simple terms, the UK government's LUP involved the creation of a financial pot by the Treasury, which would be accessible by several government departments, the Ministry of Housing, Communities and Local Government, the Scotland Office and the Wales Office, to support successful funding bids tabled by local public policy actors, primarily local authorities (HM Treasury, 2021). This new strategy for engendering a shared commitment to addressing deep-rooted territorial inequalities that have disadvantaged many of the northern constituencies involved a number of funding packages and was consequential upon the announcement by the Chancellor, Rishi Sunak, of a £100 billion capital spending programme in 2021-2. This included the aim to improve broadband, to upgrade local transport and flood defences as well as a commitment to the delivery of HS2 and other transport connectivity across the country (HM Treasury, 2021). The levelling-up dimensions of this funding, with six streams overseen by three UK government departments, is institutionally complex.

Ostensibly, the funding arrangements appear to follow a decentralisation logic. Eddie Hughes, the Parliamentary Under Secretary of State in the Ministry of Housing, Communities and Local Government stated that 'we want to devolve and decentralise to give more power to local communities, providing an opportunity for all places to level up' (HC Deb Col 180, 16 March 2021). However, in practice the devolution of power to local areas is only the case insofar as local areas need to bid for centralised funding, and the gulf between the rhetoric of devolution and decentralisation and the reality of enhanced centralisation is significant, as discussed. Moreover, recent rescaling processes have provided increased decision-making powers for urban areas (Mendez, van der Zwet, & Borowska-Waszak, 2021). So although the application process may allow for direct local inputs, all the cards are held by the UK government in terms of funding decisions.

The funding application process itself is highly politicised in that MPs will be regarded by the government as local champions for prioritising bids. The funding prospectus notes that 'when considering the weighting given to bids, the expectation is that an MP will back one bid which they see as a priority' (HM Treasury, 2021, p.7). This raises questions about which MPs will be able to access the government to state their case and be listened to. An analysis by the Financial Times found that in England 14 places that were wealthier than average were ranked in category 1 and all had at least one Conservative MP (Bounds, 2021). Areas are categorised as 1, 2 or 3, with category 1 representing places with the highest levels of identified need. Areas that fall outside of category 1 can, in theory, still receive funding but will be assessed based on deliverability, value for money, and strategic fit – all of which do not have robust indicators for them to be assessed.

Against this background, one main criticism of the government has been that the funding will be used as a political tool for maximising Conservative Party interests (Bounds, 2021). There is also the question of the capacities of local actors to fully engage in the bidding process. Such capacities are needed for areas to be able to apply for government funding in the first place. The levelling-up fund makes several assumptions about the social capital capacities available in order to complete funding applications. One of the levelling-up funding streams is the UK Community Ownership Fund, which aims to 'empower communities to protect vital community assets in their area by providing funding to take ownership over them, in support of the social wellbeing of local communities' (HM Treasury, 2021). Research into a very similar initiative in Scotland–the Community Empowerment Act 2015–has shown that community ownership initiatives are hampered by the fact that local community groups lack the resources, skills and abilities to be able to demonstrate and report on value for money (Tabner, 2018) (which is one of the criteria for the UK funding).

In terms of delivery arrangements, the UK government confirmed the following arrangements:

1. The UK will use the new financial assistance powers in the UK Internal Market Act 2020 to make the Fund available to the whole of the UK. Other vires such as the Industrial Development Act (1982) can also be used where relevant.

2. For the LUP, where appropriate, the UK Government will 'seek advice' from the devolved administrations at the shortlisting stage on projects that will be delivered in their geographical areas, including on deliverability and alignment with existing provision.

3. Final decisions will be made by HM Treasury, the Ministry of Housing, Communities and Local Government, and the Department for Transport. (UK Government, 2021)

The government indicated that summer 2021 would see the publication of some monitoring and evaluation guidance and this would provide more insights into how post-award management would take place (UK Government, 2021). However, the evaluation criteria are not built into the policy design, and this undermines the 'evaluability' of the funding awards, as we argue below. This is significant because analyses of policy interventions have often concluded that one determinant of policy failure is the lack of evaluation in the formulation process (Connolly, 2016; McConnell, 2016).

Strategic fuzziness and network complexity

In some respects, the 'levelling up' concept is fuzzy in that it means everything and nothing at the same time (Menon & Bevington, 2020). This opaqueness is mirrored in the arrangements for governance applied to the UK government's levelling up initiative. Prime Minister Boris Johnson deployed the term using broad language, referring to levels of wages, productivity, investment and opportunity and a response to 'the plea of the forgotten people and the left behind towns' (Menon & Bevington, 2020). Scholars have argued that fuzzy governance arrangements, involving a lack of clarity in lines of accountability due to a plurality of agencies being engaged in overlapping policy activities, are convenient for policy actors who might seek to avoid being held to account (Howlett, 2012; Massey, 2021).

Opaque policy processes stimulate opportunities for manoeuvring and culpability avoidance when policies fall short of their ambitions (Bache, Bartle, Flinders, & Marsden, 2015; Hood, 2020). When presenting the new Levelling-Up Prospectus in the House of Commons in March 2021 the Parliamentary Under-Secretary of State for Housing, Communities and Local Government noted that the 'cross-departmental fund represents a new approach to local investment and will end silos in Whitehall that make it difficult to take a holistic approach to the infrastructure needs in local areas' (HC Deb Col, 16 March 2021, Col 180). The problem with making such a claim is that, following serious engagement in the pre-2010 period, for some time thereafter UK governance has been marked by a lack of attention to modernisation or a 're-inventing government' agenda with the associated tools and techniques which would assist with the design and implementation of a complex and crosscutting policy initiative of the type epitomised by the LUF (see Connolly & Van der Zwet, 2021a).

Using levelling-up as a form of experimental governance to avoid silo working, with no broader modernisation or governance reform agenda, and without there being clear overseers of the policy across the three aforementioned government departments, is problematic. Indeed, the public policy literature, particularly over the past decade, has warned that the routes to policy failure are largely signposted by governance leadership deficits when it comes to the processes of decision-making and implementation of complex public policy interventions (Marsh & McConnell, 2010). It has been argued that complexity can produce fuzzy governance arrangements (i.e. when lines of accountability are unclear due to a plurality of agencies being engaged in overlapping policy activities) that are convenient for those who might seek to avoid being held to account, given that opaque policy processes stimulate opportunities for manoeuvring and culpability avoidance when policies fall short of their ambitions (Bache et al., 2015; Hood, 2020). Public policy analysts would view the LUF as a complex policy network, with associated challenges around overlapping roles and responsibilities and diffused accountabilities relating both to the policy creation and design and the delivery and implementation scenarios (Connolly & Van Der Zwet, 2021b).

The key public management, governance and public policy paradigms (see, for example, discussions in Jordan, 1990; Rhodes, 1990; Marsh & Rhodes, 1992; Rhodes,1994, 1997), have invited consideration of the implications of policy making and implementation involving complex interdependencies within different parts of the public sector, and across to private and third sector bodies and organisations. The watchwords here include policy complexity, diffusion, fragmentation and disaggregation. The LUF can be located in this context, as it involves, inter alia, at the central government level, the Treasury, the Ministry of Housing, Communities & Local Government, the Scotland Office and the Wales Office, and at the local government level multiple bidding local authorities (and associated third sector bodies), resulting in an array of ministerial and official competencies and responsibilities, a lack of clarity regarding overall 'ownership', potential for buck-passing, and significant challenges around performance management, audit and delivery.

Given that some of the funding is for infrastructure-related projects and that there are notoriously extended planning and delivery spans for these, the dangers of accountability gaps and vacuums would appear to be significant

(Massey, 2021). The lack of clarity in relation to primary responsibility for the scheme leaves the agents of accountability (at least four Commons select committees, then audit bodies, and the local authority committees) potentially struggling to identify the political and official actors whose work needs to be scrutinised. The politics of UK-devolved relations has brought a further complex dimension to this policy issue based on the fact that the Scottish and Welsh governments have reportedly considered themselves to be 'aggressively undermined' by the Westminster-controlled LUF (Batchelor, 2021).

This is because the devolved administrations (DAs), despite local authorities in their regions being candidates for the funding, have expressed a preference to make the LUF part of the devolution funding settlement and, symbolically, the LUF is seen by the DAs as a blunt and misguided mechanism for promoting the Union (Batchelor, 2021). However, while it is difficult to deny that the Conservative government is seeking policy success from levelling up, and even if intra-UK territorial politics are put to the side, it is reasonable to argue that the organisation of the policy including, as we note below, the lack of in-built evaluation of design and implementation, leaves opportunities for a degree of selectivity when it comes to claiming policy success without an evidential base. Indeed, Jonathan Holmes, a policy adviser for the The Kings Fund,[2] even suggested that the 'levelling up' language has a fluid definition and 'its meaning is in the eye of the beholder' (Holmes, 2021, p. 1). This can facilitate claims of political success, despite public policy limitations, caused in part at least by a failure to engage with the challenges associated with policy complexity, and, as we now argue, the political agenda is evident in the context of the underpinning methodology for the UK government's LUF.

Underpinning 'methodology': Part of a Political Strategy?

Early critiques of the UK government's approach to levelling up have focused, in part, on the politicisation issue, with special emphasis on the methodology selected for categorising areas by need (see Jennings et al., 2021; Newman, 2021). The government has chosen to determine eligibility based on relatively simplistic indicators grouped as need for economic recovery and growth, which include productivity unemployment and skills, as well as transport connectivity. These are not without merit in their own terms but, critically, the levels of deprivation in areas have not been included by the government (UK Government, 2021). This is problematic because the LUF methodology does not take account of deprivation within and between areas and social inequalities. The work of Holmes (2021, p. 1) illustrates this point: Improving infrastructure is a vital part of addressing inequalities, but it is not sufficient to do so entirely...There is a systemic relationship between health and deprivation, which sees people from more deprived communities experiencing worse health and shorter life-expectancy on average.

Over the past decade the gap in life expectancy between the most deprived and most affluent communities grew, and the healthy life expectancy gap between these communities is now 18.9 years for men and 19.4 years for women. Covid-19 has followed these existing fault lines in health equity, the mortality rate from the virus in the most deprived areas has been double that in the most affluent. What is more, if we overlay a map showing communities with the worst healthy life expectancies, with one highlighting the borders of the 'red wall', they aligned closely. Community studies research in England has, moreover, raised concerns about the fact that the 'funding allocated to level up is not sufficient to counteract the decade long impact of public sector cuts which have reduced the capacity of many places to capitalise on economic intervention; nor is it enough to counteract the financial impact of Covid-19 and Brexit for the most deprived places' (Institute for Community Studies, 2021, p. 5).

Beyond community research within one country, Bambra (2021, p. 4), who examined historical examples of macro-political and economic reforms in Brazil, England, Nordic countries, Germany and the USA, concluded, convincingly, that attempts to level up society cannot be divorced from the need for welfare expansion, social security safety nets, democratization processes and political incorporation, and access to healthcare (particularly for the poorest groups in society). For the UK, the attempts to level up the country have been based on an inadequate focus on health and social policy. Studies into social and health inequalities have repeatedly shown that addressing disadvantages between areas requires sustained upstream deprivation-focused policy interventions –anything else will have limited impact and become no more than an exercise in pursuing 'fantasy policy paradigms' (Scott-Samuel & Smith, 2016). The economic vulnerabilities felt by areas cannot be divorced from the accumulation of the impact of longstanding deindustrialisation on areas, which have increased deprivation and widened social and health inequalities – essentially leaving communities behind (Mackenzie, Collins, Connolly, Doyle, & McCartney, 2017).

Following the 2008 global financial crisis and the sweeping reforms to welfare in Britain post-2010, a 'decade of deprivation' has manifested itself in terms of precarious employment, increases in child poverty, and lack of affordable and social housing (Anderson, 2021). Incomes were falling even before the Covid-19 crisis; therefore those already trapped in poverty were more exposed to the economic consequences of the pandemic. Deprivation, therefore, is relevant for geographic inequalities and the levelling-up agenda, given that there is a positive correlation between income inequality, which is geographically disparate, and relative income poverty in the UK (McKnight, Duque, M, & Rucci, 2017). Compounded with this is the argument that the trade and competitiveness implications of Brexit will widen UK inter-regional inequalities but this will also be the case at the intra-regional level, because the weaker areas within broad regions generally face more severe competitiveness impacts than the more prosperous core areas within those same regions (Thissen, van Oort, McCann, Ortega-Argilés, & Husby, 2020).

Despite the importance of addressing deprivation in order to reduce inequalities the government has confirmed that they 'will not be rethinking the data or the methodology that they apply to distributing their funding' (HC Deb Col 181, 16 March 2021). The Housing, Communities and Local Government minister, confirmed in his reply to the Shadow Secretary of State for Communities and Local Government, when questioned in Parliament about the lack of inclusion of deprivation levels in the funding formula that 'I say that we decided to leave the criteria to civil servants. We set out the expectation – what we hoped to achieve – and left it to civil servants to decide the criteria' (HC Deb Col 182, 16 March 2021). This stance by the government (i.e. being clear that that formulating the methodology was the business of civil servants) provides a degree of political mileage to ministers in that they could attempt to avoid blame in the event that the LUF is found to fail in meeting its objectives.

As has been noted, 'learning to avoid blame occurs not just in a technical programme sense of greater efficiency or cost savings or congruence with prevailing policy paradigms, but also in terms of being able successfully to negotiate policy and political decision-making processes' (Howlett, 2012, p. 541). Interestingly, civil servants raised concerns about the funding methodology and were 'unhappy that they have been made to look very political' (Hill, 2021). Dr Nicola Headlam, former Head of Northern Powerhouse at the Department for Business, Energy and Industrial Strategy, who worked on the levelling-up policy, is reported to have argued that the methodology underpinning the fund was flawed given the absence of the use of Social Index of Multiple Deprivation (SIMD) saying that 'the

162

Index of Multiple Deprivation and its statistical geography were built for the task' (Bounds, 2021). The validity of the data used to profile areas has also been weakened by the fact that unemployment rates have been used as part of the decision-making processes around categorising areas in need of funding, yet pre-pandemic unemployment data is being used for the levelling-up funding allocations. The Office for Budget Responsibility has indicated that approximately 2.2 million people, or 6.5% of all workers, could be unemployed at the end of the 2021 after the end of the government's furlough scheme (the unemployment rate was 5% before the pandemic in February 2020) (Bounds, 2021).

Evaluation vagueness

Evaluation is crucial for establishing the success or failure of policy (and even the grey areas in-between). It is good governance to be able to demonstrate the social and economic value to be accrued from public investment. More broadly, the relationship between evidence and policy-making will be troubled if there is a lack of opportunities for ongoing policy learning. Yet, the government has weakened the evaluability of the LUF by taking a hands-off approach to establishing the outcomes of the funding. Studies of policy failure have shown that public value (see below for a full discussion) will not be demonstrated unless there is a reasonably high level of analytical capacity to perform the tasks associated with managing the policy process in order to implement evidence-based policymaking (Howlett, 2009; McConnell, 2018). When asked about indicators of success for the LUF, the Parliamentary Under Secretary of State confirmed that success will be for the people to decide and that there are no plans for ongoing local or national evaluations:

It will be up to local people there to determine whether that money has been spent wisely…The criteria for allocations of the funding, or applying for the funding, include need for economic recovery and growth, need for improved transport connectivity and need for regeneration I know that this is not quite what he asked, but I suggest to him that if we are going to determine the success of these projects, the British electorate will probably do that at the next general election. I look forward to seeing how that turns out. (HC Deb Col 182, 16 March 2021).

This, to an extent, and linked to the argument about the fuzziness of the government's strategy, contradicts the content of the government's levelling-up policy prospectus document, which states that 'monitoring and evaluation…will involve a combination of national-level evaluation activity with project-level monitoring and evaluation... Local authorities should set out a proportionate plan for project-level monitoring and evaluation' (HM Treasury, 2021, p. 26). Yet, the details on this are unclear, including which departments will lead or commission evaluations and if there will be extra funding for evaluation studies.

A centralised model masquerading as localism

It could be argued that the levelling-up funding initiative represented an opportunity for government to 'level-up' decision-making by giving local council leaders, leaders of mayoral combined authorities and city leaders the powers and responsibilities for making funding allocations. Local leaders would be in a better position to understand the sensitivities of their local areas and perhaps help to foster policy forums to address the ever-present inequalities of voice in communities. Inequalities are often discussed using policy language with regards to 'measures' and 'profiles', yet being subject to inequalities is an experience. Those 'left behind' may not see themselves as candidates for co-producing policy solutions (Mackenzie, Conway, Hastings, Munro, & O'Donnell, 2013). This is even more problematic when decision-making is centralised or top-down, given that the circumstances of local areas will be out of the reach of policy-makers in

Whitehall. The alternative strategy would have been for the government to work with local leaders to involve citizens and stakeholder groups to discuss existing local plans for economic regeneration and what the gaps would be in terms of short, medium and long-term funding, and then embed evaluation as part of that design process. National leadership would be more meaningful, compared to current arrangements, in terms of working with local areas to understand the feasibility and impacts of their planned projects and oversee a process rebalancing between areas (where required). This, in practice, could mean a more place-based approach with targeted funding to areas where gaps exist after having a better understanding of local needs and conditions. Instead, based upon the early indications, the most likely outcome is that the management of the LUF will remain highly centralised and will see areas compete with each other, with the very real risk that geographical inequalities will widen and tensions between areas will increase.

Missed opportunity for public value-based thinking

It could be argued that the levelling-up policy has also missed opportunities to learn the lessons of previous reviews into the performance of government in understanding the public value to be accrued (or otherwise) from Treasury-backed national policy interventions. One of the most significant drivers to promote public value across the British Government emerged in 2017 via Sir Michael Barber's report – Delivering better outcomes for citizens: Practical steps for unlocking public value (Barber, 2017). The report was commissioned by the UK Treasury to understand how the Treasury (and wider government departments) can organise themselves to deliver public value. The report introduces a 'Public Value Framework' (PVF) to encourage public managers to manage resources in order to produce better outcomes. The PVF, according to the report, promotes two main agendas. First, the goal was for the PVF to 'form the basis for the ongoing dialogue across the public sector on public value, thereby creating a common language on how to improve it' (Barber, 2017). This is based on the idea of disseminating best practice, sharing learning and producing 'new dialogues' across government departments and with the beneficiaries of policies.

The second intention of the PVF was for it to stimulate 'the agenda for periodic Public Value Reviews through which the Treasury, works in collaboration with departments' (Barber, 2017, pp. 25–26). Two years after the publication of the Barber review, a 2019 report by the House of Commons Public Accounts Committee (PAC) investigated the work of the Treasury in light of Barber's review. The PAC report noted that short-termism and a lack of joined-up approaches had remained the norm: Unless action is taken to correct these issues, the government's longstanding problems of short-term thinking, sticking plaster funding and cost-shunting will persist, resulting in poorer quality, less sustainable and joined-up services. Ultimately, this means that the needs of the public, who rely on and fund these vital services, can fall through the cracks. (Public Accounts Committee, 2019, p. 1)

In early 2021 Sir Michael Barber returned at the request of Prime Minister Boris Johnson to conduct a rapid review of Whitehall effectiveness. This was on the basis of making departments outcome-focused and more joined-up. There was even the view that perhaps Boris Johnson sought to inject some Blairite thinking into government by getting the modernisation agenda back on the policy table, given that the Covid-19 pandemic exposed the entrenched problems of silo-working across government (Diamond, 2021). The outcome of Sir Michael Barber's work has been the development of inter-departmental outcome delivery plans (Johnstone, 2021), essentially replacements for individual departmental plans, underpinned by the use of the PVF – the same approach that he sought to convince, unsuccessfully, the Treasury to adopt in the recent past.

This could have been a fruitful approach in the context of the UK government's levelling up policy, in relation to issues surrounding policy design, methodological underpinning, engagement with local leaders, and incorporation of appropriate evaluation and ongoing monitoring arrangements. However, it is clear that public value-based thinking did not feature at all in this case. In order to ensure that important policy initiatives of this type benefit from a holistic public value perspective, a wider government-wide Whitehall reform agenda is required that places public value at the heart of government decision-making (Connolly & Van der Zwet, 2021a).

Discussion and Conclusions

The LUF has been welcomed by many as a way to kick-start the recovery of the UK from the twin challenges of Brexit and the Covid-19 pandemic. As Menon and Bevington (2020) noted when the levelling-up policy was at a formative stage 'levelling-up as a political project may not necessarily be doomed to failure. For one thing, we should not underestimate the importance of political attention'. Unfortunately, the approach taken by the UK government leaves a considerable lack of clarity regarding the evidencing of reduced geographical inequalities. It might stand to reason that investing in growth, skills, transport, research and development, culture, and institutions could decrease regional inequality in the UK. Yet addressing social and health inequalities within and between areas is acutely important to level up the country.

Moreover, post-Covid-19 recovery, of which the levelling up agenda is a part, is fertile ground for social science research to have an impact. There are several potential research questions/areas for social scientists. To what extent do the values of policy actors and citizens in relation to levelling up differ across the UK? Do the values of citizens in different parts of the UK align with those of governing elites? In many senses, there is a role for building on the literature in the field of collaborative governance by integrating theories on public value theory (PVT) to frame the linkages between public values and the governance of levelling up across UK territories. Rooted in public administration scholarship, PVT underlines the importance of legitimacy and organisational capacity for achieving public values without offering normative prescriptions about the need to follow specific governance models or new public management principles.

Public value assumes that citizens create and contribute to the public sphere, for example, through the co-production of public policy. This requires public managers to open up policy processes and rebalance power relationships to give citizens a greater role in shaping policy decision-making (which is also a form of levelling up within policy spaces through citizen involvement and co-creation processes).

Social scientists also have a major role to play when it comes to investigating the extent to which policy performance, including among citizens affected by the policy, can provide what Moore (1995) refers to as legitimacy and support for policy solutions. Indeed, public value depends critically upon governance capacity. Understanding the governance of territorial policy requires an examination of the values of actors at different levels and how these shape their approach to the administration of levelling up policies across and within territories at macro (policy-making), meso (local leadership), and micro (citizen) levels. There is an opportunity for the UK government to invest in social science research to evaluate the impact of levelling-up. If this is not forthcoming, then this will be yet another indicator of policy failure in what is currently a poorly evidence-based redistributive policy in the UK.

The major weakness of the UK government's approach to levelling up has been categorised as strategic policy 'fuzziness' and a lack of appreciation of the challenges of network complexity; significant limitations within the LUF's methodological underpinning, which prioritise a political rather than a public policy agenda; vagueness on evaluation; a policy of centralisation masquerading as localism; and a missed opportunity to incorporate and embed the policy in a public value approach. In the context of the latter point, we discussed the missed opportunities that could have been addressed with more public value based leadership and thinking in government. These largely group around the lack of trust to devolve powers to local leaders, the need to embed outcomes-based evaluation at the outset, and the fact that the methodology for funding allocations is flawed due to the lack of account taken of deprivation within and between areas.

Judge (2021) has written about how the government, under Boris Johnson's leadership, has 'walked on the dark side' of scrutiny. Perhaps the LUF is a continuation of this trend in that it has been designed in such a way to allow for blame shifting, given the absence of national policy indicators for measuring success and failure. To this end, this potentially successful political project risks overshadowing what is predictably a public policy failure when it comes to reducing inequalities between areas in the UK. However, there is a major opportunity for social scientists to evaluate the LUF, and the wider agenda, on an ongoing basis in the hope that the government will listen to the evidence and adapt accordingly.

1. The Treasury, the Ministry of Housing, Communities and Local Government, and the Department for Transport.

2. The King's Fund is an English health charity that shapes health and social care policy and practice.

Disclosure statement: No potential conflict of interest was reported by the author(s). Notes on contributors: John Connolly is Professor of Public Policy at the University of the West of Scotland. Professor Robert Pyper is Emeritus Professor of Government and Public Policy at the University of the West of Scotland. Dr Arno van der Zwet is Senior Lecturer in Politics and Public Policy at the University of the West of Scotland. ORCID: John Connolly http://orcid.org/0000-0002-5563-4970. Arno van der Zwet http://orcid.org/0000-0002-0107-3290. Journal information: Print ISSN: 2158-2041 Online ISSN: 2158-205X 4 issues per year. 4 issues will be print. Contemporary Social Science features in the following abstracting and indexing databases: CommunityWise: Current Abstracts. International Political Science Abstracts. SCOPUS, SocIndex, Swets Information Service. Academy of Social Sciences and our publisher Taylor & Francis make every effort to ensure the accuracy of all the information (the "Content") contained in our publications. However, Academy of Social Sciences and our publisher Taylor & Francis, our agents (including the editor, any member of the editorial team or editorial board, and any guest editors), and our licensors make no representations or warranties whatsoever as to the accuracy, completeness, or suitability for any purpose of the Content. Any opinions and views expressed in this publication are the opinions and views of the authors, and are not the views of or endorsed by Academy of Social Sciences and our publisher Taylor & Francis. The accuracy of the Content should not be relied upon and should be independently verified with primary sources of information. Academy of Social Sciences and our publisher Taylor & Francis shall not be liable for any losses, actions, claims, proceedings, demands, costs, expenses, damages, and other liabilities whatsoever or howsoever caused arising directly or indirectly in connection with, in relation to, or arising out of the use of the Content. Terms & Conditions of access and use can be found at http://www.tandfonline.com/page/terms-and-conditions. This interdisciplinary, cross-national journal provides a forum for disseminating and enhancing theoretical, empirical and/or pragmatic research across the social sciences and related disciplines. Reflecting the objectives of the Academy of Social Sciences, it emphasises the publication of work that engages with issues of major public interest and concern across the world, and highlights the implications of that work for policy and professional practice. The journal publishes five issues per year, four of which are guest edited on specific themes with a fifth issue which is online only and open access (OA). This non-themed OA issue welcomes original papers from across the social sciences. The OA online only issue, published, from 2020 is in recognition of the fact that publishing is moving in a direction where all work is open, accessible, impactful and inclusive. Please note that authors can still publish on an OA basis in any of the themed issues Contributions are welcome in any appropriate form, including critical essays, reviews of significant topics, qualitative or quantitative empirical studies, including case studies and large-scale statistical analyses. Well documented examples of social science in action, composite reviews of sets of books and other publications are also welcome. Papers will not normally be more than 5,000 to 7,000 words. Contemporary Social Science Journal of the Academy of Social Sciences. Governing 'levelling-up' in the UK: challenges and prospects. John Connolly, Robert Pyper & Arno van der Zwet. To cite this article: John Connolly, Robert Pyper & Arno van der Zwet (2021): Governing 'levelling-up' in the UK: challenges and prospects, Contemporary Social Science, DOI: 10.1080/21582041.2021.1957495, To link to this article: https://doi.org/10.1080/21582041.2021.1957495. *CONTACT John Connolly: John.connolly@uws.ac.uk*

Chapter 9

Staying "One Step Ahead of a Racist": Expanding Understandings of the Experiences of the Covid-19 Pandemic among People from Minoritized Ethnic Groups Living in Britain

Saffron Karlsen and Rosie Nelson

Covid-19 has had a disproportionate impact on those in minoritized ethnic groups. Considerable attention has been given to evidence of ethnic inequalities in rates of infection, hospitalisation, and death. But other ways in which the pandemic experience has been affected by ethnicity have received less consideration. This paper explores the lived experiences of people in different minoritized ethnic groups living in South West England, during the United Kingdom's first pandemic lockdown, using qualitative data collected from interviews and comments provided on a survey. Perceived positive opportunities for growth were offset by anxiety and stress, which were themselves compounded by an awareness of the additional risks they experienced as members of racialized groups, and a sense that this was being ignored—or intentionally exacerbated—by the British authorities. Frustration with an incompetent and corrupt national Government was intensified by concerns regarding their racist motives. Racism in wider society undermined confidence in key public institutions, such as the NHS and the police, while also producing barriers to informal local-community pandemic responses. Only through recognition of the particular ways in which the pandemic affected those in minoritized ethnic groups, including the multiple and compounding effects of current and historical racism, will it be possible to identify avenues for transformative systemic policy change and opportunities to rebuild trust and a better post-pandemic society for all.

Introduction

The evidence regarding the disproportionate impact of the Covid-19 pandemic on those in minoritized ethnic groups living in Britain and elsewhere is irrefutable (Aldridge et al., 2020; Haque et al., 2020; Larsen et al., 2021; PHEd 2020a; 2020b; Platt and Warwick 2020a; Sze et al., 2020; WEC, 2020). In particular, studies have shown those with Bangladeshi, Black African, Black Caribbean, Indian and Pakistani ethnicities to experience higher rates of infection, hospitalisation and death compared with the white British population. But it is clear that the impact of the pandemic on society has not only been in relation to increased illness and death. Increasingly, empirical evidence has exposed other ways in which the pandemic, and the measures introduced to mitigate its effects, have disadvantaged those in minoritized ethnic groups, often by exacerbating pre-existing inequalities (Karlsen et al., 2020; Li and Heath, 2018, Longhi 2018).

For example, people in ethnic minority groups already struggling to make ends meet found themselves in occupations more vulnerable to the economic consequences of social distancing measures or less open to working at home or furlough (BSWN, 2020, Platt and Warwick, 2020a,b). The "digital divide" (and implications of overcrowded accommodation) became even more significant in a world where work and study were conducted almost entirely online (Baker et al., 2020). These negative experiences will, in turn, exacerbate persistent ethnic inequalities in health (Bambra et al., 2020; John et al., 2021; Maddock et al., 2021). For example, in the United Kingdom, people in Black, Asian (and "other white") groups reported poorer mental health and an increased sense of worry following the first pandemic lockdown1 (Barnes and Hamilton, 2020). Research from the US has also indicated higher risk of food scarcity as a consequence of the pandemic among marginalised ethnic groups which is likely to be replicated in the United Kingdom (Siddiqi et al., 2021).

Media and political debate regarding these ethnic inequalities often focused only on the immediate health consequences of the pandemic itself. Moreover, the perceived causes of these inequalities tended to prioritise explanations which focused on genetic or biological issues or the choices and behaviours characteristic of particular ethnic groups. Higher rates of Covid-19 infection were presented as being caused by cultural preferences

171

for multigenerational households, which led to overcrowding (CRED, 2021). Higher rates of death were linked to co-morbidities like diabetes and heart disease, which were perceived to be produced by biological and/ or behavioural issues. Not surprisingly, Duffy et al. (2021) found that a significant minority of the British public blamed people in minoritized ethnic groups for their own disadvantage. In the US too, "insidious and potentially racist allusions … emerge[d during discussions of the pandemic,] appearing to blame African Americans as somehow responsible for the relatively large number of cases and deaths from Covid-19 in the United States, stoking age-old tropes, and attributing morbidity and mortality to the behaviours and predispositions of BAME groups" (Bentley, 2020).

Yet consistently, the empirical evidence regarding the causes of these and other ethnic health inequalities shows that these are influenced far more greatly by societal/structural issues, than biological or cultural ones (Karlsen et al., 2019; Baumer et al., 2020; Otu et al., 2020; WEC, 2020; Simms, 2021). Endemic processes of direct and indirect racist societal exclusion operate across lives, and over generations, to limit people's access to good-quality housing, education, employment and healthcare, each of which operate to produce health and economic disadvantage independently and are also mutually reinforcing (Brynin and Guveli, 2012; Darlington-Pollock and Norman, 2017; Rafferty, 2021; Zwysen et al., 2021). The low incomes, poor living conditions, poor health and other negative experiences of parents also impact on the health and economic outcomes of their offspring, who carry this disadvantage into their own child- and adulthoods, to be further exacerbated by their own experiences of exclusion.

While we can identify a role for health conditions such as diabetes and heart disease in Covid-19 outcomes, we cannot divorce these from the impacts of lives lived on low incomes in access to healthy food or the higher levels of stress these circumstances induce. Overcrowded accommodation is an economic problem rather than a choice, and is often accompanied by issues of housing quality which will encourage respiratory and other health conditions (Darlington-Pollock and Norman, 2017). As such, these processes of exclusion concentrate those in minoritized ethnic groups in living and working conditions which expose them to greater risks of Covid-19 infection, and reduce their resilience to its more serious consequences when it occurs (Barnes and Hamilton, 2020; Brynin and Guveli, 2012; BSWN, 2020; Li and Heath, 2018; Longhi, 2020; Mamluk and Jones 2020; Platt and Warwick 2020b; Rafferty, 2021; Simms, 2021).

The United Kingdom Government continues to refute the existence of racism and its role in the generation of inequalities, including those recognised during the Covid-19 pandemic (Bamrah et al., 2021; CRED, 2021). Yet racism is a socially embedded phenomenon which plays a central role in the generation and perpetuation of these ethnic inequalities, directly and indirectly contributing to the limited life chances and premature deaths of those in minoritized ethnic groups (Nazroo and Becares, 2020; b; Gee et al., 2012; Karlsen et al., 2019; Karlsen and Nazroo 2002; Kreiger 2014; Lewis et al., 2015; Paradies et al., 2015; Priest et al., 2013; Williams 2018; Williams et al., 2019). We must recognize not only that such racisms produce the economic inequalities which explain ethnic inequalities in Covid-19 infections and their outcomes but also that interpersonal and societal racism may be exacerbated in times of social stress, with significant consequences to those it victimizes.

The more direct ways racism has affected the experience of the pandemic among racialized people living in the United Kingdom remains underexamined. There is emerging evidence, particularly from the United States, regarding the ways in which the branding of Covid-19 as a "Chinese virus" has increased exposure to inter-personal violence among those considered (East) "Asian" (Coates, 2020; Darling-Hammond et al., 2020; Dhanani and Franz, 2020), and of the negative health consequences of this on both adults and children (Cheah et al., 2020). But Black and other Asian Americans also experienced greater interpersonal racist violence during the pandemic (Ruiz et al., 2020). In the United Kingdom, racially-motivated hate crimes reported to the police rose by 12% in the year to March 2021, constituting three-quarters of the 124,091 hate crimes reported during that period (Home Office 2021). We must better understand the impact that this experience has had on its victims.

We must also recognize that racism manifests in various forms, and is not only experienced as explicitly racist verbal or physical violence or dehumanizing treatment such as that which led to the death of George Floyd from police brutality in Minneapolis, US on May 25, 2020, producing a global response so central to the pandemic experience of many, including those in this study. It is also in the more subtle everyday racisms (Essed 1992), or daily hassles, which are more difficult to measure but remain a constant feature of the lives of many people in minoritized ethnic groups (Williams et al., 2003; Karlsen and Nazroo, 2017). Indeed, racism, unlike other criminal acts, need not be experienced personally for it to produce a sense of threat. As such, racist violence should not be considered simply an attack on an individual person, but an attack on a member of a category or group, "an attack on the community as a whole" (Virdee 1995, p. 284). George Floyd's murder, and knowledge of other racist attacks or racially-motivated social exclusions, can serve to increase a sense of personal threat amongst those in racialised groups. Anticipating experiences of prejudice produces higher levels of stress (including an identifiable cardiovascular response) even where this expectation is not realised in an experience of violence (Sawyer et al., 2012). As such, simply living with the fear of being a victim of racism has found to be significantly associated with poorer health experience (Karlsen and Nazroo, 2004).

Research consistently shows the ways in which experiences of vicarious/indirect racism, and "vigilant coping"–monitoring or modifying your behaviour to protect yourself from anticipated discrimination–can directly affect mental wellbeing, with increased depression, anxiety, sleep deprivation and symptoms of post-traumatic stress disorder (Hicken et al., 2013; Himmelstein et al., 2015; Tynes et al., 2019; Chae et al., 2021). Identified physical responses to indirect racism and vigilant coping include elevated cortisol (Huynh et al., 2017) as well as higher rates of obesity (Hicken et al., 2018) and cardiovascular disease (Clark et al., 2006). The stress of vicarious racism has also been recognised in the rise in adverse health outcomes—such as elevated cortisol, or pre-term and low birthweight birth among those in racialised groups—following events which reinforce a sense of endemic racism in a society (Smart Richman and Jonassaint, 2008)–including the anti-immigration raids in Iowa, US in 2008 (Novak et al., 2017) and the presidential election of Donald Trump in 2016 (Gemmill et al., 2019).

Finally, we must recognize that racism is more than a sum of its parts. Single incidents of racism, while influential in themselves, also evoke painful memories of past racist experiences and communal histories of prejudice, which exacerbate their impact. Evidence from the Pew Research Center that, during the pandemic, Black and Asian Americans were more likely to worry that people will be suspicious of them while wearing a protective facemask in stores or other businesses (Ruiz et al., 2020) suggests that persistent racist tropes of higher criminality among certain minoritized ethnic groups continue to leach into people's daily lives. Racism identified in one domain can also raise concerns about a risk of exposure in others, particularly for incidents perpetuated by people in positions of societal responsibility. Emerging evidence from the United Kingdom indicates that people in minoritized ethnic groups were exposed to more aggressive policing during the lockdown period (Busby and Gidda, 2020; Harris et al., 2021a).

Living in areas with very high levels of police brutality have been found to be significantly and directly associated with poorer mental health and higher blood pressure and obesity, the latter both physical manifestations of extreme stress (Bor et al., 2018; Sewell et al., 2021). But Harris et al. (2021b) argue that "the new police powers [introduced during the pandemic were] adding to and exacerbating pre-existing forms of racist policing". As such, these recent experiences may also reinforce a preexisting sense of distrust in the police both among the direct victims and others in racialized groups. As a service operating on behalf of, and representing, wider structures of power in society, these experiences will also add to people's concerns regarding their risks of experiencing unfair treatment in their interactions with other statutory services as well as the extent to which they can expect protection from harm from the Government, in relation to their pandemic vulnerabilities or more generally.

This paper aims to help develop a clearer picture of the experiences of the first pandemic lockdown, using interviews conducted with, and written comments provided by, individuals who considered themselves part of a minoritized ethnic group and living in the South West region of England. While we find evidence of some positive lockdown experiences, stories are often haunted by an awareness of the existence and implications of widespread racially-motivated prejudice and ill-treatment in British society. Some participants describe personal experiences of negative treatment, but a sense of risk of exposure to racist violence also had a significant impact on people's lives. Pervasive among this sample are negative attitudes towards the pandemic responses of the British Government, and the sense that these were motivated by racism in the highest offices. Rebuilding British society in its aftermath demands that we recognise and respond to this directly.

Methods

This paper reports qualitative findings from a project exploring the pandemic experiences of people in minoritized ethnic groups living in the South West of England, conducted between June and September 2020. The project was developed in partnership with Black South West Network (BSWN), a Bristol-based Black-led racial justice charity organisation. The study comprised an online survey, distributed via the mailing lists of BSWN and other organisations based in the South West with an ethnically

175

diverse membership. The survey asked a series of questions about people's lives before and during the pandemic lockdown. Respondents to this survey were invited to participate in a follow-up semi-structured in-depth interview.

These interviews explored how participants had spent their time during lockdown, how they had been feeling, whether they had received any help they needed and their attitudes towards the activities of their local community and national and local government during this period. This paper focuses on findings from the nine people who participated in the interviews, and the 56 people (out of the 108 who responded) who provided comments on an open section of the survey. Neither the survey nor interview asked people directly about the impact of their ethnicity or racism on these experiences. As a consequence, the centrality of issues of ethnicity/"race" to these discussions/comments varies between them. However, because these issues were raised spontaneously, this offers a more realistic reflection of the importance/relevance of these issues to participants' perceptions of these experiences than might be offered by studies which ask about these issues more directly.

Pandemic restrictions prevented in-person interviews. Interviews were therefore conducted remotely—via phone, Zoom, or Microsoft Teams depending on participant preference, by a researcher presenting as a feminine white person. It is unclear whether, or how, these factors affected the findings. Interviews were only conducted in English and were between 30 and 60 min duration. Following the interviews, participants were sent a list of resources for further information and support and a £10 voucher. Interviews were audio or video recorded, dependent on platform, and uploaded to a secure server before being transcribed and deleted. Interviews were transcribed with all identifiable details anonymized. Ethical approval for the study was provided by the ethics committee of the School for Sociology, Politics and International Studies at the University of Bristol (Ref: SK050620).

The interview participants variously defined their ethnicity as: Black African, British Indian, South African/Mixed Race, Kashmiri, Black British Caribbean, Black Caribbean British, Black Caribbean, and Black British. All interview participants classified themselves as cis women and the majority were born in the United Kingdom. Two participants were aged in their mid-to late 20s, two were in their late 30s or early 40s, four were in their mid-50s and one was in their early 60s. Some participants lived alone, others with their partner and/or children. Most of the participants considered themselves relatively financially secure, and relatively unaffected by the more severe economic implications of the pandemic exposed in other research (Barnes and Hamilton, 2020). Most of them were able to work from home during the Covid-19 lockdown.

The nature of the study methodology meant that they also did not suffer from the most severe aspects of digital exclusion. These factors would suggest that exposure to the more negative aspects of the pandemic may have been limited among this group. However, several participants had been unable to find work or lost business opportunities or investments as a result of the economic slowdown coinciding with the pandemic. As such, this experience of privilege is by no means homogeneous or universal. However, these factors reinforce our awareness that, as with all qualitative research, these study findings are potentially unique to this sample and setting and cannot be generalised to other individuals or groups, in the United Kingdom or elsewhere.

The survey respondents providing comments were somewhat more diverse than those participating in the interview. Of the 56 people providing comments, six classified themselves as cis male. One person classified themselves as "Bangladeshi", five as "Black African", 13 as "Black Caribbean", two as "Black–other", three as "Chinese", eight as "Indian", two as "Mixed – Asian and white", three as "Mixed–Black African and white", seven as "Mixed – Black Caribbean and white", two as "Mixed – other", two as "other Asian", two as "Pakistani" and one as "Somali". The five people who classified themselves as "other", described their ethnicity as (variously): "Taiwanese"; "British Asian/Indian", "Filipino", "Jamaican/Indian" and "3/8 Jamaican, 1/8 Indian and 1/2 English" Their inclusion therefore helps mitigate some of the impact of bias produced by the apparent homogeneity of the interview sample.

A thematic analytical approach was used (Braun and Clarke 2006), which examined separately the themes emerging from the interview transcripts and survey comments. In each case, one author took the lead in analysing a source, whose decisions were ratified by the other. The themes from each data source were then combined for presentation. In the findings, quotes from interview participants can be identified by the prefix "IP" in their participant identifier, while survey respondents can be identified by the prefix "SR". For each quotation, we also include information on the gender, age and self-identified ethnicity of the contributor. Themes identified relate to 1) the impact of ethnicity on people's pandemic experience, 2) the impact of a heightened sense of Covid-19 risk, and 3) the causes and consequences of inadequate Government responses to the pandemic.

Results and Discussion

Many participants described the ways in which the lockdown period had provided opportunities for positive personal growth. However, the period was also associated with experiences of loss, personal difficulty and heightened emotion. For those in minoritized ethnic groups, there were additional issues associated with expectations regarding the maintenance of particular cultural traditions and absence from and fear for family living abroad. People's concerns were also exacerbated by evidence regarding the greater risk of infection and death among those in minoritized ethnic groups and a perceived lack of ability among participants to protect themselves and their family from this. People also expressed a sense of additional vulnerability to racist violence, which people felt had risen in response to the pandemic and other incidents occurring during this time. Racism from others could act as a barrier to support from their local community, while a fear of exposure to racism could also affect people's social engagement in a range of ways.

Things were made more difficult by what was ubiquitously considered the national Government's poor handling of the crisis. The measures introduced to protect people—including those specifically targeted at those in minoritized ethnic groups—were considered ineffective. Participants also described the implications of Government and media discourses which were seen to purposefully misrepresent the evidence regarding the drivers of ethnic inequalities in Covid-19 infections and deaths. Not only did this cause confusion amongst those attempting to determine and respond to their personal Covid-19 risk but was also argued to directly increase their risk of exposure to racist violence. Some participants considered the Government's dismissive attitude to be the latest manifestation of a longstanding racism among political leaders and other powerful bodies in Britain. This awareness exacerbated concerns regarding how to protect themselves from infection and their chances of receiving care if they became ill. It also reinforced a wider sense of marginalisation in and exclusion from British society.

The Impact of Ethnicity on the Pandemic Experience

Perhaps as a consequence of being largely unencumbered by the socioeconomic stresses identified as disproportionately affecting those in minoritized ethnic groups (Barnes and Hamilton, 2020; Siddiqi et al., 2021), all interview participants described positively the ways in which pandemic lockdown had offered them opportunities for personal and/or social growth. This uninterrupted time enabled people to develop new or reinvigorate old hobbies and "take stock" of and "re-evaluate" their lives. People valued having capacity to pause, be more "mindful", "slow [their] pace of life" and learn to appreciate "small achievements". Lockdown also enabled some people to engage in making special memories with significant others, and build stronger networks in their local community.

But alongside these more positive experiences, participants described various difficulties. Several participants had experienced the death of relatives and friends, from Covid-19 and other causes. Participants described loneliness and the impact of the loss of "control", freedom, valued social contacts and previously-made plans. Some lived in accommodation which was considered too "confined". Others, particularly those with young children, experienced difficulties due to a lack of outside space. Many participants described an increase in "anxiety" with the "uncertainty" brought by the pandemic, some even fearing "mental breakdown". People experienced additional stress—going into "overdrive" to manage the new complexities of carrying out ordinary tasks, like visiting the supermarket. There were also simple activities which no longer seemed possible: It has been really really hard. [...] You're not feeling the same freedom, you used to go out and chat [...] I'm really chatty–I would see people on the street and start chatting to them, but obviously you don't feel the same way. Even if you wanted [to chat], the other person might be apprehensive if she has [in case I had] Covid (IP04, Female, 42, Kashmiri)

Such findings are consistent with research on the pandemic experiences of the general population (Ettman et al., 2020; Reading Turchioe et al., 2020). However, there were particular ways in which being part of a minoritized ethnic group was considered to have impacted on people's lockdown experience. For example, some people felt that the difficulties of social distancing were exacerbated by cultural traditions encouraging more frequent social contact: Back home, you're used to family and friends coming around all the time, which is really different here (IP04, Female, 42, Kashmiri). I have an Indian background. We are all about family and keeping in touch. [...] Not seeing them every week was difficult (IP02, Female, 28, British Indian). Cultural expectations regarding the provision of care to the infirm, bereaved and deceased also could add to the mental strain of the pandemic, particularly when these traditions were not recognised or responded to by statutory services or policymakers:

Cultural expectations of many South Asian communities require different types of support during illnesses and deaths. E.g, Bangladeshi families don't cook for 3 days post any death in the family. Family and friends are expected to deliver food to the mourning family during this time. Lockdown during this pandemic has increased the burden of community care on many of us. Without any state support and the disproportionate death rates in our community puts us under unprecedented anxiety and stress (SR05, Female, 36, Bangladeshi). While the pandemic meant that opportunities for holidays and social gatherings were missed by many, the cancellation of international travel was particularly difficult for those with close family living abroad. The circumstances of the pandemic in other national contexts could also add stress: All of my mum's side are in India and […] initially it was full lockdown and then there was news of police brutality and then there was news of how bad [high] the numbers [of cases] were, people hijacking food trucks and all this. And obviously I'm just thinking, 'Oh my god! My family. What is it like for them?' (IP02, Female, 28, British Indian)

People's lockdown experiences were also affected by a fear of negative treatment. Some people described personal experiences of racially-motivated poor treatment, in this case in line with other research identifying biased policing during the pandemic (Busby and Gidda, 2020, Harris et al., 2021a; b):

I was stopped 3 times during lockdown by police and PCSO [Police Community Support Officer] while out with my 3 year old daughter, none of my white mum friends were (SR38, Female, 47, Indian).

But others described how their fear of racist victimisation had affected their lives and their mental health. Some participants reacted to these fears by adopting vigilant coping behaviours, such as reducing their social contact.

I have some friends who are of East Asian decent and they've experienced racial attacks—being made to feel like they were the cause for the pandemic. […] even though I'm African, I initially felt safer to stay home and on edge of [because I was worried about] what effect the pandemic would have on racial tensions (SR03, Female, 23, Black African).

While acknowledging that some people experienced an additional risk to which she was not exposed, SR03 also identifies a wider racism endemic to

British society which has been exacerbated by the pandemic, and of which all those in racialized groups are at risk. People's fear of exposure to racist violence also increased with lockdown restrictions on movement, a loss of witnesses potentially making violence more likely as well as reducing opportunities to respond effectively if it did.

Hate can be quite frightening, and [...] your children are walking the street at night, knowing there could be anyone like that walking on the streets. It did get quite frightening because of the isolation of the lockdown, not so many witnesses if you're on the street for any aggression or violence (IP07, Female, 53, Black Caribbean). Experiences of racism in one domain could also produce fears about negative treatment in others. In the quotation below, and as with SR03 above, the articulation of racism by members of the public produced concerns regarding the ubiquitous nature of racism in Britain, including its presence among those providing healthcare. This heightened people's sense of stress and also their perceived need for extra vigilance in behaviours to reduce the risk of infection:

With BLM [...] I found a lot of bigots, and a lot of negativity, a lot of racism [online...] which didn't make me feel confident that if I went out and asked for support, or if my health failed and I needed support and I came across someone that was really against BLM and was very angry because they'd had a protest that they were going to treat me [kindly]–so I kept myself as safe as possible because there was no way I was entering into a hospital. [...] it played on your mental health a lot. (IP07, Female, 53, Black Caribbean). Racism could directly undermine people's ability to develop supportive networks with their neighbours, which limited people's sense of available support during the lockdown:

[The] white middle-class neighbourhood helped each other. They didn't help me [...] I thought, 'Even at the lowest point, where we could all die [...] they still have that racism.' (IP07, Female, 53, Black Caribbean). In the absence of support from her local neighbourhood, IP07 established a "community" of people with similar ethnicities living in other areas. This network could not only provide the practical and emotional support she needed during the pandemic but also offered connections stemming from common experiences of social exclusion: My community is extended— Black professionals and the Black communities that I live close to, that I go to for food, warmth, emotional warmth [...] And those are the people that kept my sanity, and those are the people that understand that we are at the bottom of the chain (IP07, Female, 53, Black Caribbean). A fear of racism could also impact on someone's access to social support. IP04 describes how such anxieties had prevented them from even trying to initiate social connections:...because English is not your first language, your name isn't familiar, you probably don't talk in the same accent as people do here, so it's really difficult to adjust yourself to that kind of life. At times, when you feel those negative things [attitudes], you feel like "oh probably everybody is the same' but then when positive things happen, you start thinking 'oh no, there are still good and nice people around". [...] When somebody does a nice gesture for you, you feel overwhelmed. (IP04, Female, 42, Kashmiri).

As before, negative experiences identified in one domain increased a perceived need for vigilance in others, which led them to avoid making efforts to engage with people with whom they were unfamiliar despite the potential benefits of such relationships. While this participant does not explicitly mention racism, the "negative things" she has experienced relate to characteristics which would mark her as culturally different. Moreover, her sense of being "overwhelmed" by any "nice gestures" suggests that her sense of vulnerability to racism is significant. As discussed earlier, this may have occurred as a consequence of previous personal experiences of racist violence or through the development of a perception based on the experiences of others—or wider public discourses—that such reactions are commonly experienced by people with similar characteristics to hers.

The Impact of a Heightened Sense of Covid-19 Risk

People's pandemic anxiety was exacerbated for those, or with family, with health conditions considered to increase the risk of Covid-19 complications, particularly when they worked in a role which they could not provide at home. This concern increased with news regarding the higher prevalence of Covid-19 infections and deaths amongst those in minoritized ethnic groups.It has been a constant worry with my husband and eldest son going to work. It has been a huge worry knowing that BAME people are at a higher risk. It has just been a huge worry overall and it has battered my mental health (SR41, Female, 36, Mixed—Black Caribbean and white). Awareness of this additional health risk encouraged people to go to more extreme measures to protect themselves, even if this could exacerbate their social isolation.

I wasn't worried too much before and at the start of lockdown. However since the news of BAME people being much more likely to be impacted I have been very worried—I rarely leave the house and it has caused me anxiety for the first time in my life (SR39, Male, 37, Mixed—Black African and white). People felt that the Government's pandemic planning did not acknowledge, and might actually increase, these risks: I have had some increased anxieties since lockdown rules have relaxed and am aware of higher risks for BAME people (SR24, Female, 42, Indian). Some of the participants unable to work from home during the pandemic felt empowered to negotiate with their employers to ensure their safety at work, should this become necessary. But there was a concern that not everyone had that same capacity, or "voice". Nobody would force me to go into an office or do anything I didn't want to do [...] But like I said I'm probably in a better position than most because I've got a voice. So if you make me do something I'm not doing it and I can give you reasons why—and I'll use [my knowledge of] policy to protect myself. I think if I was more of a vulnerable person and I had to work such as a taxi driver, or a person who was working frontline in a shop and I had to work or I wouldn't get paid, it would be a different position (IP07, Female, 53, Black Caribbean).

Here, and in the quotation below, there is an awareness of the consequences of the occupational concentration which is argued to help explain ethnic inequalities in Covid-19 infections and deaths (Platt and Warwick, 2020a,b, BSWN, 2020): As an African migrant, a lot of people tend to work as healthcare assistants, nurses, doctors, so just knowing that a lot of my family members were out there on the frontline, there was anxiety on that front and hoping that they remain safe. I think the knowledge as well that there's higher prevalence in BAME communities—obviously that kind of added to the anxiety (IP01, Female, 25, Black African). These comments may suggest that all those working in such roles may be exposed to a similar risk—regardless of ethnicity. However, the comments of some survey respondents suggested a particular lack of empowerment among those in minoritized ethnic groups in some occupations which may help explain ethnic inequalities in infections and deaths even within particular occupations (Cook et al., 2020). These people argued that they had been placed at unnecessary risk by their employer in a way which was not experienced by white colleagues.

I am the only BAME employee in my service. [...] I had to raise a complaint as I felt I was being put at risk not in line with that expected of my white colleagues despite [me] having increased risk [established through a workplace risk assessment] (SR17, Female, 30, Mixed—Asian and white). I was given more responsibility to lighten the load [on] other senior members of staff [...] I was offered no flexibility [...] WFH [working from home] was only for the senior staff, whom are white (SR21, Female, 43, Indian). In addition to problems with the actions of particular employers, participants also described Government failures to provide to support to those at additional risk: that "Black people who are on the frontline have the least protection and are not given any dedicated support." (SR33, Female, 36, Black African). While the Government had introduced new measures designed to assess the risk posed to those in minoritized ethnic groups in the workplace, these measures placed additional burden on staff and could directly increase people's sense of vulnerability to infection. Moreover, some people felt that such measures were simply "tick box" exercises, which had no practical value and only served the Government by giving people the impression that were taking appropriate action when they were not:

I've had extra risk assessments at work. [...] it just became a big deal [inconvenience] anytime I did a home visit and then because I was having these extra risk assessments, it made me more nervous to do these home visits. [...] I feel like I'm just in a box and being asked for a tick-box exercise rather than anything else. (IP02, Female, 28, British Indian). This distrust in the Government's motivations was also raised in relation to other aspects of the pandemic, as we shall discuss in the next section.

The Causes and Consequences of Inadequate Government Responses to the Pandemic

Every participant expressed shock and deep frustration at the Government's handling of the pandemic, which had significantly undermined their "trust". Having family and friends living in other national contexts offered participants a particularly clear vantage point from which to recognise specific opportunities the Government had missed to act quickly and effectively in the face of rising infections and deaths, rather than waiting till "after the horse had bolted". The Government's inaction was particularly frustrating to those whose work enabled them to see first-hand the dire need for rapid action.

Don't get me started. The Government—working in the field I'm in, I saw cases [...] and we had to sit and wait for the Government to tell us what to do—by then it's too late (IP09, Female, 56, Black Caribbean). Government and media discussions regarding the causes of the pandemic—which ignored the role played by long-term Government policy in the escalation of the problem—reinforced this sense of dishonesty and corruption. Participants believed that members of the scientific community had been bribed to distort the truth, "paid back-handed to tell me rubbish". Again, these issues were particularly frustrating to those that worked in health or social care, or had friends and relatives in nursing homes or hospitals. In a nursing home [...] that's where we saw the lack of PPE [...] The media going out there ["blah blah"], we just thought "lies, lies, lies", all the way through. Then you go through anger [get angry] because obviously they then blame nursing and care staff and you knew that nursing and care staff did an incredible job.[...] So it was just the "blame game" [...] You [Government] knew it [what was happening] but [...] you were too busy covering your own asses (IP07, Female, 53, Black Caribbean).

Participants described media reports of ethnic inequalities in Covid-19 risk as particularly unhelpful and "sensationalist". As a consequence, they felt they had received little valuable information regarding the reasons for these differences, how to protect themselves or the Government's "action plan" to respond to them. This "insufficient guidance/research and action" was felt to expose "the Government's lack of priority [to protect people in ethnic minority groups] even though we appear to be the worst affected" (SR59, Female, 37, Black African). Explanations offered for ethnic inequalities in Covid-19 infections and deaths, when they occurred, were described as "disgustingly divisive". There was a concern that these had focused on genetic/biological factors and ignored the structural factors which actually explained these greater risks. For some participants, it was clear that the issue "was less about race and more about postcodes" (SR56, Female, 34, Pakistani) and other societal factors. They took this apparent distortion of the evidence as further indication of the Government's dishonesty. [The message that] 'you [those in ethnic minority groups] basically have [problems with] your metabolism or your body make-up and it's totally different [to other people's] so you're going to be high profile [at high risk] for Covid-19' was bull[shit]—we just thought "you weren't treating us properly". [...] You know it's not that [explanation. Actually,] it's lack of resources, PPE, and maybe lack of trust, lack of good quality of health[care], so there were more reasons behind it [than they were admitting] (IP07, Female, 53, Black Caribbean).

Others highlighted the shortcomings in this framing by simply asking, "Since when was a virus racist?" (SR49, Female, 34, Mixed—Black Caribbean and white). Even where these reports included greater acknowledgement of the significance of structural factors, they did not always offer sufficient analytical depth to allay people's fears or confusion: It was almost like sensationalist reporting in that 'you're more likely to die of Covid or contract Covid if you're BAME' and they didn't say why. One local reporter said, it's because these groups don't often have access to a garden. And

185

I'm like, 'well, I've always had a garden. So it was all this sort of rubbish, because the likely explanation doesn't put the Government in a good light [...] if there's no why or understanding then you're scaremongering. You're not really helping the situation. [...] I'm isolating by myself in a three-bed semi-detached [house] with a garden. I can't be the only [Black] person [like that]. So it would be interesting to see, is it BAME living in poorer conditions, you know high rise [accommodation]? What is it? (IP05, Female, 39, Black British Caribbean).

Even though this participant recognises her more privileged socioeconomic position, the media report did not support them to fully appreciate whether and how this might enable a reduced vulnerability to Covid-19 infection, or its more extreme consequences. Again, there is a perception that the Government and media would purposefully withhold information to avoid exposing their contribution to the problem. IP05 also reflected on the tendency for the Government and media to present a very homogenised, negative and biased portrayal of those in minoritized ethnic groups: I'm Black but I don't live in the poorest suburb of (area). I drive, I'm in this [higher] pay bracket, where am I? Unless I'm Black, single, single mother, on benefits, you know all the kind of negatives—I don't exist. And I go, 'well, I know I'm not unusual and there are others, so where are we (IP05, Female, 39, Black British Caribbean).

This homogenising discourse further reinforced a sense that ethnic inequalities in Covid-19 were driven by genetic/biological risks, and immune to the effects of socioeconomic and other privilege. It was also felt unhelpful for people trying to determine their own level of pandemic risk: I find that a lot of the discussion around "BAME" [Black, Asian and Minority Ethnic] during this pandemic relates to Black or Black&Asian [people], but doesn't consider other groups. [...] I feel I always have to check if I'm included or not. (SR22, Female, 45, Mixed—other). As a mixed-race person I have struggled at times to know whether and to what extent advice related to increased risk for "BAME" people applies to me (SR17, Female, 30, Mixed—Asian and white). More generally, people described how their own pandemic response had been undermined by confusing and contradictory Government messaging which forced people to make their own decisions about how to protect themselves. This distrust of the Government's motives also encouraged a perceived need for additional vigilance, to "use your [own] intelligence, not just listen to what the Government is telling you". People described seeking alternative and, what were perceived to be, more reliable sources of information on how to manage their risk than the Government was providing.

We created a bubble long before the Government told us we could because we knew we were going to have to protect ourselves. There was no way, as a Black person, I was going to take on anything that white upper-class person was going to tell me, because they weren't going to have any thoughts on my behaviour or what was going to help me (IP07, Female, 53, Black Caribbean). This distrust of the Government's motivations could also affect people's engagement with other aspects of the Government's response to the pandemic, for example in relation to the Covid-19 vaccine, voicing suspicions and concerns which have also been raised by NHS staff (Woodhead et al., 2021):

Now we're back to "[…] we want Black people to come in first and have the injections because you're at highest risk". How many idiots do you think are out there that are going to be Black–including myself–that are going to have an injection by our glorious leader [Boris Johnson] that made so many mistakes at the beginning? And then we have a glorious leader [Donald Trump] in America giving out the same message–"you're nothing, you're rubbish, I think nothing of you, but you're going to have the injection first and then we're going into Africa". (IP07, Female, 53, Black Caribbean). While it is unclear whether this concern led to a refusal to receive the vaccine, it is likely to have contributed to a greater sense of hesitancy, and additional stress amongst those receiving the vaccine. There is a strong sense here of the ways in which racism perceived in different contexts, even when experienced indirectly (eg through the comments and actions of Donald Trump), can combine to introduce/perpetuate a personal sense of vulnerability, which may even directly exacerbate a health risk, through disengagement with effective pandemic protection strategies.

Approaches which failed to acknowledge the diversity within and between minoritized ethnic groups encouraged a sense that they were inherently different from the rest of (white) British society. Participants argued that this enabled them to be presented (by the Government and media) as a threat to (the health of) British society, which could directly motivate racist violence: I don't like being classed as "BAME" […] since Covid it has underlined [reinforced] the racism [existing in Britain] where people are […] making it known [encouraging people to think] that we are carriers. "BAME" I see as classed as 'others'. (SR19, Female, 56, Black Caribbean). People felt that the pandemic had been used to try to galvanise the white

British public, through the further marginalisation of minoritized ethnic groups and to serve an anti-immigrant agenda:

Worryingly is the narrative that shifted from "white people pulling together and fighting this through", to members of the BAME community targeted as the major carriers and causing harm and being reckless. It was ironic that once the PM overcame the virus, his first point of business was tackling immigration, never mind the fact that many non-whites died looking after their elderly. [It] speaks volumes (SR44, Male, 50, Black Caribbean). As such, rather than ensuring the protection of the whole population, the Government had "turn[ed the pandemic] into a race war" (SR49, Female, 34, Mixed—Black Caribbean and white). Other events occurring during this time were also felt to have been misappropriated to reinforce this sense that those in minoritized ethnic groups are inherently problematic and dangerous. The Government and media were argued to have purposefully misrepresented the Black Lives Matter movement protests occurring in response to the death of George Floyd in order to "politicise" them and reinforce a sense that those in minoritized ethnic groups were to blame for their own difficulties, in part by minimising the attention given to the risky activities of people in other ethnic groups.

I think there's a bit of a blame sometimes—so like the Black Lives Matter protest. The news really focused on how 'this is really going to help the surge of coronavirus, the numbers are going to go up and up and up' and actually everyone on that protest was keeping their distance. They were wearing masks. As much as they could do at protests, they were following rules. And then you've got those pictures of Brighton where you've got hundreds and hundreds of people hoarding on the beach and then nothing [was said] (IP02, Female, 28, British Indian). People were also angry that this victim-blaming had enabled the Government and media to impede their ability to express their legitimate concerns about the scale of racism in Britain: "It felt like the pandemic was being used to stop people from going out to protest." (IP01, Female, 25, Black African). Like Elias et al. (2021), people did not see these negative depictions as incidents isolated from the negative treatment of people in minoritized ethnic groups in other contexts and times. People described how negative representations in relation to the pandemic replicated and were enabled by earlier discourses about those in racialised groups.

With Brexit, the racism has risen and people have been attacked [...] I've grown up with all the racism and to keep seeing it and hearing it—it just seems like it's never going to go (IP09, Female, 56, Black Caribbean). We stem from hate and we're still moving through hate. [… like] Nigel Farage who stokes things so badly and has these sheep behind him. And then you have the people who take it further, is it the Christchurch murderer who killed 50-odd people in a mosque (IP07, Female, 53, Black Caribbean).

These quotations described the legacies of racism experienced since childhood, which influence and are reproduced in later racist tropes, for example, during Brexit. They also reflect on the significant role of commentators like anti-immigrant United Kingdom Independence Party (UKIP) leader Nigel Farage and other political leaders in encouraging the racist violence perpetrated by others—the "sheep" who follow them unquestioningly, sometimes to perform acts of massacre such as the deaths of 50 people following shootings at two mosques in Christchurch, New Zealand, on March 15, 2019. It was argued that this political atmosphere presented opportunities which were then exploited by the Government during the pandemic.

So they go through [they thought] "let's just blame them [Black people] because it's easier" because at the moment, we're in the right-wing place. So let's just keep it there because people will believe that (IP07, Female, 53, Black Caribbean). The increase in (awareness of) incidents of racism during the pandemic had a significant impact on people's wellbeing. People explained "the impact of systematic racism in the world, this has affected me a lot" (SR42, Female, 56, Black—other) and that the increase in "race related attacks has been hard to watch and endure" (SR33, Female, 36, Black African). Even when occurring in contexts distant from their own, this awareness could encourage people to reflect on themselves as members of a racialized group, and the inescapable nature of and risks associated with this. Direct and indirectly experienced incidents of racism occurring during the pandemic could become "triggers" for earlier negative experiences which exacerbated people's mental distress.

The triggers from the media, BLM [Black Lives Matter protests] and BLM happening at the same time as Covid–[…] through lockdown, I've had time to reflect and through BLM I've seen a lot more of the racism that we face […] You face it daily […] Everything you do you have to think about your skin colour because you know you may be treated differently (IP07, Female, 53, Black Caribbean). Similarly, IP01 describes the way in which reflecting on previous experiences of negative treatment, motivated by experiences in relation to the death of George Floyd and the Black Lives Matter protests and ethnic inequalities in Covid-19, had produced "a lot of anger in the community" as it has exposed the persistence of these issues as a consequence of a lack of meaningful action to address them among those with the power to do so: For a lot of people it [BLM] brought up past experiences of racism which people had brushed under the carpet. I think it brought to the forefront some of the issues of racism that is experienced by Black people in particular. So, I think a related issue was obviously the higher prevalence of coronavirus deaths within the Black community. I think it added to the rhetoric of the BLM movement' (IP01, Female, 25, Black African).

The pandemic, then, as well as a specific event, became the latest manifestation of the negative treatment which those in minoritized ethnic groups had to continuously negotiate, as "second class citizen[s]". This final quote is a testament to the perpetual effort involved in maintaining resilience in the face of these constant threats of victimisation, which come from all sectors of society: They were trying to make you a victim and they didn't succeed because you were always one step ahead of them, like you [always] are, because you have to be, in work or in life. You're always one step ahead of a racist. It was just amazing the path they took. And with straight faces (IP07, Female, 53, Black Caribbean). Despite this long history, this participant still expresses disbelief that, during the Covid-19 pandemic, the British Government could behave so abominably so brazenly, ie "with straight faces", without any concern for negative repercussions. Not surprisingly, this offered them little hope for things improving in the future.

Conclusion

These findings offer a valuable insight into the experiences of people in different minoritized ethnic groups during the first Covid-19 lockdown in South-West England in 2020. Initially, some participants, shielded from the more severe financial consequences of the pandemic and its lockdown, described positive experiences including opportunities for personal growth. In itself, this may not be considered a particularly novel finding. However, it takes on new significance in light of popular discourses, referenced by our participants, which present those in racialised groups as inherently different from wider British society. Yet, the influence of "ethnicity" still looms large. A sense of greater health risk—to yourself, your friends and family and other people "like you"–developed as evidence emerged of persistent ethnic inequalities in Covid-19 infections and deaths.

These concerns were compounded by knowledge of the concentration of those in minoritized ethnic groups in exposed occupations or with particular co-morbidities. But there is also evidence of a particular sense of threat which is not rooted in the pandemic itself. That while the virus may not be "racist", the implications for people's pandemic experience of living in a society where racist victimisation is considered endemic are expressed very clearly. On top of a general sense of Government incompetence, corruption and distrust, people described a racism which infected policy and behaviour at a national level. A racist media which spun stories which deliberately delegitimised and demonised peaceful and justified protests and the ignored the actual drivers of higher infections and deaths to blame the victims. Statutory authorities who failed to protect. And a public—justified by behaviour from the top—who used the pandemic and protests as opportunities for racist violence.

The consequences of direct experience of poor treatment are easily understood. But these findings also effectively illustrate the nature of lives lived with the threat of violence, even if that threat is not always actually realised. A fear of going out in public for fear of being attacked. A fear of needing to rely on people for protection, information or care who would deliberately act to harm you, whether that be neighbours, the police, healthcare providers or the Government. Concerns which led to greater mental strain both directly and indirectly, including as a consequence of the various forms of vigilance people adopted in response. This research offers further evidence of the need to recognise the inter-connected and reinforcing nature of incidents of racism. The pandemic and other racisms experienced—vicariously or personally—at this time (including the death of George Floyd and the actions it prompted) combined to paint a stark picture of the risk experienced by all those in racialised groups, in Britain and elsewhere. These incidents also became "triggers" which forced people to reflect on their own histories as members of these groups. The pandemic, then, became not a snapshot of a time like no-other, but testament to the past and an insight into the risks of the future.

While this paper offers valuable insights into the pandemic experiences of those in minoritized ethnic groups, the sample is small and select. As such, these findings are not generalisable to a wider population and we cannot establish the extent to which these experiences may be common. In particular, the impact of vulnerability to poverty on experiences of lockdown remains a significant part of the pandemic experience of many, disproportionately those in minoritized ethnic groups. Interview participants in this study were relatively privileged in terms of career, socioeconomic position, English-language ability, citizenship/migration status, and digital connectivity. This limits the potential for this study to offer insights into this aspect of pandemic experience and this must be the focus of further research. There is also a need for further research which can explore more directly the ways in which this pandemic experience is gendered (Laster-Pirtle and Wright, 2021). That said, it may be argued that this research offers a valuable opportunity to not focus on, what one participant called, "all the negatives", approaches which may in themselves encourage the sense that those in minoritized ethnic groups are inherently different and problematic, compared with the white British majority. Moreover, these findings show that while economic security enables some potential commonalities in pandemic experience with wider British society, it does not protect people from all the health risks to which those in minoritized ethnic groups are exposed. Our findings concur with existing literature regarding the range of ways in which racism can impact on people's lives and wellbeing.

Despite centuries spent trying to find it, there remains no solid evidence that ethnic inequalities in the vast majority of health or other social and economic circumstances can be explained by physical or cultural differences between the groups. All other things being equal, the pandemic experiences of the British public should be complimentary. Our participants see this clearly. Railing against persistent victim-blaming discourses, they instead draw attention to the role of structural/societal factors: racism; a lack of economic resources, social support and effective healthcare; a reduced ability to protect yourself in the face of vulnerabilities; and people's reactions to the lack of trust these engender. If we are to have a hope of successfully building a fairer, healthier, inclusive and sustainable society in the aftermath of the pandemic, we must, as a minimum, insist that political, media and academic discourses are similarly reflective regarding the causes of these inequalities.

We must also acknowledge the centrality of racism to the experiences of many people in minoritized ethnic groups living in the United Kingdom, and elsewhere. It is a key driver of the inequalities in economic and other experience so significant for ethnic inequalities in Covid-19 infections and deaths (PHE, 2020a; Becares and Nazroo, 2020; Godlee, 2020). This research suggests that racism has also played more a direct and prominent role in the pandemic experiences of people in minoritized ethnic groups. While many of us experienced fear as Covid-19 spread around the globe, this fear was exacerbated among those who not only felt they did not have the attention of those with the power to protect them, but that they might

actually sacrifice them to save themselves. Sewell et al. (CRED, 2021) are correct to argue that people's sense of racism may be forged in history. But this research suggests that this history continues to repeat itself. For many, the pandemic has served as further evidence of the need for those in ethnic minority groups to maintain a healthy sense of distrust to survive, and be mindful that "the racist" remains close behind.

Data Availability Statement: The data presented in this article are not readily available because this would contravene the terms of the ethical agreements under which the research was conducted. Requests to access the data should be directed to SK, saffron.karlsen@bristol.ac.uk. Ethics Statement: The studies involving human participants were reviewed and approved by the SPAIS Ethics Committee, School of Sociology, Politics and International Studies, University of Bristol. The patients/ participants provided their written informed consent to participate in this study. Author Contributions; SK designed and led the project, RN was the research associate on the project and led on the data collection. Both authors contributed significantly to the analysis of the data and drafting of the manuscript. Funding; this work was supported by the Elizabeth Blackwell Institute, University of Bristol, with funding from the University's alumni and friends. Conflict of Interest: The authors declare that the research was conducted in the absence of any commercial or financial relationships that could be construed as a potential conflict of interest. Publisher's Note: All claims expressed in this article are solely those of the authors and do not necessarily represent those of their affiliated organizations, or those of the publisher, the editors and the reviewers. Any product that may be evaluated in this article, or claim that may be made by its manufacturer, is not guaranteed or endorsed by the publisher. Acknowledgments; with thanks to the anonymous reviewers for their insightful comments on an earlier draft of this manuscript. With thanks to the Black South West Network (BSWN) for their partnership in this project, and to our participants for their valuable contributions. Footnotes ; Lockdown is the cessation of all non-essential activities to slow the spread of Covid-19. In the United Kingdom, this saw strict limits imposed on people's activities both within and outside of their homes, including both what they could do and who they could spend time with. The first United Kingdom lockdown was applied on 23 March 2020, lasting until 4 July 2020, although regional/territory specific approaches were introduced after this time. Subsequent national lockdowns were implemented in October 2020 and January 2021, although with differing degrees of impact (e.g., regarding whether or not educational establishments were affected) and territorial time frames. Open Access Publisher and Open Science Platform. ORIGINAL RESEARCH article. Front. Social. 01 November 2021 | https://doi.org/10.3389/fsoc.2021.730313. Our journals are led and peer-reviewed by editorial boards of over 100,000 top researchers. Covering more than 900 academic disciplines, we are one of the largest and highest-cited publishers in the world. To date, our freely accessible research articles have received over 1 billion views and downloads and 1.6 million citations. We strive to continuously empower *the academic community with innovative solutions that improve how science is published, evaluated and communicated to researchers, innovators and the public. Our mission is to make science open. Research is the foundation of modern society and it's thanks to advances in science that we enjoy longer, healthier and more prosperous lives than ever before in human history. We want to build on successful science and make it even more powerful by ensuring it is openly available. This way, society will be able to generate more knowledge and accelerate innovation, health and prosperity for all. Keywords: Covid-19, coronavirus, ethnicity, health, inequality, race, racism. Citation: Karlsen S and Nelson R (2021) Staying "One Step Ahead of a Racist": Expanding Understandings of the Experiences of the Covid-19 Pandemic Among People From Minoritized Ethnic Groups Living in Britain. Front. Sociol. 6:730313. doi: 10.3389/fsoc.2021.730313. Received: 24,June, 2021; Accepted: 11 October 2021; Published: 01 November 2021. Edited by: Sin Yi Cheung, Cardiff University, United Kingdom. Reviewed by: Renee Luthra, University of Essex, United Kingdom Arjan de Haan, International Development Research Centre, Canada James Laurence, The University of Manchester, United Kingdom. Copyright © 2021 Karlsen and Nelson. This is an open-access article distributed under the terms of the Creative Commons Attribution License (CC BY). The use, distribution or reproduction in other forums is permitted, provided the original author(s) and the copyright owner(s) are credited and that the original publication in this journal is cited, in accordance with accepted academic practice. No use, distribution or reproduction is permitted which does not comply with these terms. *Correspondence: Saffron Karlsen, saffron.karlsen@bristol.ac.uk. Disclaimer: All claims expressed in this article are solely those of the authors and do not necessarily represent those of their affiliated organizations, or those of the publisher, the editors and the reviewers. Any product that may be evaluated in this article or claim that may be made by its manufacturer is not guaranteed or endorsed by the publisher.*

Notes to Chapters

Chapter-1: The United Kingdom in Danger of Becoming a Failed State

1. Robert I. Rotberg, in his well-written book "Failed States, Collapsed States, Weak States: Causes and Indicators.

2. Ibid

3. M. Weir, "International Encyclopaedia of the Social & Behavioural Sciences,-2001

4. K.W. Moore, in his comment (International Encyclopaedia of the Social & Behavioural Sciences, 2001

5. Associate Professor of Law, University of Virginia School of Law, Rosa Ehrenreich Brookst (Failed States, or the State as Failure? The University of Chicago Law Review, Volume 72 Fall 2005 Number-4, the University of Chicago.

6. Failed or Fragile States in International Power Politics, Mr. Nussrathullah W. Said, City College of New York, 2013

7. Stewart Patrick in his paper (Working Paper Number 73, January 2006. Weak States and Global Threats: Assessing Evidence of "Spill overs". Centre for Global Development.

8. Heather Rawling in the Socialist newspaper analysis, (Poverty increasing. Welfare state in crisis. Do we need a new Beveridge Report?-28 April 2021.

9. Christopher Ansell, Eva Sørensen & Jacob Torfing in their research paper (The COVID-19 pandemic as a game changer for public administration and leadership? The need for robust governance responses to turbulent problems-2020.

10. Robert I. Rotberg in his well-written book "Failed States, Collapsed States, and Weak States: Causes and Indicators

11. Ibid

12. Failed or Fragile States in International Power Politics", Mr. Nussrathullah W. Said (City College of New York, 2013

13. Stewart Patrick in his paper (Working Paper Number 73 January 2006. Weak States and Global Threats

14. Grant Walton. Risks of corruption to state legitimacy and stability in fragile situations-U4 Issue-May 2012 No 3, Anti-Corruption Resource Centre

15. BBC (February 2021

16. Ibid

17. Vivien Lowndes, Alison Gardner in their research paper (Local Government under the Conservatives: Super-austerity, devolution and the 'smarter state', Institute of Local Government Studies-2016

18. Karlo Basta & Ailsa Henderson. 2021. Multinationalism, Constitutional Asymmetry and COVID: UK Responses to the Pandemic, Nationalism and Ethnic Politics.

19. Mark Sandford, (Is this the way to English devolution? Voice, delegation, levelling up? UK in a Changing Europe, 06 Sep 2021.

20. Mario Silva (Failed and Failing States: Causes and Conditions-June 2012

21. Nicola McEwen, Michael Kenny, Jack Sheldon and Coree Brown Swan in their recent paper (Reforming Intergovernmental Relations in the United Kingdom, November 2018

22. In May 2021, Sir David Lidington in his lecture on the future of British constitution and function of the Union of four provinces warned that future of the country is in danger.

23. The Wales government published a report full of protestation and complaints against the attitude of Westminster (Reforming our Union: Shared governance in the UK June 2021. The 2nd edition of the Welsh Government's views on the reforms needed to put the Union on a sustainable footing for the future.

24. Michael Kenny, Philip Rycroft and Jack Sheldon, Union at the Crossroads: Can the British state handle the challenges of devolution? The Constitution Society-2021

25. The Wales government report (Reforming our Union: Shared governance in the UK June 2021

26. Chief Minister of Wales, Mark Drakeford expressed concern over the attitude of Whitehall towards provinces and future of the Union. In his commentary in the foreword of the report of his administration (Reforming our Union: Shared Governance in the UK-2021.

27. 25 January 2021, former Prime Minister Gordon Brown warned that the public's trust in the way the UK is run was breaking down. Al Jazeera

28. Ibid

29. On 28 October, 2021, in his Expatica article, analyst and expert Gary Buswell has highlighted system of government

30. Martin Ivens. Japan Times, 27 May, 2020

31. 25, January 2021, Al Jazeera

32. Ibid

33. on 25 January 2021, Gavin Esler in his article (Is the UK really about to become a 'failed state'? The National News

34. John Ryan in his article. The UK economy is paying a heavy price for Johnson's hubris, February 24th, 2021

35. The SIPRI Yearbook 2002: The challenges of security sector reform. By, Dylan Hendrickson and Andrzej Karkoszka

36. Press TV, (Brexit is propelling Britain towards the door marked 'failed state'-24 September 2021), analysts John Wight

37. Luke Raikes and Dr. Arianna Giovannini, in their joint paper (The Progressive Policy Think Tank 20 November, 2019

38. 15 July, 2021, Prime Minister Boris Johnson speech

39. Japan Times, Martin Iven, Britain's prime minister has centralized power, but he doesn't seem to want to use it-May 27, 2020

40. 18 April 2019, journalist Lyra McKee was killed by the new IRA' gunman

41. Ibid

42. First Minister Arlene Foster said PSNI Chief Constable Simon Byrne should resign over the force's handling of the funeral of senior republican Bobby Storey in June

43. BBC, 07 April 2021

44. Ibid

45. Tom Fowdy (07 April 2021

Chapter 2: Domestic Governance, Intelligence Diversity, and Surveillance

1. 11 March, 2021, BBC, Home Office tests web-spying powers with help of UK internet firms

2. The CAGE article-13 July, 2016

3. Mariana Mazzucato, Rainer Kattel, Giulio Quaggiotto and Milica Begovic, in their research paper, (United Nations Development Programme: COVID-19 and the Need for Dynamic State Capabilities: An International Comparison.

4. Stop spying on US, Musa Khan Jalalzai

5. Global Britain in a Competitive Age: The Integrated Review of Security, Defence, Development and Foreign Policy-16 March 2021

6. Nuclear Madness. Musa Khan Jalalzai

7. Dr Javier Argomaniz, Dr Oldrich Bures and Dr Christian Kaunert (A decade of EU Counterterrorism and Intelligence: A critical assessment.

8. Editors of The U.K.'s Changing Democracy notes

9. Ibid

10. Intelligence and Security Committee-13 November 2021

11. Intelligence and Security Committee of Parliament, in its report, (Diversity and Inclusion in the UK Intelligence Community Presented to Parliament pursuant to section 3 of the Justice and Security Act 2013, 18 July 2018)

12. Ibid

13. Ibid

14. Daniel W. B. Lomas in his research paper on diversity in the UK intelligence agencies, (ForgetJamesBond: diversity, inclusion and the UK's intelligence agencies, Intelligence and National Security, 36:7, 995-1017, DOI:10.1080/0 2684527.2021.1938370.

15. Ibid

16. Regulation of Investigatory Power Act 2000

17. Part-11 and Part-111 of the Regulations of Investigatory Power Act of 2000-RIPA

18. Mass Surveillance programs by British and European intelligence services

19. Ibid

20. "Don't Spy on US," coalition policy paper, September 2014

21. December 2012 to January 2013, MUSCULAR collected 181 million records, while INCENSER, another WINDSTOP program, collected over 14 billion records

22. 01 July, 2015, the Investigatory Powers Tribunal (IPT), which investigates

23. Ibid

24. Ibid

25. Ibid

26. Ibid

27. Ibid

28. Ibid

29. Ibid

30. Ibid

31. Ibid

32. Ibid

33. 07 October 2020, the Register Kieren McCarthy

34. November 2015, the UK government promulgated Investigatory Powers Bill

35. 06 November 2015, Investigatory Power Bill

36. 20 June 2018, in a speech in Brussels, the GCHQ Chief Jeremy Fleming's statement was evident of his irritation about the dilapidating security crisis

37. National Security Capability Review. 2018

38. 04 June 2018 version, the U.K. Counter-Terrorism Strategy

39. Ibid

40. Ibid

41. From January to June 2019, more than 100 people in England were killed, and 100 more were injured

42. Snoopers Charter Surveillance (SCS) and the government's war on civilian privacy

43. National policing digital strategy: Digital, data and technology strategy-2020-2030

44. The Home Office National Centre for Policing Excellence

45. National Centre for Scientific Research, Paris, France, Dr Hager Ben Jaffel and Senior Lecturer, University of Sunderland, Dr Jeremy Pearson, (Intelligence, Law Enforcement and Brexit-26 Feb 2021

46. Ibid

47. Ibid

48. Iinar research paper underlined crucial aspects of the NSC and its significance to national security. Institute for Government research associates Dr. Joe Devanny and Josh Harris asserted.

49. Ibid

50. Ibid

51. Clare Dyer in his BMJ commentary (on 15 June 2020, Covid-19: Woman whose father died in care home launches legal review over government's "litany of failures".

52. 05 November 2020, Prime Minister Boris Johnson imposed a second national lockdown

53. Jeff Harris, (Global Research, October 30, 2020

54. 04 Nov, 2020, Prime Minister Boris Johnson was branded "petty" after he walked out of the House of Commons as soon as his predecessor former

Prime Minister Theresa May started presenting her criticism of his handling of Covid-19 restrictions.

55. 06 November 2020, Lockdown Sceptics quoted an article of Professor Carl Heneghan and Dr Tom Jefferson from the Oxford Centre for Evidence-Based Medicine in Daily Telegraph criticizing government's failures in presenting clear, honest, reliable data to justify its decisions.

56. Ibid

Chapter 3: Facial Recognition Technology, Biological Terrorism and Mass surveillance

1. OpenDemocracy-30 March 2020
2. Gordon Corera (April 2020
3. 11 November 2020, European Union Agency for Law Enforcement Cooperation
4. Ibid
5. 03 November 2020, BBC report
6. 17 November 2020, the UK Counter Terrorism Policing launched new ACT Early safeguarding website and advice line, and said they were listening and offer help and advice
7. Cate Pye and Nick Newman (An opportunity to enact long-lasting change to UK Defence and National Security, Bringing Ingenuity of Life
8. Global Security Review paper (COVID-19 and the Increasing Risk of Terrorism, 02 October, 2020
9. Nafeez Ahmed (Coronavirus exposes who Britain's national security industry is designed to protect – not the public, 21 March 2020.

Chapter 4: ForgetJamesBond: diversity, inclusion and the UK's intelligence agencies. Daniel W. B. Lomas

1. Brown, "MI6 recruiting foreign-born spies for first time to improve diversity".
2. https://twitter.com/ChiefMI6/status/1362733197449170953?s=20 ≥ For just some of the coverage, see Warrell, "MI6 chief apologises for historical ban on gay employees"; Sabbagh, "MI6 boss apologises for past ban on LGBT staff"; and Bunkall, "MI6 chief apologises for LGBT+ ban that "blighted lives and shattered dreams".
3. Maurice, "Queer spies reveal homophobic legacy of MI6's "illogical" LGBT+ ban – and how far things have come".
4. Rayment, "MI6 spy chiefs advertising for part-time James Bonds who "must love to travel""; Dickinson, "MI6 looking for part-time James Bond-style spies to 'spice up dull lives."

5.   https://twitter.com/ChiefMI6/status/1355822524823646208 >

6.   McCrisken, "James Bond, Ian Fleming and intelligence," 807.

7.   MacAskill, "James Bond would not get job with real MI6, says spy chief".

8.   Shahan, "Spying Gender: Women in British intelligence, 1969–1994", 2.

9.   Proctor, Female Intelligence, 256.

10. "Would you ever like to work for GCHQ, MI5 or MI6 (Britain's security services)?".

11. "Would you rather be in MI5 (the secret services focused on Britain) or MI6 (the secret services focused on British interests around the world)?"

12. Moran and Murphy, "Intelligence studies then and now," 1.

13. See Bean and Fischer. "Queering intelligence studies" and Shahan, ""Don't keep mum"".

14. Van Puyvelde and Curtis, "Standing on the Shoulders of Giants,"1048. See also Johnson and Shelton, "Thoughts on the State of Intelligence Studies,"109–120; Johnson and Phythian, "Intelligence and National Security at Thirty," 7. On the subject of diversity and intelligence generally, read Callum, "The case for cultural diversity in the Intelligence Community"; and Martin, "America's Evolution of Women and Their Roles in the Intelligence Community," 99–109.

15. Rimington, Open Secret.

16. See Andrew, Defence of the Realm; Ferris, Behind the Enigma, 437–52.

17. Jeffery, MI6.

18. For an example see Smith, The Hidden History of Bletchley Park; Toy and Smith, "Women in the shadow war," 688–706; Hubbard-Hall and O'Sullivan, "Wives of Secret Agents," 181–207; Pattinson, Behind Enemy Lines.

19. Beach, "No Cloaks, No Daggers," 212; and Shahan, ""Don't keep mum"," 2.

20. Alleyne-Lawler, "MI6 speaks to diversity dashboard".

21. On the impact of stereotype in the US, see Zegart, "Spytainment," 599–622.

22. See Van Puyvelde, "Women and black employees at the Central Intelligence Agency".

23. "Diversity and Inclusion".

24. Diversity and Inclusion: Examining Workforce Concerns Within the Intelligence Community.

25. See Southern, Homosexuality at the Foreign Office, 1967–1991; Southern, Black Skin, Whitehall: Race and the Foreign Office, and Women and the Foreign Office.

26. On the work of the ISC see Gaskarth, Secrets and Spies and Bochel, Defty and Kirkpatrick, Watching the Watchers.

27. HC. 633, 12–3, 15. The committee also did not publish a 2014–15 report thanks to the May 2015 General Election and the delay in appointing a new committee even though the committee has a statutory requirement to publish annual reports (see Defty, "Coming in from the cold," 31). 1010 D. W. B. LOMAS

28. HC. 1297, 19–20.

29. Senior Civil Service is "the most senior grade of the civil service made up of the senior management team" ('Grade structures of the civil service').

30. Cm 8403, 65–6.

31. HC. 970, 9. For some of the coverage of the report read Helm, "Spying has been an old boys' club for too long".

32. Cm. 8455, 9.

33. HC. 547, 40–1. On groupthink, see Omand, How Spies Think, 122–5.

34. HC. 970, 2. Read MacAskill, "Look to Mumsnet for new recruits, British intelligence agencies told".

35. HC. 970, p. iv.

36. Ibid., 22–3.

37. Ibid., 37–9.

38. Mission Critical: Why Inclusion is a National Security Issue and What You Can do To Help, 2, 7–

39. Alleyne-Lawler, "MI6 speaks to the Diversity Dashboard".

40. Director's Speech at CyberUK 2018.

41. "MI5 host a meeting of the 30% Club in Thames House".

42. HC. 1297, 1.

43. "Gender balance in the civil service".

44. "Dataset: Civil Service Statistics".

45. Ferris, Behind the Enigma, 719.

46. HC. 1297, 14.

47. Cm. 8403, 65.

48. HC. 444, 14.

49. HC. 1297, 14–15.

50. Cm. 9696, 2.

51. HC. 1297, Diversity and Inclusion.

52. Ibid., 29–30. On vetting see Scott, "The contemporary vetting landscape".

53. Private information.

54. Cm. 8403, 66.

55. See Beesley, The Official History of the Cabinet Secretaries, 555–6; West, "The UK's Not Quite so Secret Services,"23–30.

56. Urban, UK Eyes Alpha, 266.

57. Cm. 6864, 17.

58. Private Information.

59. See note 53 above.

60. Cowell, "Britain's Secret Service Indeed! Spy on It on Its Web site".

61. "MI6 ad for operational officers".

62. Andrew, Defence of the Realm, 791.

63. Lowe and Pemberton, The Official History of the British Civil Service, 115–121.

64. Ibid., 298–9.

65. Read Deavanny and Haddon, Women and Whitehall and McCarthy, Women of the World.

66. Andrew, Defence of the Realm, 549.

67. Ibid., 550.

68. Corera, The Art of Betrayal, 101–2. On Park read Hayes, Queen of Spies.

69. Rimington, Open Secret, 170.

70. Private Information.

71. Private Information.

72. Andrew, Defence of the Realm, 774; Rimington, Open Secret, 222.

73. Hayes, Daphne Park, 245.

74. Private Information.

75. See note 53 above.

76. Private Information.

77. "SIS is celebrating International Women's Day!"

78. Macintyre, "Revealed: women who sprang Gordievsky from KGB clutches". Pettit is referred to as Veronica Price in Macintyre, The Spy and the Traitor.

79. Private Information.

80. Tomlinson, The Big Breach, 46.

81. See note 53 above.

82. "SIS is celebrating International Women's Day!". There is some debate over when the 'bar' ended in SIS; Haynes suggests it only ended in the 1980s (see Hayes, Queen of Spies, 244). On the FCO bar read McCarthy, Women of the World, 283–90. Andrew, Defence of the Realm, 550.

83. Private Information.

84. McCarthy, Women of the World, 296; Women and the Foreign Office, 20.

85. Wintour, "New UK Ambassador".

86. Private Information.

87. Private Information.

88. Private Information and Ferris, Behind the Enigma, 448.

89. Omand, "Bonsall"; and Private Information.

90. Private Information.

91. Read Ferris, Behind the Enigma.

92. Muir, "MI6."

93. Ibid., 457.

94. Private Information.

95. Private Information.

96. See Taylor, "Race, parochialism and politics," 135–46; and "Profile: Lord Taylor of Warwick".

97. Private Information.

98. Private Information.

99. Private Information.

100. Harris, "Configurations of Racism," 3.

101. TNA: CSC 5/1139, Somerville to Hayes, 27 February 1956.

102. TNA: CAB 134/3256, SM (0) 2nd Meeting, 24 May 1967.

103. Read Lomas, "Crocodiles in the Corridors," 20.

104. "GCHQ hiring bar is upheld".

105. Norton-Taylor, "Soldier's court action over GCHQ post fails".

106. Hewitt, The British War on Terror, 109.

107. Cm. 5542, 26.

108. Cm. 5837, 14.

109. Cm. 6510, 20–21.

110. Ibid., 1.

111. See "Percentage of BAME staff in whole civil service and senior civil service, 1990–2020".

112. Cm. 6864, 21.

113. Dodd and Norton-Taylor, "Al-Qaida plan to infiltrate MI5 revealed".

114. Private Information.

115. Private Information.

116. Sengupta, "MI5 recruitment drive will focus on Asians"; "Asian MI5 and MI6 officers speak".

117. Cm. 7542, 25.

118. "Asian MI5 and MI6 officers speak".

119. Lappard, ""Racism" at GCHQ is undermining fight against terror".

120. Taylor, "GCHQ spared having inner workings made public".

121. Hewitt, The British War on Terror, 108.

122. Arthanayake, "Why GCHQ needs to fix its diversity problem".

123. "Why British Asians should consider a career in intelligence"; "Recruiting diverse talent to protect modern Britain".

124. Private Information.

125. Lomas and Murphy, "Security or Scandal?," 72–91.

126. See Drabble, Angus Wilson, 100.

127. Cmd. 9715, 3.

128. Andrew, Defence of the Realm, 398.

129. Ibid., 399.

130. TNA: CAB 134/3256, SM(O)(67)19, Security Implications of the Sexual Offences Act, 1967.

131. Corera, "The challenge of being gay and an MI6 spy".

132. Moore, Margaret Thatcher: The Authorised Biography, Volume Three, 257.

133. Historical Institutional Abuse Inquiry (HIAI) KIN-104288, memo to Sir Robert Armstrong, 31 March 1980.

134. HIAI: KIN-104317, Smith to Armstrong, 19 February 1981.

135. "Director GCHQ's speech at Stonewall Workplace Conference – as delivered".

136. TNA: CAB 134/4564, PSC(81)3, Security policy in regard to homosexuality, 28 April 1981.

137. PREM 19/1634, 'Report of the Security Commission, December 1981' reproduced in Lomas, 'Security, scandal and the Security Commission Report 1981', 745; Ferris, Behind the Enigma, 460.

138. Cmnd. 9923, p. 10.

139. TNA: CAB 134/4743, The Security Implications of Transvestism and Transsexuality, 9 March 1983.

140. Private Information.

141. Private Information.

142. Entry for 13 March 1990 in Wright, Behind Diplomatic Lines, 221. On the end of the bar Southern, Homosexuality at the Foreign Office and Lomas and Murphy, "Security or Scandal?".

143. Hansard, HC. Deb, 23 July 1991, Vol. 195, Cols. 474 W.

144. Norton-Taylor, "Gay spies allowed to come in from the Cold".

145. See note 131 above.

146. Maurice, "Queer spies reveal homophobic legacy of MI6's "illogical" LGBT+ ban".

147. HC. 1297, 15.

148. "Population of England and Wales".

149. "Male and Female Populations".

150. See note 117 above

151. HC. 1297, 25.

152. See note 53 above.

153. Cm. 9696, 1.

154. Secret Intelligence Service: Gender Pay Gap 2019, p. 2.

155. Secret Intelligence Service: Gender Pay Gap 2020, p. 2.

156. HC. 1297, 14.

157. See Secret Intelligence Service: Gender Pay Gap 2020, p. 3, MI5 Gender Page Gap 2020, p. 2, GCHQ Gender Pay Gap 2020, p. 6.

158. On this see Navigating the Labyrinth.

159. Private Information.

160. Haynes, "Women are great spies. We save the world and we pick up the children".

161. Private Information. See also Macintyre, "Move over 007, this is a job for a women".

162. Kerbaj, "Pay attention, 007: next real-life M will be a woman".

163. Private Information.

164. See Lomas, "Different Perspectives," 23.

165. See HC. 1297, 35–6.

166. Private Information.

167. "MI5 employed employer of the year by Stonewall".

168. "The Times Top 50 Employers for Women"

169. "Women in STEM". On diversity and cyber, read Decrypting Diversity.

170. Galpin, "GCHQ staff teach"; Lost for Words, 29–30.

171. See Skapinker, "How to remedy Britain''s language deficit curse"; Pozniak, "For Queen and Country". 172. HC. 1297, 25.

173. Private Information.

174. "Recruiting Diverse Talent to Protect Modern Britain".

175. "Location of new GCHQ site in Manchester revealed".

176. Cm. 6864, 21.

177. Johnson, "MI5 seeks "older, wiser women"".

178. Elliott, "GCHQ pleased with Tom Clancy campaign".

179. Cm. 7807, 10.

180. Private Information.

181. McLoughlin, Ward and Lomas, "Hello, world," 233–51.

182. McCallum, "To keep Britain safe".

183. Bunkall, "MI6 releases cinema advert in attempt to recruit more diverse candidates".

184. Corera, "MI6 airs TV ads to recruit more women and ethnic minorities".

185. "News: New SIS "Barbershop Advert" released on YouTube and Google display".

Printed Primary Sources

Alleyne-Lawler, Omar. 2017. "MI6 speaks to the Diversity Dashboard." October 25. https://www.blackhistorymonth.org. uk/article/section/civil-service-careers/mi6-speaks-bhm/

Cm. 5542. Intelligence and Security Committee: Annual Report, 2001-2002, June 2002.

Cm. 5837. Intelligence and Security Committee: Annual Report, 2002-2003, June 2003.

Cm. 6510. Intelligence and Security Committee: Annual Report, 2004-2005, April 2005.

Cm. 6864. Intelligence and Security Committee: Annual Report 2005-2006, June 2006.

Cm. 7542, Intelligence and Security Committee: Annual Report 2007-2008, March 2009.

Cm. 7807. Intelligence and Security Committee: Annual Report 2008-2009, March 2010.

Cm 8403. Intelligence and Security Committee: Annual Report, 2011-2012, July 2012.

Cm. 8455. Government Response to the Intelligence & Security Committee's Annual Report, 2011-12, November 2012.

Cm. 9696. Government response to the Intelligence and Security Committee of Parliament Report on Diversity and Inclusion in the Intelligence Community, September 2018.

Cmd. 9715. Statement on the Findings of the Conference of Privy Councillors on Security, March 1956. "Dataset: Civil Service Statistics." https://www.ons.gov.uk/employmentandlabourmarket/peopleinwork/publicsectorper son-nel/datasets/civilservicestatistics

Decrypting Diversity: Diversity and Inclusion in Cyber Security. KPMG and NCSC, July 2020. https://www.ncsc.gov.uk/report/diversity-and-inclusion-in-cyber-security-report .

"Director GCHQ's speech at Stonewall Workplace Conference–as delivered." 15 April 2016. https://www.gchq.gov.uk/speech/director-gchq-s-speech-at-stonewall-workplace-conference—as-delivered

"Director's Speech at CyberUK 2018." 2018. April 12. https://www.gchq.gov.uk/speech/director-cyber-uk-speech-2018

"Diversity and Inclusion: Examining Workforce Concerns Within the Intelligence Community." January 2017. https://www.dni.gov/files/documents/Newsroom/IC_EEOD_Barriers_Analysis.pdf .

"GCHQ Gender Pay Gap 2020." https://www.gchq.gov.uk/news/gender-pay-gap-2020 .

"Gender balance in the civil service."https://www.instituteforgovernment.org.uk/explainers/gender-balance-civilservice

HC. 444. Intelligence and Security Committee of Parliament: Annual Report, 2015–2016, July 2016.

HC. 633. Intelligence and Security Committee of Parliament: Annual Report 2018-2019, 21 July 2020.

HC. 970. Women in the UK Intelligence Community: a report by the Intelligence and Security Committee of Parliament, 5 March 2015.

HC. 1297. Intelligence and Security Committee of Parliament: Diversity and Inclusion in the UK Intelligence Community, July 2018.

HC. 1692. Intelligence and Security Committee: Annual Report, 2017-2018.

"Location of new GCHQ site in Manchester revealed." 20 October 2019. https://www.gchq.gov.uk/news/location-of-new -gchq-site-in-manchester-revealed

McCallum, Ken. 2021. "To keep Britain safe, MI5 is becoming more open." The Telegraph, April 22.

"MI5 Gender Pay Gap 2020." https://www.mi5.gov.uk/news/mi5-publishes-gender-pay-gap-report-2020

Mission Critical: Why Inclusion is a National Security Issue and What You Can do To Help.

Navigating the Labyrinth: Socio-economic background and career progression within the Civil Service, The Social Mobility Commission, May 2021. https://www.gov.uk/government/publications/navigating-the-labyrinth

"News: New SIS "Barbershop Advert" released on YouTube and Google display." 24 January 2019. https://www.sis.gov. uk/barbers-shop-advert.html .

"Percentage of BAME staff in whole civil service and senior civil service, 1990-2020." https://www.instituteforgovern ment.org.uk/charts/ethnicity-whole-and-senior-civil-service

"Regina v Secretary of State for Foreign and Commonwealth Affairs ex parte Manelfi: Admn 25 October 1996."

Tomlinson, Richard. The Big Breach: From Top Secret to Maximum Security. Moscow: Narodny Variant Publishers, 2000.

"Recruiting Diverse Talent to Protect Modern Britain." 14 November 2016. https://www.gchq.gov.uk/information/recruiting-diverse-talent-protect-modern-britain

Rimington, Stella. Open Secret: The Autobiography of the Former Director-General of MI5. London: Arrow, 2002.

Secret Intelligence Service Gender Pay Gap Report, 2019. https://www.sis.gov.uk/media/1405/sis-gender-pay-gap.pdf

Secret Intelligence Service Gender Pay Gap Report, 2020. https://www.sis.gov.uk/media/1476/sis-gender-pay-gap.pdf

"The Times Top 50 Employers for Women." 28 April 2018. https://appointments.thetimes.co.uk/article/the-times-top-50-employers-for-women-2018/

"Women in STEM: Percentages of Women in STEM subjects." 22 January 2021. https://www.stemwomen.co.uk/blog/ 2021/01/women-in-stem-percentages-of-women-in-stem-statistics .

"Would you ever like to work for GCHQ, MI5 or MI6 (Britain's security services)?." 2019. YouGov.co.uk, April 8. https://yougov.co.uk/topics/politics/survey-results/daily/2019/04/08/684cd/1 >

"Would you rather be in MI5 (the secret services focused on Britain) or MI6 (the secret services focused on British interests around the world)?." 2019.

YouGov, June 19. https://yougov.co.uk/topics/politics/survey-results/daily/2019/06/19/cb25d/3

Wright, Patrick. Behind Diplomatic Lines: Relations with Ministers. London: Biteback, 2018.

Bibliography

Andrew, C. Defence of the Realm: The Authorised History of MI5. London: Allen Lane, 2009.

Arthanayake, N. 2016. "Why GCHQ Needs to Fix Its Diversity Problem." BBC News, November 22.

Beach, J. "No Cloaks, No Daggers: The Historiography of British Military Intelligence." In Intelligence Studies in Britain and the US: Historiography since 1945, edited by C. R. Moran and C. J. Murphy. Edinburgh: Edinburgh University Press, 2013 pp. 202-221.

Bean, H., and M. Fischer. 2021. "Queering Intelligence Studies." Intelligence & National Security, March.

Beesley, I. The Official History of the Cabinet Secretaries, 1947 – 2002. Oxon: Routledge, 2017.

Bochel, H., A. Defty, and J. Kirkpatrick. Watching the Watchers: Parliament and the Intelligence Services. Houndmills: Palgrave, 2014.

Brown, L. 2021. "MI6 Recruiting Foreign-born Spies for First Time to Improve Diversity." The Times, February 10.

Bunkall, A. 2017. "MI6 Releases Cinema Advert in Attempt to Recruit More Diverse Candidates." Sky News, March 3.

Bunkall, A. 2021. "MI6 Chief Apologises for LGBT+ Ban that "Blighted Lives and Shattered Dreams"." Sky News, February 19.

Callum, R. "The Case for Cultural Diversity in the Intelligence Community." International Journal of Intelligence and

CounterIntelligence 14, no. 1 (2001): 25–48. doi:10.1080/08850600150501317.

Corera, G. The Art of Betrayal: Life and Death in the British Secret Service. London: Weidenfeld & Nicholson, 2011.

Corera, G. 2018. "MI6 Airs TV Ads to Recruit More Women and Ethnic Minorities." BBC News, May 24.

Corera, G. 2021. "The Challenge of Being Gay and an MI6 Spy." BBC News, February 28.

Cowell, A. 2005. "Britain's Secret Service Indeed! Spy on It on Its Web Site." The New York Times, October 14.

Damien, V. P. 2020. "Women and Black Employees at the Central Intelligence Agency: From Fair Employment to Diversity Management." Cambridge Review of International Affairs, December.

Deavanny, J., and C. Haddon. 2015. Women and Whitehall. September.

Defty, A. "Coming in from the Cold: Bringing the Intelligence and Security Committee into Parliament." Intelligence & National Security 34, no. 1 (2019): 22–37. doi:10.1080/02684527.2018.1513441.

Dickinson, I. 2021. "MI6 Looking for Part-time James Bond-style Spies to "Spice up Dull Lives"." Daily Star, January 30.

Dodd, V., and R. Norton-Taylor. 2006. "Al-Qaida Plan to Infiltrate MI5 Revealed." The Guardian, 4 July

Drabble, M. Angus Wilson: A Biography. London: Secker & Warburg, 1995.

Elliott, P. 2008. "GCHQ Pleased with Tom Clancy Campaign." January 22.

Ferris, J. Behind the Enigma: The Authorised History of Britain's Secret Cyber-intelligence Agency. London: Bloomsbury, 2020.

Galpin, R. 2011. "GCHQ Staff Teach "Future Spies" in Schools." BBC News, March 9.

Gaskarth, J. Secrets and Spies: UK Intelligence Accountability after Iraq and Snowden. Washington, DC: Brookings Institute Press/Chatham House, 2020.

"GCHQ Hiring Bar Is Upheld." 1996. The Independent, October 25.

Harris, C. "Configurations of Racism: The Civil Service, 1945–60." Race & Class 33, no. 1 (1991): 1–30. doi:10.1177/030639689103300101.

Hayes, P. Queen of Spies: Daphne Park, Britain's Cold War Spymaster. London: Duckworth Overlook, 2016.

Haynes, D. 2014. "Women are Great Spies. We Save the World and We Pick up the Children." The Times, March 31.

Helm, S. 2015. "Spying Has Been an Old Boys' Club for Too Long." The Telegraph, March 6.

Hewitt, S. The British War on Terror: Terrorism and Counter-terrorism on the Home Front since 9/11. London: Continuum, 2008.

Hubbard-Hall, and O'Sullivan. "Wives of Secret Agents: Spyscapes of the Second World War and Female Agency."

International Journal of Military History and Historiography 39, no. 2 (2019): 181–207. doi:10.1163/24683302-03902003.

Jeffery, K. MI6: The History of the Secret Intelligence Service, 1909–1949. London: Bloomsbury, 2010.

Johnson, L. K., and M. Phythian. "Intelligence and National Security at Thirty." Intelligence & National Security 31, no. 1 (2016): 1–7. doi:10.1080/0268452 7.2016.1104011.

Johnson, L. K., and A. M. Shelton. "Thoughts on the State of Intelligence Studies: A Survey Report." Intelligence & National Security 28, no. 1 (2013): 109–120. doi:10.1080/02684527.2012.748368.

Johnson, P. 2005. "MI5 Seeks "Older, Wiser Women"." The Telegraph, May 10.

Kelly, J. 2016. "The Era When Gay Spies Were Feared." BBC News, January 20.

Kerbaj, R. 2018. "Pay Attention, 007: Next Real-life M Will Be a Woman." The Times, April 29.

Lappard, D. 2010. "'Racism' at GCHQ Is Undermining Fight against Terror." The Sunday Times, 11 July.

Lomas, D. 2020. "Different Perspectives." Janes Intelligence Review, August.

Lomas, D. "Security, Scandal and the Security Commission Report, 1981." Intelligence & National Security 35, no. 5 (2020):734–750. doi:10.1080/0268452 7.2020.1740387.

Lomas, D. "Crocodiles in the Corridors: Security Vetting, Race and Whitehall, 1945–1968." Journal of Imperial & Commonwealth History 49, no. 1 (2021): 148–177. doi:10.1080/03086534.2019.1648231.

Lomas, D. W. B., and C. J. Murphy. "Security or Scandal? Homosexuality and the Foreign Office, 1945 – 1991." In The Bridge in the Park: The Five Eyes and Cold War CounterIntelligence, edited by Molinaro, 72–91. Toronto: University of Toronto Press, 2021.

Lost for Words: The Need for Languages in UK Diplomacy and Security. London: British Academy, November 2013.

Lowe, R., and H. Pemberton. The Official History of the British Civil Service: Reforming the Civil Service, Vol. II, the Thatcher and Major Revolutions, 1982–97. Abingdon: Routledge, 2020.

MacAskill, E. 2016. "James Bond Would Not Get Job with Real MI6, Says Spy Chief." The Guardian, December 8.

MacAskill, E. 2015. "Look to Mumsnet for New Recruits, British Intelligence Agencies Told." The Guardian, March 5.

Macintyre, B. The Spy and the Traitor: The Greatest Espionage Story of the Cold War. London: Viking, 2018.

Macintyre, B. 2019. "Move over 007, This Is a Job for a Women." The Times, May 18.

Macintyre, B. 2020. "Revealed: Women Who Sprang Gordievsky from KGB Clutches." The Times, March 24.

Martin, A. J. "America's Evolution of Women and Their Roles in the Intelligence Community." Journal of Strategic Security 8, no. 3 (2015): 99–109. doi:10.5038/1944-0472.8.3S.1479.

McCarthy, H. Women of the World: The Rise of the Female Diplomat. London: Bloomsbury, 2014.

McCrisken, T. "James Bond, Ian Fleming and Intelligence: Breaking down the Boundary between the "Real" and the "Imagined"." Intelligence & National Security 33, no. 6 (2018). pp. 804-821.

McLoughlin, L., S. Ward, and D. W. B. Lomas. ""Hello, World": GCHQ, Twitter and Social Media Engagement." Intelligence & National Security 35, no. 2 (2020): 233–251. doi:10.1080/02684527.2020.1713434.

"MI5 Host a Meeting of the 30% Club in Thames House." https://www.mi5.gov.uk/news/mi5-host-meeting-of-30-club-in -thames-house

"MI5 Wins BDF Disability Smart Award." 24 October 2019. https://www.mi5.gov.uk/news/mi5-wins-bdf-disability-smartaward

"MI6 Ad for Operational Officers." 2006. BBC News, April 27.

Moore, C. Margaret Thatcher: The Authorised Biography, Vol. 3: Herself Alone. London: Allen Lane, 2019.

Moran, C. R., and C. J. Murphy. "Intelligence Studies Then and Now." In edited by Moran and Murphy, Intelligence Studies in Britain and the US pp. 1-15.

Muir, H. 2017. "MI6, Why Would Minorities Spy for a Society They Don't Feel Part Of?." The Guardian, March 3.

Norton-Taylor, R. 1996. "Soldier's Court Action over GCHQ Post Fails." The Guardian, October 26.

Norton-Taylor, R. 1997. "Gay Spies Allowed to Come in from the Cold." The Guardian, May 26.

Omand, D. 2018. "Bonsall, Sir Arthur Wilfred [Bill] (1917 – 2014)." Oxford Dictionary of National Biography, February 15.

Omand, D. How Spies Think: Ten Lessons of Intelligence. London: Viking, 2020.

Pattinson, J. Behind Enemy Lines: Gender, Passing and the Special Operations Executive in the Second World War. Manchester: Manchester University Press, 2007.

Powys Maurice, E. 2021. "Queer Spies Reveal Homophobic Legacy of MI6's "Illogical" LGBT+ Ban – And How Far Things Have Come." PinkNews, February 19.

Pozniak, H. 2011. "For Queen and Country." The Independent, October 23.

Proctor, T. M. Female Intelligence: Women and Espionage in the First World War. New York: New York University Press, 2006.

"Profile: Lord Taylor of Warwick." 2001. BBC News, April 30. http://news.bbc. co.uk/1/hi/uk_politics/1304393.stm

Rayment, S. 2021. "MI6 Spy Chiefs Advertising for Part-time James Bonds Who "Must Love to Travel"." The Mirror, January 30.

Sabbagh, D. 2021. "MI6 Boss Apologises for past Ban on LGBT Staff." The Guardian, February 19.

Scott, P. "The Contemporary Vetting Landscape." Intelligence & National Security 35, no. 1 (2020): 54–71. doi:10.1080/02684527.2019.1665688.

Sengupta, K. 2004. "MI5 Recruitment Drive Will Focus on Asians." The Independent, February 24.

Shahan, J. 2019. "Spying Gender: Women in British Intelligence, 1969 – 1994." thesis submitted to the Department of International Relations, Aberystwyth.

Shahan, J. 2021. ""Don't Keep Mum": Critical Approaches to Narratives of Women Intelligence Professionals." Intelligence & National Security, March.

"SIS Is Celebrating International Women's Day!." 8 March 2019 https://www.sis. gov.uk/sis-is-celebrating-internationalwomens-day.html

Skapinker, M. 2020. "How to Remedy Britain's Language Deficit Curse." Financial Times, January 14.

Smith, C. The Hidden History of Bletchley Park: A Social and Organisational History, 1939–1945. Houndmills: Palgrave Macmillan, 2015.

Southern, J. 2017. "Homosexuality at the Foreign Office, 1967-1991." History Notes, July 19.

Southern, J. 2018. "Black Skin, Whitehall: Race and the Foreign Office." History Notes, October 21.

Taylor, J. 2012. "GCHQ Spared Having Inner Workings Made Public after "Racism" Case Is Settled Out of Court at the Last Minute." The Independent, September 11.

Taylor, S. "Race, Parochialism and Politics: The General Election in Cheltenham." New Community 22, no. 1 (1996): 135–146.

Toy, R. F., and C. Smith. "Women in the Shadow War: Gender, Class and MI5 in the Second World War." Women's History

Review 27, no. 5 (2018): 688–706. doi:10.1080/09612025.2017.1345714.

Urban, M. UK Eyes Alpha: The inside Story of British Intelligence. London: Faber & Faber, 1997.

Van Puyvelde, D., and S. Curtis. ""Standing on the Shoulders of Giants": Diversity and Scholarship in Intelligence Studies." Intelligence & National Security 31, no. 7 (2013. pp. 1040-1054).

Warrell, H. 2021. "MI6 Chief Apologises for Historical Ban on Gay Employees." The Financial Times, February 19.

West, N. "The UK's Not Quite so Secret Services." International Journal of Intelligence and CounterIntelligence 18, no. 1 (2005): 23–30. doi:10.1080/08850600590882038.

"Why British Asians Should Consider a Career in Intelligence." 28 June 2018 https://www.gov.uk/government/speeches/why-british-asians-should-consider-a-career-in-intelligence

Wintour, P. 2021. "New UK Ambassador to France Means Women Hold All Key Postings." The Guardian, April 29.

"Women and the Foreign Office." 2018. History Notes, October 20.

Zegart, A. "Spytainment: The Real Influence of Fake Spies." International Journal of Intelligence and CounterIntelligence 23, no. 4 (2010): 599–622. doi:10.1080/08850607.2010.501635.

Chapter 5 Executive Accountability and National Security. Lorna Woods OBE, Lawrence McNamara, Judith Townend

1   Shortcomings had long been identified; for example HC Deb vol 222 cols 131-138 29 March1993; HC Deb vol 222 col 940 15 April 1993

2   Cabinet Office Ministerial Code (August 2019), paras [1.3] and [1.7] at https://www.gov.uk/government/publications/ministerial-code. All URLs last visited 11 August 2020 unless other-wise noted.

3   For example on the role of the judiciary, including special advocates and closed material procedures: D. Feldman, 'Human Rights, Terrorism and Risk: The Role of Politicians and Judges'[2006] Public Law 364; J. Ip, 'The Rise and Spread of the Special Advocate' [2008] Public Law 717; G. van Harten, 'Weaknesses of adjudication in the face of secret evidence' (2009) 13 International Journal of Evidence and Proof 1; A. Kavanagh, 'Special Advocates, Control Orders and the Right to a Fair Trial' (2010) 73 MLR 836; A. Tomkins, 'Justice and Security in the United Kingdom' (2014) 47 Israel Law Review 305; C. Walker and G. Lennon (eds), Routledge Handbook of Law and Terrorism (London & New York, NY: Routledge, 2015) esp ch 8, B. Dickson, 'Terror-ism and Legal Accountability' and ch 18, D. Jenkins, 'The Handling and Disclosure of Sensitive Intelligence: Closed Material Procedures and Constitutional Change in the Five Eyes Nations'. Chamberlain QC, 'Special Advocates and Amici Curiae in National Security Proceedings in the United Kingdom' (2018) 68 University of Toronto Law Journal 496; L. Graham, 'Statutory secret trials: the judicial approach to closed material procedures under the Justice and Security Act 2013' (2019) 38 Civil Justice Quarterly 189. On review mechanisms: D. Anderson, 'The In-dependent Review of Terrorism Laws' [2014] Public Law 403; J. Blackbourn, 'Evaluating the Independent Reviewer of Terrorism

Legislation' (2014) 67 Parliamentary Affairs 955; K. Roachand C. Forcese, 'Bridging the National Security Accountability Gap: A Three-Part System to Modernize Canada's Inadequate Review of National Security' Ottawa Faculty of Law Work-ing Paper 2016-05, 31 March 2016. On oversight of the intelligence agencies: J. Ip, 'Terrorismlaws and constitutional accountability' in Walker and Lennon, ibid, 99; S. McKay and J. Moran, 'Surveillance Powers and the Generation of Intelligence within the law' in Walker and Lennon, this note, above, 133; T. Hickman and A. Tomkins, 'National security law and the creep of se-crecy: a transatlantic tale' in L. Lazarus, C. McCrudden and N. Bowles (eds), Reasoning Rights:Comparative Judicial Engagement (London: Hart, 2014). The most notable recent attempt to bringthese together has been P. Scott, The National Security Constitution (London: Hart, 2018). Scott'sthematic choices are citizenship, justiciability, secrecy and sovereignty. See also P. Scott, 'Hybridinstitutions in the national security constitution: the case of the Commissioners' (2019) 39 LegalStudies 432.

4   For example Joined Cases C-293/12 and C-594/12 Digital Rights Ireland v Minister for Communications, Marine and Natural Resources et al ECLI: EU:C:2014:238; Joined Cases C-203/15and C-698/15 Tele2 Sverige AB v Postoch telestyrelsen and Secretary of State for the Home Department v Tom Watson and Others, ECLI:EU:C:2016:970; Big Brother Watch v UK (Appl 58170/13,62322/14), judgment 13 September 2018 (this judgment has been referred to the Grand Cham-ber).

5   For example Malone v UK [1984] ECHR 10 (Malone); Halford v UK [1997] ECHR 32. Principles relating to oversight and approval are also found in the wider European context: for example Fundamental Rights Agency, Surveillance by intelligence services: fundamental rights safeguards and remedies in the EU, Vol 1: Member States' legal frameworks (Vienna: European Union Agency for Fundamental Rights, 2017).

6   Law Commission of England and Wales, Protection of Official Data: A Consultation Paper Consultation Paper No 230 (2017) (Law Commission, Consultation Paper).

7   Law Commission of England and Wales, Protection of Official Data Report No 395 (2020) (Law Commission Report).

8   M. Rush, Parliament Today (Manchester: Manchester University Press, 2005) 3; HC Political and Constitutional Reform Committee, Role and Powers of the Prime Minister HC 351 (2014) para[52].

9   Resolution on Ministerial Responsibility, HC Deb vol 292 col 1046-1047 19 March 1997;Ministerial Code n 2 above para [1.3(b)]. R. Brazier, Ministers of the Crown (Oxford: Clarendon Press, 1997) 261-270.

10   In addition to general obligations, see for example Ministerial Code, ibid paras [1.3(d)], [9.1].

11   HC Deb vol 238 col 153 22 February 1994.

12 Telecommunications Act 1984, s 94(1), (5)

13 Telecommunications Act 1984, s 94(2A), as amended by the Communications Act 2003.

14 HL Deb vol 449 col 1161 20 March 1984 (Lord Mackay of Clashfern).

15 Malone v UK n5above.

16 HC Deb vol 33 col 89 29 November 1982 (Bob Cryer MP).

17 Intelligence Services Act 1994, s 3(2)(c); Privacy International v Secretary of States for Foreign and Commonwealth Affairs and Ors [2018] UKIPTrib IPT 15_110_CH (23 July 2018) at [73]-[77].

18 Report of the Joint Committee on the Draft Communications Data Bill HL 79 HC 479 (2012) para[2].

19 Home Affairs Select Committee, Report on Regulation of Investigatory Powers Act 2000 HC 711(2014) para [15].

20 This is implicit from the arguments put forward in Privacy International v Secretary of States for Foreign and Commonwealth Affairs and Ors [2016] UKIPTrib 15_110-CH (17 October 2016) at[13].

21 This problem was recognised in D. Anderson QC, A Question of Trust: Report of the Investigatory Powers Review (June 2015) para [13.31], albeit in the context of RIPA 2000, Part 1.

22 Half Yearly Report of the Interception of Communications Commissioner (Sir Anthony May) HC 308(16 July 2015) 13-14.

23 Malone n 5 above; HC Deb vol 77 col 298 15 April 1993.

24 Interception of Communications Act 1985, s 8.

25 See for example HC Deb vol 38 col 782 6 March 2000 (Anne Widdecombe MP); HC Deb vol381 cols 793-794 6 March 2000 (Harry Cohen MP).

26 Anderson, n 21 above, para [6.102].

27 Security Service Act 1989, s 4; Intelligence Services Act 194, s 8.

28 HC Deb vol 238 col 157 (and more generally cols153-244) 22 February 1994 (Douglas HurdMP).

29 The Intelligence Service Commissioner had been asked in 2010 to oversee on an extra-statutory basis the activities of GCHQ in relation to s 94 directions, but even the fact of that oversight was not made known until 2015 (Report of the Intelligence Services Commissioner for 2015 (Sir Mark Waller) HC 459 (8 September 2016)), 5. Responsibility was transferred to the IoCC in January 2015. Report of the Interception of Communications Commissioner (Sir Anthony May) HC 1113 (12 March 2015), section 10; Half-yearly Report of the Interception of Communications Commissioner (Sir Anthony May) n 22 above, section 4; Report of the Interception of Communications Commissioner

(Sir Stanley Burnton): Review of directions given under section 94 of the Telecommunications Act 1984. Priorto 2015,the position was opaque.The IoCC had earlier provided 'limited non-statutory oversight of [part of the safeguards relating to] one particular set of section 94 directions' (emphasis inoriginal) and could say no more about that oversight: Half-yearly Report of the Interception of Communications Commissioner (Sir Anthony May) ibid, para [4.6]-[4.7]. However, it is clear that oversight arrangements were limited, partial, did not challenge the interpretation of s 94, and did not cover all s 94 directions: Report of the Interception of Communications Commissioner (Sir Stanley Burnton): Review of directions given under section 94 of the Telecommunications Act 1984, sections 4-5. See also Anderson, n 21 above, para [6.104] and the Privacy International litigation notes 17 and 20 above.

30   Half-yearly Report of the Interception of Communications Commissioner (Sir Anthony May) ibid,para[4.8].

31   RIPA 2000, s 58(4), (6).

32   This point was recognised in debates relating to the Intelligence Services Bill: HC Deb vol 238col 153-244 22 February 1994.

33   RIPA 2000, s 58(7).

34   Protection of Freedoms Act 2012, s 20.

35   Protection of Freedoms Act 2012, s 34.

36   Protection of Freedoms Act 2012, s 21(5).

37   Commissioner for the Retention and Use of Biometric Material, Annual Report 2019, iii.

38   Home Secretary, Amber Rudd MP, 'Investigatory Powers Commissioner establishes oversight regime' 1 September 2017 at https://www.gov.uk/government/news/investigatory-powers-commissioner-establishes-oversight-regime.

39   Anderson, n 21 above, paras [6.103] - [6.104], [12.79] et seq.

40   Investigatory Powers Act 2016, s 234(7).

41   HL Deb vol 774 col 630 19 July 2016.

42   Investigatory Powers Commissioner's OĂce, Annual Report 2017 HC 1780 (31 January 2019).

43   Investigatory Powers Commissioner's OĂce, Annual Report 2018 HC 67 (5 March 2020), 62.

44   Anderson, n 21 above, para [6.103].

45   Law Commission, Consultation Paper n 6 above, para [7.103] et seq.

46   ibid para [7.115].

47   Law Commission Report n 7 above, para [10.9].

48 Goodwin v United Kingdom (1996) 22 EHRR 123; Financial Times Ltd and Others v the United Kingdom (2010) 50 EHRR 46; Sanoma Uitgevers BV v Netherlands (2010) 30 BHRC318; Becker v Norway [2017] ECHR 834. See L. Woods, L. McNamara and J. Townend,'Law Commission Consultation on the Protection of OĂcial Data (CP 230): Response'at https://infolawcentre.blogs. sas.ac.uk/Áles/2017/06/Law-Commission-Consultation-on-the-Protection-of -OĂcial-Information-Woods-McNamara-Townend-09062017-Ánal-online.pdf .

49 Law Commission Report n 7 above, para [10.36](3).

50 Such concerns had some years earlier led the (then) government to reject the wider use of theInterception Commissioner when RIPA 2000 was being enacted: HL Deb vol 615 col 386 13July 2000 (Lord Bach).

51 Justice and Security Act 2013, s 2.

52 Justice and Security Act 2013, s 1. More generally see H. Bocehl, A. Defty and J Kirkpatrick'"New Mechanisms of Independent Accountability": Select Committees and Parliamentary Scrutiny of the Intelligence Services' (2015) 68 Parliamentary AÆairs 314; A. Defty, 'Coming in from the cold: bringing the Intelligence and Security Committee into Parliament' (2019) 34 Intelligence and National Security 22.

53 A Democratic Licence to Operate: Report of the Independent Surveillance Review RUSI Whitehall Re-port 2-15 (July 2015), paras [4.101]-[4.102].

54 Home AÆairs Select Committee, Counter-Terrorism HC 231 (30 April 2014), para [157] and An-nex B [26] et seq. See also Lord MacDonald, 'Proper Parliamentary Oversight of the SecurityServices is Desperately Needed' FA Mann Lecture, December 2013 at http://www.democraticaudit.com/wp-content/uploads/2013/12/FAMann-lecture2.pdf . The risk of intel-ligence powers being used for political purposes is widely recognised: see for example European Parliament, Parliamentary Oversight of Security and Intelligence Agencies in the European Union PE453.207 (2011) 88-89.

55 Intelligence and Security Committee of Parliament Detainee Mistreatment and Rendition: 2001-2010 HC 1113 (28 June 2018); Intelligence and Security Committee of Parliament, DetaineeMistreatment and Rendition: Current Issues HC 1114 (28 June 2018).

56 Intelligence and Security Committee of Parliament, UK Lethal Drones Strikes in Syria HC 1152(26 April 2017); Intelligence and Security Committee of Parliament, Annual Report 2016-17HC 655 (20 December 2017) 105-106; Intelligence and Security Committee of Parliament Detainee Mistreatment and Rendition: 2001-2010 ibid para [236]; HL Deb vol 799 cols 81GC-83GC (Marquess of Lothian), 87GC (Lord Anderson of Ipswich), 95GC-97GC (Lord Paddick)9 Sep 2019.

57 Justice and Security Act 2013, Sched 1, para 4.

58 John Hayes MP, answering written questions from David Davis MP, ElectronicSurveillance: Written question – 16310, 16312, 16313, 13 November 2015 athttps://www.parliament.uk/business/publications/written-questions-answers-statements/written-question/Commons/2015-11-13/16310/.

59 Intelligence and Security Committee of Parliament, Privacy and Security: A modern and transparent legal framework HC 1075 (12 March 2015).

60 Justice and Security Act 2013, s 3(1), (7). Confidential reports may also be made directly to the Prime Minister.

61 Justice and Security Act 2013, s 3(4)

62 Privacy and Security n 59 above, 100. Redaction markings are explained in the preface to the report.

63 There is a Memorandum of Understanding between the ISC and the government about thespeed of response; the government does not always comply – see for example Intelligence andSecurity Committee of Parliament, Annual Report 2017-18 HC 1692 (22 November 2018) para[1].

64 HC Deb vol 667 col 647 5 November 2019 (Dominic Grieve QC MP); HL Deb vol 800 col1097 19 November 2019 (Lord Anderson of Ipswich).

65 Intelligence and Security Committee of Parliament, Russia HC 632 (21 July 2020).

66 See for example Intelligence Services Bill [Lords], 2nd Reading, HC Deb vol 238 col 153-24422 February 1994, especially the concerns raised by Jack Cunningham MP, col 165 et seq.

67 Investigatory Powers Act 2016, s 236.

68 For example XLtdv Morgan Grampian (Publishers Limited) [1991] 1 AC 1, 48; Duport Steel v Sirs [1980] 1 WLR 142, 157; R (on the application of UNISON) v Lord Chancellor [2017] UKSC51 at [68] per Lord Reed; Lord Neuberger, Lord Mance, Lord Kerr, Lord Wilson and Lord Hughes agreeing; R (on the application of Miller) v The Prime Minister [2019] UKSC 41 at [46]-[47]; Constitutional Reform Act 2005, s 3.

69 For example much of what we know about the operation of s 94 has emerged in court pro-ceedings; Privacy International v Secretary of State for Foreign & Commonwealth Aﬀairs and Ors n17above, esp at [6]; Report of the Interception of Communications Commissioner (Sir Stanley Burnton):Review of directions given under section 94 of the Telecommunications Act 1984 HC 33 (7 July 2016)para [8.17].

70 R v Secretary of State for Foreign & Commonwealth, ex parte Bancoult (No 2) [2008] UKHL 61;R (Abbasi) v Secretary of State for Foreign and Commonwealth Aﬀairs [2002] EWCA Civ 1598;Council of Civil Service Unions v Minister for the Civil Service [1985] AC 37 (the GCHQ case); T.Poole, 'United Kingdom: The royal prerogative' (2010) 8 I.Con 146; A.

Tomkins 'Deaning and Delimiting National Security' (2002) 118 LQR 200, 202-203; Mohamed, R (on the application of)v Secretary of State for Foreign & Commonwealth Aæairs [2010] EWCA Civ 65 at [44] per Judge LCJ;at [129], [131]-[135],[154], [189]-[191] per Neuberger MR; at [208], [262], [285],[290], [295] per May PQBD; Lord Kerr, "'Only Parliament can do that"? The reliance of British jurisprudence on the common law in the national security context' [2015] Civil Justice Quarterly 244, 247.

71 Terrorism Act 2000, s 5; The Proscribed Organisations Appeal Commission (Procedure) Rules 2007, SI 2007/1286.

72 The Employment Tribunal is a fourth example and warrants more detailed and critical attention than can be given in this article. In particular, in national security matters it is subject to Ministerial direction in ways that the others are not: The Employment Tribunals (Constitution and Rules of Procedure) Regulations 2013, SI 2103/1237, reg 94.

73 Terrorism Act 2000, ss 5, 6.

74 RIPA 2000, s 67(8), however this was narrowly interpreted in Privacy International v Investigatory Powers Tribunal [2019] UKSC 22.

75 Investigatory Powers Act 2016, s 242 (inserting s 67A into RIPA 2000)

76 The background is well explained in HC Constitutional Aæairs Committee, The Operation of the Special Immigration Appeal Commission (SIAC) and the use of Special Advocates HC 323-I (3 April 2005) esp ch 4. See also Chamberlain, n 3 above, 496-503.

77 Chahal v United Kingdom (1997) 23 EHRR 413;Constitutional Aæairs Committee,The Operation of the Special Immigration Appeal Commission ibid.

78 The Proscribed Organisations Appeal Commission (Procedure) Rules 2007, SI 2007/1286.

79 The Investigatory Powers Tribunal Rules 2018 introduced (r 10(4)) a presumption towards open hearings where possible, confirming the approach the IPT had developed for itself; of the Investigatory Powers Tribunal Rules 2000, r 9(6), that stated 'The Tribunal's proceedings,including any oral hearings, shall be conducted in private'.

80 Special Immigration Appeals Commission (Procedure) Rules 2003, as amended.

81 Al Rawi v The Security Service and others [2011] UKSC 34.

82 ibid,for example at [69] per Lord Dyson, at [71]-[74] per Lord Hope, at [86]-[87] per Lord Brown),at [95] per Lord Kerr.

83 Cabinet Oǎce, Justice and Security Green Paper Cmd 8194 (2011) ch 2; the Justice and Security Bill was subsequently introduced in 2012.

84 Nicholas Blake QC (later Mr Justice Blake and, since retirement, a Judicial Commissioner under the IPA), evidence to the Joint Committee on Human Rights, cited in Justice and Security Green Paper: Response to Consultation from Special Advocates 16 December 2011, para [12] at http://webarchive. nationalarchives.gov.uk/20140911100308/http://consultation.cabinet.gov.uk/ justiceandsecurity/wp-content/uploads/2012/09_Special%20Advocates.pdf. Chamberlain,n 3 above, 505-508, looks at the concerns in some detail.

85 Ministry of Justice, Use of Closed Material Procedure Reports at https://www. gov.uk/government/collections/use-of-closed-material-procedure-reports; L. McNamara and D. Lock, Closed mate-rial procedures under the Justice and Security Act 2013: A review of the ärst report by the Secretary ofState (with supplement) (London: Bingham Centre for the Rule of Law, December 2014).

86 Guardian News and Media Ltd & Ors v R & Incedal [2016] EWCA Crim 11; Guardian News &Media Ltd v Incedal & Bouhadjar [2014] EWCA Crim 1861.

87 Guardian News and Media Ltd v AB & CD, [2014] EWCA Crim (B1) (12 June 2014) at [16], [19];Dominic Casciani, 'Erol Incedal: The Trial We Couldn't Report' BBC.co.uk 26 March 2015 athttps://www.bbc.com/news/ uk-31989581.

88 Incedal [2016] EWCA Crim 11, n 86 above.

89 ibid at [75]. For a non-terrorism national security case see R (on the application of Wang Yam)(Appellant) v Central Criminal Court and another (Respondents) [2015] UKSC 76 (Wang Yam); on appeal from [2014] EWHC 3558 (Admin); Yam v United Kingdom (2020) ECHR 31295/11;[2020] All ER (D) 55 (Jan).

90 P. Scott, 'An inherent jurisdiction to protect the public interest: from PII to "secret trials"' (2016)27 King's Law Journal 259, 265-266.

91 ibid, 271.

92 The courts in England and Wales have recently established a library of closed judg-ments: 'Practice Direction: Closed Judgments' 14 January 2019 at https:// www.judiciary.uk/announcements/practice-direction-closed-judgments/. Its scope, however, is very un-clear: L. McNamara, 'Closed judgments: security, accountability and court processes' UK Human Rights Blog, 25 January 2019 at https://ukhumanrightsblog.com/2019/01/25/closed-judgments-security- accountability-and-court-processes/.

93 H. Irving and J. Townend, 'Censorship and National Security: Information Control in the Sec-ond World War and Present Day' [2016] History & Policy at http://www.historyandpolicy.org/index.php/policy-papers/papers/ censorship-and-national-security-information-control.

94 Law Commission, Consultation Paper n 6 above, para [5.41]. Law Commission Report n 7 above,para [7.65]; see also paras [7.63] and

[7.88] where the Commission states that the 'primary focus'is to be on the administration of justice, though it is not clear whether that means open justice(noting also an apparent typo in the reference to Recommendation 24, as it appears clearly tobe a reference to the text of Recommendation 29).

95   Law Commission Report ibid, para [7.65].

96   Law Commission, Consultation Paper, n 6 above, para [5.53]; Law Commission Report ibid,para [7.83].

97   Law Commission, Consultation Paper ibid, para [5.59], emphasis added.

98   Law Commission Report n 7 above, para [7.87].

99   ibid, paras [7.90]-[7.100].

100   By way of disclosure, parts of our own evidence was among one strand cited by the Commission in its report: ibid, paras [7.94]-[7.95].

101   Law Commission, Consultation Paper n 6 above, para [5.52]. It retained this view in the report: ibid, para [7.83]. The report cites our statement that the JSA dispenses with open justice (para[7.95]) but does not engage with that.

102   Justice and Security Act 2013, s 6(5). Moves to incorporate open justice considerations into the Bill, after inclusion at Lords committee stage, were later defeated: HL Deb vol 740 col 1812-1860 21 November 2012; Public Bill Committee Proceedings, 5 February 2013, Amendment 55; Hansard HC Deb vol 559 col 685-752 4 March 2013.

103   The Incedal approach could, however, present other implications for access to justice. This was contended in Wang Ya m n 89 above,in which the appellant (unsuccessfully) argued, under Article 34 ECHR, that he should be permitted to refer to in camera material relating to his defence in his application to the European Court of Human Rights.

104   Wilson v Minister for Aboriginal and Torres Strait Islander Aﬀairs [1996] HCA 18 at [30] per Kirby J,dissenting; for a critique of the public confidence rationale, see E. Handsley, 'Public confidence in the judiciary: A red herring for the separation of judicial power' (1998) 20 Sydney Law Review 183.

105   Mistretta v United States 488 US 361 (1989), 407; Wilson v Minister for Aboriginal and Torres Strait Islander Affairs ibid at [25] per Brennan CJ, Dawson, Toohey, McHugh and Gummow JJ; Grollo vPalmer (1995) 184 CLR 348, 365 per Brennan CJ, Deane, Dawson and Toohey JJ; R v Kirby exparte Boilermakers' Society of Australia (1956) 94 CLR 254; Hilton v Wells (1985) 157 CLR 57; F. Wheeler,'The use of federal judges to discharge executive functions' (1996) 11 Australian Institute of Administrative Law Forum 1; P. Emerton and H.P. Lee, 'Judges and non-judicial functions in Australia' in H.P. Lee (ed), Judiciaries in Comparative Perspective (New York, NY: CUP, 2011).

106 Select Committee on Public Administration, Government by Inquiry Vol 1, HC 51-1 (2004).

107 S. Sedley, 'Public Inquiries: A Cure or a Disease?' (1989) 52 MLR 469; J. Beatson, 'Should judges conduct inquiries' (2005) 121 LQR 221; Select Committee on Public Administration, ibid, speech 3.

108 Lord Thomas of Cwmgiedd, 'The future of public inquiries' [2015] Public Law 225, 234-235.

109 ibid, 234.

110 ibid, 235.

111 For example Wilson v Minister for Aboriginal and Torres Strait Islander Aﬀairs n 104 above.

112 Regulators form part of the executive branch of government having the responsibility for implementation and oversight of policy, mainly against private actors, sometimes having a quasi-judicial function in the determination of breach of rules (whether as a result of the regulator's investigation or as a result of complaints by third parties), and will generally be independent. That independence cannot easily be overridden even on the grounds of national security: R(on the application of VIP Communications Ltd) v Secretary of State for the Home Department and the Office of Communications [2019] EWHC 994 (Admin) on the interpretation of Communications Act 2003, s 5.

113 There is a contrast here with commissioners established under the Protection of Freedoms Act 2012; they are not required to be judges but they are not focussed on oversight of SIAs.

114 We note that the Biometrics Commissioner,who need not be a judge,may make decisions about retention and use in individual cases but not about warrants: Protection of Freedoms Act 2012,s 20.

115 Investigatory Powers Act 2016, s 227(2).

116 Investigatory Powers Act 2016, s 227(3)-(4), 228(2)-(3).

117 Investigatory Powers Act 2016, s 228(4).

118 Report of the Joint Committee on the Draft Investigatory Powers Bill HL 93, HC 651 (11 February 2016), paras [594]-[597]; the removal proposals were strengthened after the Joint Committee reported.

119 Lord Judge, Oral Evidence to the Joint Committee on the Investigatory Powers Bill HC 651(2 December 2015), Q 59 at https://www.parliament.uk/documents/joint-committees/draft-investigatory-powers-bill/oral-evidence-draft-investigatory-powers-committee.pdf ; seealso Report of the Joint Committee on the Investigatory Powers Bill , ibid, paras [580]-[588].

120 Zakharov v Russia [2015] ECHR 1065, [257]-[260].

121 Sir Stanley Burnton, Oral Evidence to the Joint Committee on the Investigatory Powers Bill n 119above, Q 57.

122 Lord Thomas of Cwmgiedd, n 108 above, 234-235.

123 Investigatory Powers Act 2016, ss 23, 77, 89, 108, 140, 159, 179, 208, 252-254. They include approving warrants issued by the executive for interception, identification or confirmation of journalistic sources, retention of communications data, equipment interference, bulk interception and acquisition, bulk personal datasets, and general 'national security notices' that require a telecommunications operator to 'take such specfied steps as the Secretary of State considers necessary in the interests of national security'.

124 For example Investigatory Powers Act 2016, s 23.

125 Investigatory Powers Act 2016, s 2.

126 Anderson, n 21 above, [14.47]-[14.57]

27 For example Investigatory Powers Act 2016, ss 2(4), 23(2) and its references to ss 2, 20, 21.

128 Investigatory Powers Act 2016, s 2.

129 Investigatory Powers Act 2016, s 227 (definitions), s 229, esp s 229(6); Explanatory notes, 'Commentary on provisions of the Act', para [640].

130 Lord Pannick QC, 'Safeguards provide a fair balance on surveillance powers' The Times 12November 2015.

131 IPCO Press release,18 October 2017 at https://www.ipco.org.uk /docs/ JC%20Announcement%2020171018.pdf

132 Investigatory Powers Act 2016, s 229(4).

133 IPCO now has responsibility for the Consolidated Guidance to Intelligence OÄcers and Service Personnel on the Detention and Interviewing of Detainees Overseas,and on the Passing and Receipt of Intelligence Relating to Detainees, and oversight over UK-US Data Access Agreement,but is not involved in approving requests: The Functions of the Investigatory Powers Commissioner (Oversight of the Data Access Agreement between the United Kingdom and the United States of America and of functions exercisable under the Crime (Overseas Production Orders)Act 2019) Regulations 2020 (draft at the time of writing).

134 Law Commission Report n 7 above, paras [8.66]-[8.128].

135 ibid, para [8.127].

Chapter 6: Scottish independence after Brexit: Eve Hepburn, Michael Keating and Nicola McEwen

Brown, A. (2017). 'The dynamics of frame-bridging: exploring the nuclear discourse in Scotland', Scottish Affairs, 26(2), pp.194-211. https://www.euppublishing.com/doi/abs/10.3366/scot.2017.0178

Brown, A. (2019) Devolution, climate change and the climate emergency. https://www.centreonconstitutionalchange.ac.uk/news-and-opinion/devolution-climatechange-and-climate-emergency

Burns et al (2019) 'De-Europeanising or disengaging? EU environmental policy and Brexit', Environmental Politics, 28(2), pp.271–292. https://www.tandfonline.com/doi/full/10.1080/09644016.2019.1549774

Committee on Climate Change (2020) Building a resilient recovery from the COVID-19 crisis to Roseanna Cunningham MSP. https://www.theccc.org.uk/publication/letter-building-a-resilient-recovery-from-the-covid-19-crisis-to-roseanna-cunninghammsp/

Copeland, P. (2016) 'Europeanisation and de-Europeanisation in UK employment policy: changing governments and shifting agendas', Public Administration, 94(4),pp.1124-1139. https://onlinelibrary.wiley.com/doi/abs/10.1111/padm.12283, Gove, M. (2017) The unfrozen moment – delivering a Green Brexit, speech. https://gov.uk/government/speeches/the-unfrozen-moment-delivering-a-green-brexit

Haf, S et al (2019) 'Distributing Power? Community energy projects' experiences of planning, policy and incumbents in devolved nations of Scotland and Wales', Journal of Environmental Planning and Management, vol.62, No.6, pp.921-938. https://www.tandfonline.com/doi/abs/10.1080/09640568.2018.1453490

Harvey, P. (2019) 'Smacking and fracking results show the Greens aren't all talk', The National (4th October). https://www.thenational.scot/news/17945987.smackingfracking-results-show-greens-arent-talk/

Savaresi, Annalisa (2020) 'Environmental Governance in Scotland after EU Exit', SPICe SB20-02. https://sp-bpr-en-prod-cdnep.azureedge.net/published/2020/1/9/Environmental-Governance-in-Scotland-after-EU-Exit/SB%2020-02.pdf

Scottish Government (2017) Scottish Energy Strategy: the future of energy in Scotland. https://www.gov.scot/publications/scottish-energy-strategy-future-energyscotland-9781788515276/pages/2/

Scottish Government (2019a) Scotland's place in Europe: assessment of the revised EU withdrawal agreement and political declaration. https://www.gov.scot/publications/scotlands-place-europe-assessment-revised-withdrawal-agreement-political-declaration/

Scottish Government (2019b) Protecting Scotland's Future: the Government's Programme for Scotland 2019-2020. https://www.gov.scot/publications/protectingscotlands-future-governments-programme-scotland-2019-20/pages/3/

Scottish Government (2020) Environment after Brexit (protection and legislation) February 2020. https://www.mygov.scot/brexit-environment/

Scottish Parliament (2019) Climate Change (Emissions Reduction Targets) (Scotland) Act 2019. http://www.legislation.gov.uk/asp/2019/15/enacted

Scottish Parliament (2020) Roseanna Cunningham Questions and Answers. https://www.scottishparliament.tv/meeting/portfolio-questions-virtual-environment-climatechange-and-land-reform-june-4-2020

The Guardian (26/6/2019) Scotland 'at risk of losing environmental protection after Brexit'. https://www.theguardian.com/uk-news/2019/jun/26/ensure-brexit-does-notderail-environment-law-warn-scots-activists

UK Government (2020) Our approach to the Future Relationship with the EU, UK Government, 27 February. https://www.gov.uk/government/publications/our-approachto-the-future-relationship-with-the-eu

Chapter 7: Contesting Sovereignty and Borders: Northern Ireland, Devolution and the Union. Mary C. Murphy & Jonathan Evershed

Barry, J. (2017, July 6). From power sharing to power being shared out. Green European Journal. Retrieved July 26, 2020, from https://www.greeneuropeanjournal.eu/from-power-sharing-to-power-being-shared-out/

Birrell, D., & Heenan, D. (2017). The continuing volatility of devolution in Northern Ireland: The shadow of direct rule. The Political Quarterly, 88(3), 473–479. https://doi.org/10.1111/1467-923X.12391

Budd, L. (2015). The consequences for the Northern Ireland economy from a United Kingdom exit from the European Union, Briefing Note: CETI/OU, 2/15, March.

Byrne, S. (2001). Consociational and civic society approaches to peacebuilding in Northern Ireland. Journal of Peace Research, 38(3), 327–352. https://doi.org/10.1177/0022343301038003004

Cochrane, F. (2020). Breaking peace: Brexit and Northern Ireland. Manchester University Press.

Connelly, T. (2018) Brexit and Ireland: The dangers, the opportunities and the inside story of the Irish response. Penguin.

Connelly, T. (2020, February 29). Dangerous game: The deepening standoff over the Irish Protocol. RTÉ News. Retrieved July 25, 2020, from https://www.rte.ie/news/analysis-and-comment/2020/0229/1118290-brexitblog-tony-connelly/

Connolly, E., & Doyle, J. (2019). Brexit and the changing international and domestic perspectives of sovereignty over Northern Ireland. Irish Studies in International Affairs, 30, 217–233. https://doi.org/10.3318/isia.2019.30.13

Cramer, C. (2006). Civil war is not a stupid thing: Accounting for violence in developing countries. C. Hurst & Co.

Curtis, J. (2014). Human rights as war by other means: Peace politics in Northern Ireland. University of Pennsylvania Press.

DeYoung, E. (2018). Girdwood Barracks: Power, planning and politics in a post-ceasefire city [Doctoral dissertation, University of Liverpool]. https://livrepository.liverpool.ac.uk/3021323/

Donaghy, P. (2019). A 'likely' story - The Secretary of State needs to explain under what circumstances he would hold a border poll. Slugger O'Toole, 11 September. Retrieved March 5, 2021. https://sluggerotoole.com/2019/09/11/a-likely-story-the-secretary-of-state-needs-to-explain-under-what-circumstances-he-would-hold-aborder-poll/

Donaghy, P. (2020). The mystery of the 'shy nationalists' - online and face-to-face polling on Irish unity continues to give different results. Slugger O'Toole, 19 February. Retrieved March 5, 2021. https://sluggerotoole.com/2020/02/19/the-mystery-of-the-shy-nationalists-online-and-face-to-face-polling-on-irish-unity-continuesto-give-different-results/

Drakeford, M. (2019, May 9). The future of devolution: The UK after Brexit – Keynote speech. Institute for Government. https://www.instituteforgovernment.org.uk/events/future-devolution-uk-after-brexit-keynote　　-speech-mark-drakeford

Eggins, B. (2015). History and hope: The alliance party of Northern Ireland. The History Press Ireland.

Evershed, J. (2018). Ghosts of the Somme: Commemoration and culture war in Northern Ireland. University of Notre Dame Press.

Evershed, J. (2021). Making it up as we go along: Brexit and constitutional politics in Britain and Ireland. In M.

Holmes & K. Simpson (Eds.), Ireland and the European Union: Economic, political and social crises. Manchester University Press.

Farrell, M. (1980). Northern Ireland: the orange state. Pluto Press.

Farren, S. (2010). The SDLP: the struggle for agreement in Northern Ireland. Four Courts Press.

Farrington, C. (2001). Ulster unionist political divisions in the late twentieth century. Irish Political Studies, 16(1), 49–71.

Finlay, A. (2001). Defeatism and northern protestant 'identity'. Global Review of Ethnopolitics, 1(2), 3–20. https://doi.org/10.1080/14718800108405094

Gallagher, J. (2012). Intergovernmental relations in the UK: Co-operation, competition and constitutional change. The British Journal of Politics and International Relations, 14(2), 198–213. https://doi.org/10.1111/j.1467-856X.2011.00485.x

Garry, J., & Coakley, J. (2016, October 15). Brexit: Understanding why people voted as they did in the choice of a lifetime. News Letter. https://www.news-letter.co.uk/news/brexit-understanding-why-people-voted-theydid-choice-lifetime-1190201

Gaskell, J., Stoker, G., Jennings, W., & Devinees, D. (2020). Covid-19 and the blunders of our governments: Long-run system failings aggravated by political choices. The Political Quarterly, early view. https://doi.org/10.1111/1467-923X.12894

Gormley-Heenan, C., & Aughey, A. (2017). Northern Ireland and Brexit: Three effects on 'the border in the mind'. The British Journal of Politics and International Relations, 19(3), 497–511. https://doi.org/10.1177/1369148117711060

Guelke, A. (2003). Civil Society and the Northern Ireland Peace Process. Voluntas, 14(1), 61–78.

Hall, A. (2018). Incomplete peace and social stagnation: Shortcomings of the Good Friday Agreement. Open Library of Humanities, 4(2), 1–31. https://doi.org/10.16995/olh.251

Hayes, B. C., McAllister, I., & Dowds, L. (2005). The erosion of consent: Protestant disillusionment with the 1998 Northern Ireland agreement. Journal of Elections, Public Opinion and Parties, 15(2), 147–167. https://doi.org/10.1080/13689880500178690

Hayward, K. (2018). The pivotal position of the Irish border in the UK's withdrawal from the European Union. Space and Polity, 22(2), 238–254. https://doi.org/10.1080/13562576.2018.1505491

Hayward, K., & McManus, C. (2019). Neither/nor: The rejection of unionist and nationalist identities in post-agreement Northern Ireland. Capital & Class, 43(1), 139–155. https://doi.org/10.1177/0309816818818312

Hayward, K., & Murphy, M. C. (2018). The EU's influence on the peace process and agreement in Northern Ireland in light of Brexit. Ethnopolitics, 17(3), 276–291. https://doi.org/10.1080/17449057.2018.1472426

Hayward, K., Phinnemore, D., Komarova, M., Campbell, C., & Greer, J. (2020). Anticipating and meeting new multilevel governance challenges in Northern Ireland after Brexit. The UK in a Changing Europe.

Henderson, A., Jeffery, C., Wincott, D., & Wyn Jones, R. (2017). How Brexit was made in England. The British Journal of Politics and International Relations, 19(4), 631–646. https://doi.org/10.1177/1369148117730542

House of Lords European Union Committee (HL EC). (2020). The Protocol on Ireland: Northern Ireland, HL 2019–2021 (66). The Stationery Office.

Irish Government. (2020). Programme for government: Our shared future.

Irish Times. (2020, July 20). SDLP forum on united Ireland will seek unionist input. Irish Times. https://www.irishtimes.com/news/politics/sdlp-forum-on-united-ireland-will-seek-unionist-input-1.4308238

Jeffery, C. (2007). The unfinished business of devolution: Seven unanswered questions. Public Policy and Administration, 22(1), 92–108. https://doi.org/10.1177/0952076707071506

Jeffery, C. (2009). Devolution in the United Kingdom: Problems of a piecemeal approach to constitutional change. Publius: The Journal of Federalism, 39(2), 289–313. https://doi.org/10.1093/publius/pjn038

Kenny, M.,& Sheldon, J. (2020). When planets collide: The British conservative party and the discordant goals of delivering Brexit and preserving the domestic union, 2016–2019. Political Studies, early access. https://doi.org/10.1177/0032321720930986

Matthews, F. (2017). Whose mandate is it anyway? Brexit, the constitution and the contestation of authority'. The Political Quarterly, 88(4), 603–611. https://doi.org/10.1111/1467-923X.12419

McAuley, J. W. (2010). Ulster's last stand: Reconstructing unionism after the peace process. Irish Academic Press.

McBride, S. (2019). Burned: The inside story of the 'Cash-for-Ash' scandal and Northern Ireland's secretive new elite. Merrion Press.

McCann, D., & McGrattan, C. (Eds.). (2017). Sunningdale, the ulster workers' council strike and the struggle for democracy in Northern Ireland. Manchester University Press.

McEwen, N. (2020). Negotiating Brexit: power dynamics in British intergovernmental relations. Regional Studies, early access. https://doi.org/10.1080/00343404.2020.1735000

McEwen, N., Kenny, M., Sheldon, J., & Brown Swan, C. (2020). Intergovernmental relations in the UK: Time for a radical overhaul? The Political Quarterly, early access. https://doi.org/10.1111/1467-923X.12862

McGarry, J., & O'Leary, B. (2004). Northern Ireland: consociational engagements. Oxford University Press.

McKinnion, D. (2015). Devolution, state restructuring and policy divergence in the UK. The Geographical Journal,181(1), 47–56.

McLoughlin, P. J. (2010). John Hume and the revision of Irish nationalism. Manchester University Press.

Morrow, D. (2012). The rise (and fall?) of reconciliation in Northern Ireland. Peace Research, 44(1), 5–36.

Morrow, D. (2017). Reconciliation and after in Northern Ireland: The search for a political order in an ethnically divided society. Nationalism and Ethnic Politics, 23(1), 98–117. https://doi.org/10.1080/13537113.2017.1273688

Murphy, M. C. (2018). Europe and Northern Ireland's future: Negotiating Brexit's unique case. Agenda Publishing.

Murphy, M. C., & Evershed, J. (2020). Between the devil and the DUP: The Democratic Unionist Party and the politics of Brexit. British Politics, 15(4), 456–477.

Murtagh, B., & Shirlow, P. (2012). Devolution and the politics of development in Northern Ireland. Environment and Planning C: Government and Policy, 30(1), 46–61. https://doi.org/10.1068/c10216r

Nagle, J. (2009). Potemkin village: Neoliberalism and peacebuilding in Northern Ireland. Ethnopolitics, 8(2), 173–190. https://doi.org/10.1080/17449050802593275

Nagle, J. (2014). From the politics of antagonistic recognition to agonistic peacebuilding: An exploration of symbols and rituals in divided societies. Peace and Change, 39(4), 468–494.

Nagle, J. (2018). Between conflict and peace: An analysis of the complex consequences of the Good Friday Agreement. Parliamentary Affairs, 71(2), 395–416. https://doi.org/10.1093/pa/gsx030

Nolan, P., Bryan, D., Dwyer, C., Hayward, K., Radford, K., & Shirlow, P. (2014). The flag dispute: Anatomy of a protest. Queen's University Belfast.

O'Callaghan, M. (2006). Genealogies of partition: History, history-writing and 'the troubles' in Ireland. Critical Review of International Social and Political Philosophy, 9(4), 619–634. https://doi.org/10.1080/13698230600942091

Oxford Economics. (2016). Assessing the economic implications of Brexit: Executive summary. Oxford Economics Limited.

Rice, C. (2020, May 23). A road to nowhere? The UK's approach to implementing the NI protocol. The UK in a Changing Europe. Retrieved July 25, 2020, from https://ukandeu.ac.uk/a-road-to-nowhere-the-uksapproach-to-implementing-the-ni-protocol/

Sandford, M., & Gormley-Heenan, C. (2020). 'Taking back control', the UK's constitutional narrative and Schrodinger's devolution. Parliamentary Affairs, 73(1), 108–126. https://doi.org/10.1093/pa/gsy039

Shirlow, P. (2001). Devolution in Northern Ireland/ulster/the north/six counties: Delete as appropriate. Regional Studies, 35(8), 743–752. https://doi.org/10.1080/00343400120084722

Springford, J. (2015, April 7). Disunited kingdom: Why 'Brexit' endangers Britain's poorer regions. CER Policy Brief. http://www.cer.eu/publications/archive/policy-brief/2015/disunited-kingdom-why-'brexit'-endangersbritain's-poorer-reg

Tannam, E. (2018). Intergovernmental and cross-border civil service cooperation: The Good Friday Agreement and Brexit. Ethnopolitics, 17(3), 243–262. https://doi.org/10.1080/17449057.2018.1472422

Tannam, E. (2020, July 2). Shared Island? There's hope for British–Irish intergovernmental relations. LSE Blog. https://blogs.lse.ac.uk/brexit/2020/07/02/shared-island-theres-hope-for-british-irish-intergovernmental-relations/

Taylor, R. (2008). The Belfast agreement and the limits of consociationalism. In C. Farrington (Ed.), Global change, civil society and the Northern Ireland peace process: Implementing the political sentiment (pp. 183–198). Palgrave Macmillan.

Teague, P. (2019). Brexit, the Belfast Agreement and Northern Ireland: Imperilling a fragile political bargain. The Political Quarterly, 90(4), 690–704. https://doi.org/10.1111/1467-923X.12766

Todd, J. (1987). Two traditions in unionist political culture. Irish Political Studies, 2(1), 1–26. https://doi.org/10. 1080/07907188708406434

Todd, J. (2015). The vulnerability of the Northern Ireland settlement: British Irish relations, political crisis and Brexit. Études Irlandaises, 40(2), 61–73. https://doi.org/10.4000/etudesirlandaises.4734

Todd, J. (2020). Unionisms and the challenges of change. Irish Political Studies, 35(3), 335–355. https://doi.org/ 10.1080/07907184.2020.1816374

Tonge, J. (2000). From Sunningdale to the Good Friday Agreement: Creating devolved government in Northern Ireland. Contemporary British History, 14(3), 39–60. https://doi.org/10.1080/13619460008581593

Tonge, J. (2020). Beyond unionism versus nationalism: The rise of the alliance party of Northern Ireland. The Political Quarterly, early access. https://doi.org/10.1111/1467-923X.12857

Tonge, J., Braniff, M., Hennessey, T., McAuley, J. W., & Whiting, S. A. (2014). The democratic unionist party: From protest to power. Oxford University Press.

Tonge, J., Braniff, M., Hennessey, T., McAuley, J. W.,&Whiting, S. A. (2019). The ulster unionist party: Country before party? Oxford University Press.

Tonge, J., & Evans, J. (2018). Northern Ireland: double triumph for the democratic unionist party. Parliamentary Affairs, 71(Suppl. 1), 139–154. https://doi.org/10.1093/pa/gsx067

Whiting, M. (2017). Sinn Féin and the IRA: From revolution to moderation. Edinburgh University Press. Whyte, J. (1983). How much discrimination was there under the unionist regime 1921–1968? In T. Gallagher & J. O'Connell (Eds.), Contemporary Irish studies (pp. 1–36). Manchester University Press.

Wilson, S. (2020, July 16). The United Kingdom will not be free from European Union until the Northern Ireland protocol is replaced. Belfast Newsletter. https://www.newsletter.co.uk/news/opinion/columnists/sammy-wilso-nunited-kingdom-will-not-be-free-european-union-until-northern-ire-land-protocol-replaced-2915002

Wincott, D. (2018). Brexit and the state of the United Kingdom. In P. Diamond, P. Nedergaard, & B. Rosamond (Eds.), The Routledge handbook of the politics of Brexit (pp. 15–26). Routledge.

Wincott, D., Davies, G., & Wager, A. (2020). Crisis, what crisis? Conceptualizing crisis, UK pluri-constitutionalism and Brexit politics. Regional Studies, early access. https://doi.org/10.1080/00343404.2020.1805423

Woodwell, D. (2005). The 'troubles' of Northern Ireland: Civil conflict in an economically well developed state. In P. Collier & N. Sambanis (Eds.), Understanding civil war: Evidence and analysis, volume II: Europe, Central Asia and other regions (pp. 161–190). World Bank.

YouGov. (2019, November 11). Four in ten mainland Britons don't care about Northern Ireland. https://yougov.co.uk/topics/politics/articles-reports/2019/11/11/four-ten-mainland-britons-dont-care-about-northern

YouGov. (2020, April 22). Brits increasingly don't care whether Northern Ireland remains in UK. https://yougov.co.uk/topics/politics/articles-reports/2020/04/22/brits-increasingly-dont-care-whether-northern-irel

Chapter 8: Governing 'levelling-up' in the UK: challenges and prospects. John Connolly, Robert Pyper & Arno van der Zwet

1. Anderson, H. (2021). After a decade of deprivation, we need policies that prioritise recovery for families in poverty. Joseph Rowntree Foundation. Retrieved March 31, 2021, from https://www.jrf.org.uk/press/afterdecade-deprivation-we-need-policies-prioritise-recovery-families-poverty [Google Scholar]

2. Bache, I., Bartle, M., Flinders, G., & Marsden, G. (2015). Blame games and climate change: Accountability, multi-level governance and carbon management. The British Journal of Politics and International Relations, 17(1), 64–88. doi: 10.1111/1467-856X.12040 [Crossref], [Web of Science °], [Google Scholar]

3. Baldini, G., Bressanelli, E., & Gianfreda, S. (2020). Taking back control? Brexit, sovereignism and populism in Westminster (2015–17). European Politics and Society, 21(2), 219–234. doi: 10.1080/23745118.2019.1632584 [Taylor & Francis Online], [Google Scholar]

4. Bambra, C. (2021). Levelling up: Global examples of reducing health inequalities. Scandinavian Journal of Public Health, 1–6. [PubMed], [Web of Science ®], [Google Scholar]

5. Barber, M. (2017). Delivering better outcomes for citizens: practical steps for unlocking public value. Commissioned by HM Treasury. https://www.gov.uk/government/news/sirmichael-barber-report-into-improving-value-in-public-spending-published [Google Scholar]

6. Batchelor, T. (2021). Boris Johnson 'aggressively undermining' Wales and Scotland with levelling up fund, say devolved governments. https://www.independent.co.uk/news/uk/politics/boris-johnson-devoluton-fund-walesscotland-b1807210.html [Google Scholar]

7. Bounds, A. (2021). Levelling up bias in favour of tory seats. Financial Times. Retrieved March 31, 2021,fromhttps://www.ft.com/content/d485da2a-5778-45ae-9fa8-ca024bc8bbcf?fbclid=IwAR1Zng7heRN0RTxXckLgJ9x8kI0ItxVy pb92rZ32IpRuq7sOSrb6qzFCLLU [Google Scholar]

8. Brien, P. (2020). Briefing paper: The UK shared prosperity fund. London: House of Commons Library. [Google Scholar]

9. Connolly, J. (2016). Contribution analysis as an approach to enable public managers to demonstrate public value. International Journal of Public Sector Management, 29(7), 690–707. doi: 10.1108/IJPSM-12-2015-0225 [Crossref], [Web of Science ®], [Google Scholar]

10. Connolly, J., & Van der Zwet, A. (2021a). Public value management, governance and reform in Britain. Switzerland: Palgrave. [Crossref], [Google Scholar]

11. Connolly, J., & Van Der Zwet, A. (2021b). Public value in Britain: A 'post-new public management' environment? In Public Value Management, Governance and Reform in Britain (pp. 15–44). Cham: Palgrave Macmillan. [Crossref], [Google Scholar]

12. Curtice, J. (2019). General election 2019: What's behind the conservative victory? Retrieved March 27, 2021. https://www.bbc.co.uk/news/election-2019-50774061 [Google Scholar]

13. Davenport, A., & Zaranko, B. (2020). IFS Green Budget 2020. Institute for Fiscal Studies. Retrieved March 27, 2021. https://www.ifs.org.uk/uploads/Green-Budget-2020-Levelling-up-where-and-how.pdf [Google Scholar]

14. Diamond, P. (2021). 'What Michael Barber's appointment tells us about Whitehall reform and the 'science' of delivery'. British Politics and Policy at LSE. Retrieved June 1, 2021, from https://blogs.lse.ac.uk/politicsandpolicy/michael-barberappointment-whitehall-reform/ [Google Scholar]

15. Ferry, M. (2021). Pulling things together: Regional policy coordination approaches and drivers in Europe. Policy and Society, 1–21. http://doi.org/10.1080/14494035.2021.1934985 [Web of Science ®], [Google Scholar]

16. Forth, T. (2021). Regional inequalities post-Brexit: Levelling-up? UK in a Changing Europe, https://ukandeu.ac.uk/regional-inequalities-and-brexit/ [Google Scholar]

17. HC Deb Col. (16 March 2021). Col 180, Vol 691. [Google Scholar]

18. HC Deb Col. (16 March 2021). Col 181, Vol 691. [Google Scholar]

19. HC Deb Col. (16 March 2021). Col 182, Vol 691. [Google Scholar]

20. Hill, J. (2021). Exclusive: Councils mull legal action over levelling-up fund exclusions. Retrieved March 29, 2021, from https://www.lgcplus.com/finance/exclusive-councils-mull-legal-action-overlevelling-up-fund-exclusions-29-03-2021/ [Google Scholar]

21. HM Treasury. (2021). Levelling-up fund: Prospectus, pp. 2–3. Retrieved March 27, 2021, from https://assets.publishing.service.gov.uk/government/uploads/system/uploads/attachment_data/file/966138/Levelling_Up_prospectus.pdf [Google Scholar]

22. Holmes, J. (2021). 'Levelling up' – from slogan to strategy. The Kings Fund. https://www.kingsfund.org.uk/blog/2021/04/levelling-up-slogan-strategy [Google Scholar]

23. Hood, C. (2020). The blame game: Spin, bureaucracy, and self-preservation in government, 2020. New Jersey: Princeton University Press. [Google Scholar]

24. Howlett, M. (2009). Policy analytical capacity and evidence-based policy-making: Lessons from Canada. Canadian Public Administration, 52(2), 153–175. doi: 10.1111/j.1754-7121.2009.00070_1.x [Crossref], [Web of Science ®], [Google Scholar]

25. Howlett, M. (2012). The lessons of failure: Learning and blame avoidance in public policymaking. International Political Science Review, 33(1), 539–555. doi: 10.1177/0192512112453603 [Crossref], [Google Scholar]

26. Hutton, W. (2021). Britain must harness the social sciences to fight post-pandemic deprivation. The Guardian. Retrieved May 26, 2021. https://www.theguardian.com/commentisfree/2021/apr/15/britain-harness-socialsciences-covid-pandemic-deprivation [Google Scholar]

27. Institute for Community Studies. (2021). "Why don't they ask us?" The role of communities in levelling up', ICS Working Paper 2 – Fixing Local Economies, The Young Foundation. Retrieved July 14, 2021, from https://www.youngfoundation.org/wp-content/uploads/2021/07/ICS-WHY-DONT-THEY-ASK-US-compressed.pdf [Google Scholar]

28. Jennings, W., McKay, L., & Stoker, G. (2021). The politics of levelling up. The Political Quarterly, 92(2), 302–311. doi: 10.1111/1467-923X.13005 [Crossref], [Web of Science ®], [Google Scholar]

29. Johnstone, R. (2021). Goodbye single departmental plans, hello outcome delivery plans: new system to monitor Whitehall performance revealed. Civil Service World. Retrieved March 24. https://www.civilserviceworld.com/news/article/goodbye-single-departmental-plans-hello-outcome-delivery-plans-new-system-to-monitor-whitehall-performance-revealed [Google Scholar]

30. Jordan, G. (1990). Sub-governments, policy communities and networks: Refilling the old bottles? Journal of Theoretical Politics, 2(3), 319–338. doi: 10.1177/0951692890002003004 [Crossref], [Google Scholar]

31. Judge, D. (2021). Walking the dark side: Evading parliamentary scrutiny. The Political Quarterly. https://onlinelibrary.wiley.com/doi/full/10.1111/1467-923X.12983 [Crossref], [Google Scholar]

32. Loney, M. (1983). Community against government. London: Heinemann Educational Books. [Google Scholar]

33. Mackenzie, M., Collins, C., Connolly, J., Doyle, M., & McCartney, G. (2017). Working-class discourses of politics, policy and health: 'I don't smoke; I don't drink: The only thing wrong with me is my health'. Policy & Politics, 45(2), 231–249. doi: 10.1332/030557316X14534640177927 [Crossref], [Web of Science ®], [Google Scholar]

34. Mackenzie, M., Conway, E., Hastings, A., Munro, M., & O'Donnell, C. (2013). Is 'candidacy' a useful concept for understanding journeys through public services? A critical interpretive literature synthesis. Social Policy & Administration, 47(7), 806–825. doi: 10.1111/j.1467-9515.2012.00864.x [Crossref], [Web of Science ®], [Google Scholar]

35. MacKinnon, D., Tomaney, J., & Pike, A. (2021, June 3). 'Left Behind Places': A geographical etymology, presentation at the regions in recovery festival. Retrieved from https://events.rdmobile.com/Lists/Details/1132652 [Google Scholar]

36. Marsh, D., & McConnell, A. (2010). Towards a framework for establishing policy success. Public Administration, 88(2), 564–583. doi: 10.1111/j.1467-9299.2009.01803.x [Crossref], [Web of Science ®], [Google Scholar]

37. Marsh, D., & Rhodes, R. A. W. (1992). Policy networks in British government. Oxford: Clarendon Press. [Crossref], [Google Scholar]

38. Massey, A. (2021). Accountability and networks: Mind the gap. In J. Connolly and A. van der Zwet (Eds.), Public value management, governance and reform in Britain (pp. 201–225). Cham: Palgrave Macmillan. [Crossref], [Google Scholar]

39. McConnell, A. (2016). A public policy approach to understanding the nature and causes of foreign policy failure. Journal of European Public Policy, 23(5), 667–684. doi: 10.1080/13501763.2015.1127278 [Taylor & Francis Online], [Web of Science °], [Google Scholar]

40. McConnell, A. (2018). Rethinking wicked problems as political problems and policy problems. Policy & Politics, 46(1), 165–180. [Web of Science °], [Google Scholar]

41. McKnight, A., Duque, M., M, M., & Rucci, M. (2017). Double trouble: A review of the relationship between UK poverty and economic inequality. Retrieved March 31, 2021, from https://policypractice.oxfam.org/resources/double-trouble-a-review-of-the-relationship-between-ukpoverty-and-economic-ine-620373/ [Crossref], [Google Scholar]

42. Mendez, C., van der Zwet, A., & Borowska-Waszak, S. (2021). Rescaling urban development policy in the EU: The impact of integrated place-based approaches in cohesion policy. Regional Studies, 1–12. [Web of Science °], [Google Scholar]

43. Menon, A., & Bevington, M. (2020). Will Johnson really be able to level up? Retrieved March 31, 2021, from https://ukandeu.ac.uk/will-johnson-really-be-able-to-level-up/ [Google Scholar]

44. Moore, M. H. (1995). Creating public value: Strategic management in government. Harvard University Press. [Google Scholar]

45. Newman, J. (2021). The ambiguous ideology of levelling Up. The Political Quarterly, 92(2), 312–320. doi: 10.1111/1467-923X.13010 [Crossref], [Web of Science °], [Google Scholar]

46. Northern Ireland Executive. (2021). Programme for government 2021. Retrieved July 21, 2021, from https://www.northernireland.gov.uk/programmegovernment-pfg-2021 [Google Scholar]

47. Scottish Government (2021). Growing the economy. Retrieved July 21, 2021, from https://www.gov.scot/policies/economic-growth/ [Google Scholar]

48. Public Accounts Committee. (2019, January 30). House of commons committee of public accounts: Improving government planning and spending. Seventy-Eighth Report of Session 2017–19. [Google Scholar]

49. Rhodes, R. A. (1990). Policy networks: A British perspective. Journal of Theoretical Politics, 2(3), 293–317. doi: 10.1177/0951692890002003003 [Crossref], [Google Scholar]

50. Rhodes, R. A. (1994). The hollowing out of the state: The changing nature of the public service in Britain. The Political Quarterly, 65(2), 138–151. doi: 10.1111/j.1467-923X.1994.tb00441.x [Crossref], [Web of Science °], [Google Scholar]

51. Rhodes, R. A. W. (1997). Understanding governance: Policy networks, governance, reflexivity and accountability. Buckingham: Open University Press. [Google Scholar]

52. Scott-Samuel, A., & Smith, K. E. (2016). Fantasy paradigms of health inequalities: Utopian thinking? Social Theory & Health, 163(3), 418–436. [Google Scholar]

53. Scott, M. (2017). Loney, M. (1983). Community against government: British community development project, 1968–78 (studies in social policy and welfare), Heinemann Educational Books, London, UK. CDP (1981). The costs of industrial change, CDP publications, Newcastle Upon tyne, UK. Community Development Journal, 52(2), 313–318. doi: 10.1093/cdj/bsx005 [Crossref], [Google Scholar]

54. Tabner, K. (2018). Scottish community empowerment: Reconfigured localism or an opportunity for change? Concept, 9(1), 11. [Google Scholar]

55. Thissen, M., van Oort, F., McCann, P., Ortega-Argilés, R., & Husby, T. (2020). The implications of Brexit for UK and EU regional competitiveness. Economic Geography, 1–25. http://doi.org/10.1080/00130095.2020.1820862 [Web of Science °], [Google Scholar]

56. Tomaney, J., & Pike, A. (2020). Levelling up? The Political Quarterly, 91(1), 43–48. doi: 10.1111/1467-923X.12834 [Crossref], [Web of Science °], [Google Scholar]

57. UK Government. (2021). Levelling up fund: Prioritisation of places methodology note. Retrieved March 27, 2021, from https://www.gov.uk/government/publications/levelling-up-fund-additionaldocuments/levelling-up-fund-prioritisation-of-places-methodology-note [Google Scholar]

58. Wager, A., Bale, T., Cowley, P., & Menon, A. (2021). The death of May's law: Intra-and inter-party value differences in Britain's labour and conservative parties. Political Studies, 1–23. [Web of Science °], [Google Scholar]

Chapter 9: Staying "One Step Ahead of a Racist": Expanding Understandings of the Experiences of the Covid-19 Pandemic among People from Minoritized Ethnic Groups Living in Britain. Saffron Karlsen and Rosie Nelson

Aldridge, R. W., Lewer, D., Katikireddi, S. V., Mathur, R., Pathak, N., Burns, R., et al. (2020). Black, Asian and Minority Ethnic groups in England are at increased risk of death from COVID-19: indirect standardisation of NHS mortality data. Wellcome Open Res. 5, 88. doi:10.12688/wellcomeopenres.15922.2

PubMed Abstract | CrossRef Full Text | Google Scholar

Baker, C., Hutton, G., Christie, L., and Wright, S. (2020). COVID-19 and the Digital divide London: UK Parliament. Available at: https://post.parliament.uk/covid-19-and-the-digital-divide/.

Google Scholar

Bambra, C., Riordan, R., Ford, J., and Matthews, F. (2020). The COVID-19 pandemic and health inequalities. J. Epidemiol. Community Health 74, 964–968.

CrossRef Full Text | Google Scholar

Bamrah, J. S., Chakravorty, I., and Singhal, P. (2021). The Sewell Report Risks Turning the Clock Back on the fight against Racism in the UK BMJ. https://blogs.bmj.com/bmj/2021/04/12/the-sewell-report-risks-turning-the-clock-back-on-the-fight-against-racism-in-the-uk/.

Google Scholar

Barnes, A., and Hamilton, M. (2020). Coronavirus and the social impacts on Different ethnic groups in the UK: 2020 London: Office for National Statistics. Release date 14 December 2020 https://www.ons.gov.uk/peoplepopulationandcommunity/culturalidentity/ethnicity/articles/coronavirusandthesocialimpactsondifferentethnicgroupsintheuk/2020.Google Scholar

Baumer, T., Phillips, E., Dhadda, A., and Szakmany, T. (2020). Epidemiology of the First Wave of COVID-19 ICU Admissions in South Wales-The Interplay Between Ethnicity and Deprivation. Front. Med. (Lausanne) 7, 569714. doi:10.3389/fmed.2020.569714PubMed Abstract | CrossRef Full Text | Google Scholar

Becares, L., and Nazroo, J. Y. (2020). Racism is the Root Cause of Ethnic Inequities in COVID-19 Discover Society. https://archive.discoversociety.org/2020/04/17/racism-is-the-root-cause-of-ethnic-inequities-in-covid19/. Google Scholar

Bentley, G. R. (2020). Don't blame the BAME: Ethnic and structural inequalities in susceptibilities to COVID-19. Am. J. Hum. Biol. 32 (5), e23478. doi:10.1002/ajhb.23478.PubMed Abstract | CrossRef Full Text | Google Scholar

Black South West Network (BSWN) (2020). Impact of COVID-19 on BAME Led Businesses. Organisations & Communities Bristol:BSWN available at https://static1.squarespace.com/static/594948a7414fb5804d2b4395/t/5ec3e e32a5b5c27385219625/1589898876817/Covid19_Report_v2_compressed. pdf. Google Scholar

Bor, J., Venkataramani, A. S., Williams, D. R., and Tsai, A. C. (2018). Police killings and their spillover effects on the mental health of black Americans: a population-based, quasi-experimental study. Lancet 392 (10144), 302–310. doi:10.1016/S0140-6736(18)31130-9. PubMed Abstract | CrossRef Full Text | Google Scholar

Brynin, M., and Güveli, A. (2012). Understanding the ethnic pay gap in Britain. Work, Employment Soc. 26 (4), 574–587. doi:10.1177/0950017012445095. CrossRef Full Text | Google Scholar

Busby, M., and Gidda, M. (2020). BAME people fined more than white population under Coronavirus laws the Guardian. Available at: https://www.theguardian.com/world/2020/may/26/bame-people-fined-more-than-white-population-under-coronavirus-laws. Google Scholar

Chae, D. H., Yip, T., Martz, C. D., Chung, K., Richeson, J. A., Hajat, A., et al. (2021). Vicarious Racism and Vigilance During the COVID-19 Pandemic: Mental Health Implications Among Asian and Black Americans. Public Health Rep. 136 (4), 508–517. doi:10.1177/00333549211018675 PubMed Abstract | CrossRef Full Text | Google Scholar

Cheah, C. S. L., Wang, C., Ren, H., Zong, X., Cho, H. S., and Xue, X. (2020). COVID-19 Racism and Mental Health in Chinese American Families. Pediatrics 146 (5), e2020021816. doi:10.1542/peds.2020-021816. PubMed Abstract | CrossRef Full Text | Google Scholar

Clark, R., Benkert, R. A., and Flack, J. M. (2006). Large arterial elasticity varies as a function of gender and racism-related vigilance in Black youth. J. Adolesc. Health 39 (4), 562–569. doi:10.1016/j.jadohealth.2006.02.012. PubMed Abstract | CrossRef Full Text | Google Scholar

Coates, M. (2020). Covid-19 and the rise of racism. BMJ 369, m1384. doi:10.1136/bmj.m1384. PubMed Abstract | CrossRef Full Text | Google Scholar

Commission on Race and Ethnic Disparities (CRED) (2021). Commission on Race and Ethnic Disparities. The Report. Available at: https://www.gov.uk/government/publications/the-report-of-the-commission-on-race-and-ethnic-disparities. Google Scholar

Cook, T., Kursumovic, E., and Lennane, S. (2020). Exclusive: Deaths of NHS staff from Covid-19 analysed Health Services Journal. Available at: https://www.hsj.co.uk/exclusive-deaths-of-nhs-staff-from-covid-19-analysed/7027471. Google Scholar

Darling-Hammond, S., Michaels, E. K., Allen, A. M., Chae, D. H., Thomas, M. D., Nguyen, T. T., et al. (2020). After "The China Virus" Went Viral: Racially Charged Coronavirus Coverage and Trends in Bias Against Asian Americans. Health Educ. Behav. 47 (6), 870–879. doi:10.1177/1090198120957949. PubMed Abstract | CrossRef Full Text | Google Scholar

Darlington-Pollock, F., and Norman, P. (2017). Examining ethnic inequalities in health and tenure in England: A repeated cross-sectional analysis. Health Place 46, 82–90. doi:10.1016/j.healthplace.2017.04.011 PubMed Abstract | CrossRef Full Text | Google Scholar

Dhanani, L. Y., and Franz, B. (2020). Unexpected public health consequences of the COVID-19 pandemic: a national survey examining anti-Asian attitudes in the USA. Int. J. Public Health 65, 747–754. doi:10.1007/s00038-020-01440-0. PubMed Abstract | CrossRef Full Text | Google Scholar

Duffy, B., Hewlett, K., Hesketh, R., Benson, R., and Wager, A. (2021). Unequal Britain: Attitudes to Inequalities after Covid-19. London: KCL. https://www.kcl.ac.uk/policy-institute/assets/unequal-britain.pdf. Google Scholar

Elias, A., Ben, J., Mansouri, F., and Paradies, Y. (2021). Racism and nationalism during and beyond the COVID-19 pandemic. Ethnic Racial Stud. 44 (5), 783–793. doi:10.1080/01419870.2020.1851382. CrossRef Full Text | Google Scholar

Ettman, C. K., Abdalla, S. M., Cohen, G. H., Sampson, L., Vivier, P. M., and Galea, S. (2020). Prevalence of Depression Symptoms in US Adults Before and During the COVID-19 Pandemic. JAMA Netw. Open 3 (9), e2019686. doi:10.1001/jamanetworkopen.2020.19686. PubMed Abstract | CrossRef Full Text | Google Scholar

Gee, G. C., Walsemann, K. M., and Brondolo, E. (2012). A Life Course Perspective on How Racism May Be Related to Health Inequities. Am. J. Public Health 102, 967–974. doi:10.2105/AJPH.2012.300666. CrossRef Full Text | Google Scholar

Gemmill, A., Catalano, R., Casey, J. A., Karasek, D., Alcalá, H. E., Elser, H., et al. (2019). Association of Preterm Births Among US Latina Women With the 2016 Presidential Election. JAMA Netw. Open 2 (7), e197084. doi: PubMed Abstract | CrossRef Full Text | Google Scholar

Godlee, F. (2020). Racism: the other pandemic. Bmj 369, m2303. doi:10.1136/bmj.m2303. CrossRef Full Text | Google Scholar

Haque, Z., Becares, L., and Treloar, N. (2020). Over-Exposed and Under-Protected: The Devastating Impact of COVID-19 on Black and Minority Ethnic Communities in Great Britain. London: Runnymede Trust.https:/www.runnymedetrust.org/uploads/Runnymede%20Covid19%20Survey%20report%20v3.pdf.Google Scholar

Harris, S., Joseph-Salisbury, R., Williams, P., and White, L. (2021). A Threat to public safety: policing, Racism and the Covid-19 pandemic London. London, United Kingdom: Institute of Race Relations. Available at: https://irr.org.uk/wp-content/uploads/2021/09/A-threat-to-public-safety-v3.pdf. Google Scholar

Harris, S., Joseph-Salisbury, R., Williams, P., and White, L. (2021). A Collision of Crises: Racism, policing, and the COVID-19 pandemic London: Institute of Race Relations. Available at: https://www.runnymedetrust.org/uploads/projects/CoDE%20Briefings/Runnymede%20CoDE%20A%20Collision%20of%20Crises%20FINAL.pdf. Google Scholar

Hicken, M. T., Lee, H., Ailshire, J., Burgard, S. A., and Williams, D. R. (2013). "Every shut eye, ain't sleep": The role of racism-related vigilance in racial/ethnic disparities in sleep difficulty. Race Soc. Probl. 5, 100–112. doi:10.1007/s12552-013-9095-9. PubMed Abstract | CrossRef Full Text | Google Scholar

Hicken, M. T., Lee, H., and Hing, A. K. (2018). The weight of racism: Vigilance and racial inequalities in weight-related measures. Soc. Sci. Med. 199, 157–166. doi:10.1016/j.socscimed.2017.03.058. PubMed Abstract | CrossRef Full Text | Google Scholar

Himmelstein, M. S., Young, D. M., Sanchez, D. T., and Jackson, J. S. (2015). Vigilance in the discrimination-stress model for Black Americans. Psychol. Health 30 (3), 253–267. doi:10.1080/08870446.2014.966104. PubMed Abstract | CrossRef Full Text | Google Scholar

Home Office (2021). Official Statistics: Hate Crime, England and Wales, 2020 to 2021. Available at: https://www.gov.uk/government/statistics/hate-crime-england-and-wales-2020-to-2021/hate-crime-england-and-wales-2020-to-2021. Google Scholar

Huynh, V. W., Huynh, Q. L., and Stein, M. P. (2017). Not just sticks and stones: Indirect ethnic discrimination leads to greater physiological reactivity. Cultur Divers. Ethnic Minor. Psychol. 23 (3), 425–434. doi:10.1037/cdp0000138. PubMed Abstract | CrossRef Full Text | Google Scholar

John, J. R., Curry, G., and Cunningham-Burley, S. (2021). Exploring ethnic minority women's experiences of maternity care during the SARS-CoV-2 pandemic: a qualitative study. BMJ Open 11, e050666. doi:10.1136/bmjopen-2021-050666. PubMed Abstract | CrossRef Full Text | Google Scholar

Karlsen, S., and Nazroo, J. Y. (2004). Fear of racism and health. J. Epidemiol. Community Health 58 (12), 1017–1018. doi:10.1136/jech.2004.020479. PubMed Abstract | CrossRef Full Text | Google Scholar

Karlsen, S., and Nazroo, J. Y. (2017). "Measuring And Analyzing "Race," Racism, And Racial Discrimination," in Methods in Social Epidemiology. Editors J. M. Oakes, and J. S. Kaufmann (San Francisco: Jossey-Bass). Google Scholar

Karlsen, S., and Nazroo, J. Y. (2002). Relation between racial discrimination, social class, and health among ethnic minority groups. Am. J. Public Health 92 (4), 624–631. doi:10.2105/ajph.92.4.624. PubMed Abstract | CrossRef Full Text | Google Scholar

Karlsen, S., Roth, M., and Becares, M. (2019). "Understanding the influence of ethnicity on health," in Understanding 'race' and ethnicity. Editors S. Chattoo, K. Atkin, G. Craig, and R. Flynn (Bristol: Policy Press). Google Scholar

Karlsen, S., Nazroo, J. Y., and Smith, N. R. (2020). Ethnic, Religious and Gender Differences in Intragenerational Economic Mobility in England and Wales. Sociology 54 (5), 883–903. doi:10.1177/0038038520929562. CrossRef Full Text | Google Scholar

Krieger, N. (2014). Discrimination and Health Inequities. Int. J. Health Serv. 44 (4), 643–710. doi:10.2190/HS.44.4.b. CrossRef Full Text | Google Scholar

Larsen, T., Bosworth, M., and Nafilyan, V. (2021). Updating ethnic Contrasts in Deaths involving the Coronavirus (COVID-19), England: 24 January 2020 to 31 March 2021 London: Office for National Statistics. Release date 26 May 2021 https://www.ons.gov.uk/peoplepopulationandcommunity/birthsdeathsandmarriages/deaths/articles/updatingethniccontrastsindeathsinvolvingthecoronaviruscovid19englandandwales/24january2020to31march2021. Google Scholar

Laster Pirtle, W. N., and Wright, T. (2021). Structural Gendered Racism Revealed in Pandemic Times: Intersectional Approaches to Understanding Race and Gender Health Inequities in COVID-19. Gend. Soc. 35 (2), 168–179. doi:10.1177/08912432211001302. CrossRef Full Text | Google Scholar

Lewis, T. T., Cogburn, C. D., and Williams, D. R. (2015). Self-reported experiences of discrimination and health: scientific advances, ongoing controversies, and emerging issues. Annu. Rev. Clin. Psychol. 11 (1), 407–440. doi:10.1146/annurev-clinpsy-032814-112728. PubMed Abstract | CrossRef Full Text | Google Scholar

Li, Y., and Heath, A. (2018). Persisting disadvantages: a study of labour market dynamics of ethnic unemployment and earnings in the UK (2009-2015). J. Ethnic Migration Stud. 46 (5), 857–878. doi:10.1080/1369183x.2018.1539241. CrossRef Full Text | Google Scholar

Longhi, S. (2020). A longitudinal analysis of ethnic unemployment differentials in the UK. J. Ethnic Migration Stud. 46 (5), 879–892. doi:10.1080/1369183x.2018.1539254. CrossRef Full Text | Google Scholar

Maddock, J., Parsons, S., Di Gessa, G., Green, M. J., Thompson, E. J., Stevenson, A. J., et al. (2021). Inequalities in healthcare Disruptions during the Covid-19 pandemic: Evidence from 12 UK population-Based longitudinal studies, 06, 21258546. (Note that this article is a preprint and has not been peer-reviewed.).medRxiv08

Nazroo, J. Y., and Becares, L. (2020). Ethnic inequalities in COVID-19 mortality: A Consequence of persistent Racism. London: Runnymede Trust. Available at: https://www.runnymedetrust.org/uploads/Runnymede%20CoDE%20COVID%20briefing%20v3.pdf.Google Scholar

Novak, N. L., Geronimus, A. T., and Martinez-Cardoso, A. M. (2017). Change in birth outcomes among infants born to Latina mothers after a major immigration raid. Int. J. Epidemiol. 46 (3), 839–849. doi:10.1093/ije/dyw346. PubMed Abstract | CrossRef Full Text | Google Scholar

Otu, A., Ahinkorah, B. O., Ameyaw, E. K., Seidu, A. A., and Yaya, S. (2020). One country, two crises: what Covid-19 reveals about health inequalities among BAME communities in the United Kingdom and the sustainability of its health system. Int. J. Equity Health 19 (1), 189. doi:10.1186/s12939-020-01307-z. PubMed Abstract | CrossRef Full Text | Google Scholar

Paradies, Y., Ben, J., Denson, N., Elias, A., Priest, N., Pieterse, A., et al. (2015). Racism as a Determinant of Health: A Systematic Review and Meta-Analysis. PLoS ONE 10 (9), e0138511. doi:10.1371/journal.pone.0138511. PubMed Abstract | CrossRef Full Text | Google Scholar

Platt, L., and Warwick, R. (2020b). COVID-19 and Ethnic Inequalities in England and Wales. Fisc Stud. 41, 259–289. doi:10.1111/1475-5890.12228. PubMed Abstract | CrossRef Full Text | Google Scholar

Platt, L., and Warwick, R. (2020a). Are Some Ethnic Groups More Vulnerable to COVID-19 than Others. London: The Institute for Fiscal Studies. www.ifs.org.uk/uploads/Are-some-ethnic-groups-more-vulnerable-to-COVID-19-than-others-V2-IFSBriefing-Note.pdf. Google Scholar

Priest, N., Paradies, Y., Trenerry, B., Truong, M., Karlsen, S., and Kelly, Y. (2013). A systematic review of studies examining the relationship between reported racism and health and wellbeing for children and young people. Soc. Sci. Med. 95, 115–127. doi:10.1016/j.socscimed.2012.11.031. PubMed Abstract | CrossRef Full Text | Google Scholar

Public Health England (PHE) (2020a). Beyond the Data: Understanding the Impact of COVID-19 on BAME Groups. London. https://assets.publishing.service.gov.uk/government/uploads/system/uploads/attachment_data/file/892376/COVID_stakeholder_engagement_synthesis_beyond_the_data.pdf. Google Scholar

Public Health England (PHE) (2020b). Disparities in the Risk and Outcomes of COVID-19. London. https://assets.publishing.service.gov.uk/government/uploads/system/uploads/attachment_data/file/892085/disparities_review.pdf. Google Scholar

Rafferty, A. (2021). Ethnic penalties in graduate level over-education, unemployment and wages: evidence from Britain Work. Employment Soc. 26 (6), 987–1006. Google Scholar

Reading Turchioe, M., Grossman, L. V., Myers, A. C., Pathak, J., and Creber, R. M. (2020). Correlates of Mental Health Symptoms Among US Adults During COVID-19, March-April 2020. Public Health Rep. 136 (1), 97–106. doi:10.1177/0033354920970179. PubMed Abstract | CrossRef Full Text | Google Scholar

Richman, L. S., and Jonassaint, C. (2008). The Effects of Race-related Stress on Cortisol Reactivity in the Laboratory: Implications of the Duke Lacrosse Scandal. Ann. Behav. Med. 35 (1), 105–110. doi:10.1007/s12160-007-9013-8. PubMed Abstract | CrossRef Full Text | Google Scholar

Ruiz, N. G., Horowitz, J., and Tamir, C. (2020). Many Black and Asian Americans Say They Have Experienced Discrimination Amid the COVID-19 Outbreak

Pew Research Center. Available at: https://www.pewresearch.org/social-trends/2020/07/01/many-black-and-asian-americans-say-they-have-experienced-discrimination-amid-the-covid-19-outbreak/.Google Scholar

Sawyer, P. J., Major, B., Casad, B. J., Townsend, S. S., and Mendes, W. B. (2012). Discrimination and the Stress Response: Psychological and Physiological Consequences of Anticipating Prejudice in Interethnic Interactions. Am. J. Public Health 102, 1020–1026. doi:10.2105/AJPH.2011.300620. CrossRef Full Text | Google Scholar

Sewell, A. A., Feldman, J. M., Ray, R., Gilbert, K. L., Jefferson, K. A., and Lee, H. (2021). Illness spillovers of lethal police violence: the significance of gendered marginalization. Ethnic Racial Stud. 44 (7), 1089–1114. doi:10.1080/0 1419870.2020.1781913. CrossRef Full Text | Google Scholar

Siddiqi, S. M., Cantor, J., Dastidar, M. G., Beckman, R., Richardson, A. S., Baird, M. D., et al. (2021). SNAP Participants and High Levels of Food Insecurity in the Early Stages of the COVID-19 Pandemic. Public Health Rep. 136 (4), 457–465. PubMed Abstract | CrossRef Full Text | Google Scholar

Simms, A. (2021). COVID-19, Black jurisdictions, and budget constraints: how fiscal footing shapes fighting the virus. Ethnic Racial Stud. 44 (5), 836–850. doi:10.1080/01419870.2020.1859576. CrossRef Full Text | Google Scholar

Sze, S., Pan, D., Nevill, C. R., Gray, L. J., Martin, C. A., Nazareth, J., et al. (2020). Ethnicity and clinical outcomes in COVID-19: A systematic review and meta-analysis. EClinicalMedicine 29, 100630. doi:10.1016/j.eclinm.2020.100630. PubMed Abstract | CrossRef Full Text | Google Scholar

Tynes, B. M., Willis, H. A., Stewart, A. M., and Hamilton, M. W. (2019). Race-related traumatic events online and mental health among adolescents of color. J. Adolesc. Health 65 (3), 371–377. doi:10.1016/j.jadohealth.2019.03.006. CrossRef Full Text | Google Scholar

Williams, D. R., Lawrence, J. A., Davis, B. A., and Vu, C. (2019). Understanding how discrimination can affect health. Health Serv. Res. 54 Suppl 2, 1374–1388. doi:10.1111/1475-6773.13222. PubMed Abstract | CrossRef Full Text | Google Scholar

Williams, D. R., Neighbors, H. W., and Jackson, J. S. (2003). Racial/ethnic discrimination and health: findings from community studies. Am. J. Public Health 93 (2), 200–208. doi:10.2105/ajph.93.2.200,

PubMed Abstract | CrossRef Full Text | Google Scholar

Williams, D. R. (2018). Stress and the Mental Health of Populations of Color: Advancing Our Understanding of Race-related Stressors. J. Health Soc. Behav. 59 (4), 466–485. doi:10.1177/0022146518814251. PubMed Abstract | CrossRef Full Text | Google Scholar

Williams, D. R., Lawrence, J. A., and Davis, B. A. (2019). Racism and Health: Evidence and Needed Research. Annu. Rev. Public Health 40 (1), 105–125. doi:10.1146/annurev-publhealth-040218-043750 PubMed Abstract | CrossRef Full Text | Google Scholar

Women and Equalities Committee (WEC), House of Commons (2020). Unequal Impact? Coronavirus and BAME people Third Report of Session 2019–21 London. House of Commons https://committees.parliament.uk/publications/3965/documents/39887/default/.Google Scholar

Woodhead, C., Onwumere, J., Rhead, R., Bora-White, M., Chui, Z., Clifford, N., et al. (2021). Race, ethnicity and COVID-19 vaccination: a qualitative study of UK healthcare staff. Ethn. Health, 1–20. doi:10.1080/13557858.2021.1936464

Zwysen, W., Di Stasio, V., and Heath, A. (2021). Ethnic minorities are less likely to find good work than their white British counterparts, even when born and educated in the UK. LSE British Politics and Policy Blog. Available at: https://blogs.lse.ac.uk/politicsandpolicy/ethnic-penalties-and-hiring-discrimination/.

Index

P

PINWALE 43

POKERFACE 43, 57

Progressive Unionist Party 32

Proscribed Organisations Appeal
Commission 105, 221

Public Health of England (PHE) 53

R

Regulations of Investigatory Power Act
of 2000 42, 198

Rosa Ehrenreich Brookst 11, 195

S

Sarah Dix 4, 15

Security and intelligence agencies
(SIAs) 94

Security Sector Reforms (SSR) 37, 63

Security Service (MI5) 68

Snoopers Charter Surveillance 51, 199

Social Index of Multiple Deprivation
162

Special Immigration Appeals Commission 105, 221

T

Talibanization 9

TEMPORA 42, 43, 57, 63

Trade and Cooperation Agreement
122

Traditional Unionist Voice 32

W

Weak States 9, 13, 195, 196

WINDSTOP 43, 198

X

XKEYSCORE 43, 57

About the Author

Musa Khan Jalalzai is a journalist and research scholar. He has written extensively on Afghanistan, terrorism, nuclear and biological terrorism, human trafficking, drug trafficking, and intelligence research and analysis. He was an Executive Editor of the Daily Outlook Afghanistan from 2005-2011, and a permanent contributor in Pakistan's daily *The Post, Daily Times*, and *The Nation, Weekly the Nation*, (London). However, in 2004, US Library of Congress in its report for South Asia mentioned him as the biggest and prolific writer. He received Masters in English literature, Diploma in Geospatial Intelligence, University of Maryland, Washington DC, certificate in Surveillance Law from the University of Stanford, USA, and diploma in Counter terrorism from Pennsylvania State University, California, the United States.

CPSIA information can be obtained
at www.ICGtesting.com
Printed in the USA
LVHW090236160122
708529LV00002B/10